THE DEAD SEA SCROLLS AND THE BIBLE

The Dead Sea Scrolls
and the Bible

James C. VanderKam

WILLIAM B. EERDMANS PUBLISHING COMPANY

GRAND RAPIDS, MICHIGAN / CAMBRIDGE, U.K.

Published 2012 by
Wm. B. Eerdmans Publishing Co.
2140 Oak Industrial Drive N.E., Grand Rapids, Michigan 49505 /
P.O. Box 163, Cambridge CB3 9PU U.K.

Printed in the United States of America

18 17 16 15 14 13 12   7 6 5 4 3 2 1

Library of Congress Cataloging-in-Publication Data

VanderKam, James C.
The Dead Sea scrolls and the Bible / James C. VanderKam.
p.   cm.
"Six of the seven chapters in The Dead Sea scrolls and the Bible
began as the Speaker's Lectures at Oxford University, delivered
during the first two weeks of May 2009" — Introd.
Includes bibliographical references.
ISBN 978-0-8028-6679-0 (pbk.: alk. paper)
1. Dead Sea scrolls.   2. Dead Sea scrolls — Relation to the Old Testament.
3. Dead Sea scrolls — Relation to the New Testament.
4. Judaism — History — Post-exilic period, 586 B.C.–210 A.D.   I. Title.

BM487.V255   2012
221.4′4 — dc23

2011029919

www.eerdmans.com

Contents

Introduction

S ix of the seven chapters in *The Dead Sea Scrolls and the Bible* began as the Speaker's Lectures at Oxford University, delivered during the first two weeks of May 2009. For the published form of the lectures, I have changed the first person address of the speeches to the third person, entered many minor alterations into the texts, and supported the statements in the texts with footnotes.

I am grateful to John Barton of Oriel College for the invitation to be the Speaker's Lecturer. In the invitation he suggested that the lectures be devoted to topics in the Dead Sea Scrolls. I took that suggestion in a broad sense — surveying some of the many ways in which the scrolls enlighten one's reading of the Bible, also understood in a broad sense as including the Hebrew Bible/Old Testament and the New Testament. In fact, the New Testament is an important resource for several of the chapters. This is a position it naturally occupies as a near-contemporary, largely Jewish witness to practices, procedures, beliefs, and debates in the late Second Temple period.

The purpose of the lectures themselves and also of their published form is to provide up-to-date, accessible overviews of major subjects in the area of the scrolls and the Bible, especially ones that have interested me over the last several decades. Each of them covers central topics in scrolls research and inquires about the significance of the data for material in the Bible. In particular, I have attempted to think through the implications of the scrolls for their time and in their contexts by asking questions such as: What is the information available, what are the problems connected with it, and what possibilities are raised by it? In approaching the areas covered in the lectures and now in the chapters of this book, I have drawn upon my previous work, revised, updated, and added to it, while also drawing upon the many studies written by colleagues and friends in the busy field of scrolls research. Given the nature of the book, it is not my purpose to provide full bibliographical coverage but rather to make a selection from the nearly innumerable publications in order to furnish the reader with documentation and indications where further information may be found.

The first chapter, "The 'Biblical' Scrolls and Their Implications," begins with a survey of the manuscript copies of books that eventually became part of the Hebrew Bible, citations of those books, and other evidence for their texts in the Judean Desert finds; but it is more concerned with providing specific examples from the manuscripts and with exploring where the newer data lead. Chapter 2, "Commentary on Older Scripture in the Scrolls," focuses on a major preoccupation of the authors — explaining the meaning of older, authoritative works for their time. Included are studies of the sources of interpretation — whether in the Hebrew Bible or other, older works — on which the writers could draw and the ways in which they went about handling these more ancient texts. The third chapter, "Authoritative Literature According to the Scrolls," deals with the assumptions that drove the scrolls writers and the ways in which they indicate which ancient texts functioned authoritatively at a time when there was not, as nearly as one can tell, a canon of scripture in the strict sense of the term. In Chapter 3 New Testament information is adduced as helpful comparative evidence from roughly the same historical period.

The fourth chapter contains an essay that was not delivered as one of the Speaker's Lectures. "New Copies of Old Texts" is a study of various Jewish compositions that were known before the scrolls discoveries (made between 1947 and 1956) but of which fragmentary copies from the original language texts have turned up in the caves at Qumran. The works covered are *Jubilees, Aramaic Levi*, the *Book of the Giants*, the Wisdom of Ben Sira, Tobit, *Enoch* (especially the Greek fragments from cave 7 that may contain bits of the Epistle of Enoch), the Epistle of Jeremiah, and Psalms 151, 154, and 155. All of these works, apart from *Aramaic Levi*, have found a place in the Bibles of various groups — even the *Book of the Giants* among the Manichees — and for that reason can be said to fall under the overall rubric of *The Dead Sea Scrolls and the Bible*.

In Chapter 5, "Groups and Group Controversies in the Scrolls," I turn to the question of whether the scrolls deal with the three "sects" that Josephus mentioned — Pharisees, Sadducees, and Essenes — and what they say about them, if they do mention them. The texts plainly, in my opinion, speak of the first and last of these groups, using specific names for both, while the evidence is weaker for the presence of Sadducees, though there is evidence for a "Sadducean" approach to law in the scrolls. Once again New Testament passages are summoned as comparative material.

The final two chapters are directed principally at places in the Gospels, Acts, and letters of Paul where the scrolls provide illumination that enriches the reading of those texts. The sixth chapter, "The Dead Sea Scrolls and the New Testament Gospels," examines several pericopes and topics (e.g., messianism, legal matters) that benefit the student of the New Testament in understanding phenomena in the texts. The last chapter, "The Dead Sea Scrolls, the Acts of the Apostles, and the Letters of Paul," offers analyses of the first chapters of Acts that exhibit profound parallels with the scrolls, along with some differences, and a number of issues in Pauline studies (scriptural interpretation, 2 Cor. 6:14–7:1, works of the law) in connection with material in the scrolls.

I wish to thank all in Oxford who made my visit and my wife Mary's stay for the second week such a memorable and enjoyable one: John Barton, as noted, who issued the invitation but was prevented by family matters from being present as he intended; Paul Joyce of St. Peter's College, who ably stepped in and also hosted us at his college; the Rev. Peter Southwell of Queen's College, Markus Bockmuehl of Keble College and his wife Celia, Christopher Rowland of Queen's College, and John Day of Lady Margaret Hall, all of whom served as hosts for meals; Alison Salvesen, Martin Goodman, and Fergus Millar, who welcomed me to the Oriental Institute; and Geza Vermes, a longtime fellow devotee of the scrolls. I am also grateful to Mrs. Elizabeth Macallister, administrative officer in the Theology Faculty, for making such good plans for our visit, and to Kevin Cathcart and Nick King, S.J., for welcoming us to Campion Hall.

In preparing the book I have received assistance from Sara Ferry, who also was a helpful and eager font of knowledge about Oxford. As he has so often, Gene Ulrich has been a generous source of information about the "biblical" scrolls and subjects related to them. My wife Mary has taken the time to read over the chapters and offer suggestions for improving them. Sarah Schreiber, a doctoral student at the University of Notre Dame, deserves lavish praise for her indispensable, expert help in reading the proofs and preparing the index — all done with the utmost good cheer. Once again I am grateful to Eerdmans for publishing my work and for their skill in doing so.

JAMES C. VANDERKAM

Abbreviations

EDSS	*Encyclopedia of the Dead Sea Scrolls,* ed. L. H. Schiffman and J. C. VanderKam. 2 vols. New York, 2000
GAP	Guides to Apocrypha and Pseudepigrapha
HDR	Harvard Dissertations in Religion
HS	*Hebrew Studies*
HSM	Harvard Semitic Monographs
HTR	*Harvard Theological Review*
HUCM	Monographs of the Hebrew Union College
ICC	International Critical Commentary
IEJ	*Israel Exploration Journal*
JBL	*Journal of Biblical Literature*
JBLMS	Journal of Biblical Literature Monograph Series
JJS	*Journal of Jewish Studies*
JR	*Journal of Religion*
JSJSup	Journal for the Study of Judaism Supplement
JSOTSup	Journal for the Study of the Old Testament: Supplement Series
JSP	*Journal for the Study of the Pseudepigrapha*
JSPSup	Journal for the Study of the Pseudepigrapha: Supplement Series
JSSSup	Journal of Semitic Studies Supplement
LCL	Loeb Classical Library
LD	Lectio divina
LHB/OTS	Library of Hebrew Bible/Old Testament Studies
LSTS	Library of Second Temple Studies
NICNT	New International Commentary on the New Testament
NovTSup	Supplements to Novum Testamentum
NRSV	New Revised Standard Version
NTOA	Novum Testamentum et Orbis Antiquus
NTS	*New Testament Studies*
OTL	Old Testament Library
PAAJR	*Proceedings of the American Academy of Jewish Research*
RB	*Revue biblique*
RevQ	*Revue de Qumran*
SBLEJL	Society of Biblical Literature Early Judaism and Its Literature
SBLMS	Society of Biblical Literature Monograph Series
SBLSCS	Society of Biblical Literature Septuagint and Cognate Studies
SBLTT	Society of Biblical Literature Texts and Translations
SBT	Studies in Biblical Theology

SDSSRL	Studies in the Dead Sea Scrolls and Related Literature
SNTSMS	Society for New Testament Studies Monograph Series
STDJ	Studies on the Texts of the Desert of Judah
StPB	Studia post-biblica
SVTP	Studia in Veteris Testamenti pseudepigraphica
TDNT	*Theological Dictionary of the New Testament,* ed. G. Kittel and G. Friedrich. 10 vols. Grand Rapids, 1964-1976
Text	*Textus*
TSAJ	Texte und Studien zum antiken Judentum
VT	*Vetus Testamentum*
VTSup	Supplements to Vetus Testamentum

CHAPTER 1

The "Biblical" Scrolls and Their Implications

For many the first response to the question about the value of the Dead Sea Scrolls to modern biblical studies would be the copies of scriptural works found among them. The fact that many copies of books that later became part of the Hebrew Bible are represented among the fragments removed from the caves at Qumran has been trumpeted about as their greatest contribution to contemporary analysis and appreciation of the Bible. There have been numerous surveys of the scrolls finds that have been labeled "biblical," and the present chapter adds to that survey — but just briefly. It is worth covering the entire corpus if only because the situation has continued to change slightly right up to the present. More space will be devoted to examining the implications of these unquestionably significant finds.

It is a fact that, among the more than 900 manuscripts identified by editors of the scrolls, approximately 200-210 qualify as copies of one or more scriptural books (although the status of the books in question is not always clear) — that is, copies of works which at some, apparently later time became parts of the Hebrew Bible.[1] If one adds those discovered at other Judean Desert sites, the number jumps to approximately 230. The historical period in which the scrolls from the Qumran caves were transcribed begins in the third century B.C.E. and continues to the first century C.E., with most of them having been copied in the first century B.C.E. or

---

1. The remains of these copies have been gathered by Eugene Ulrich into a single volume: *The Biblical Qumran Scrolls: Transcriptions and Textual Variants* (VTSup 134; Leiden: Brill, 2010).

the first C.E.[2] They come from a time many centuries before the earliest representative of the Masoretic Text (= MT, ca. 900 C.E.) and the most ancient codex of the Old Greek translation (= LXX, 4th century C.E.). It is likely that the Qumran copies reflect the situation with respect to the text of scriptural books not only at the small site of Qumran but also throughout the land of Israel, as some of the scrolls — certainly the earliest ones — were brought to Qumran from elsewhere.

NUMBER OF COPIES FROM THE QUMRAN CAVES

Only one of the many scriptural scrolls can be called complete, apart from a few scraps: 1QIsa[a] contains the entire book of Isaiah. All of the other representatives of "biblical" books are fragmentary to one degree or another, usually to a very high degree. Except for one, every book in the Hebrew Bible is represented by at least one fragment among the Dead Sea Scrolls; the missing one is, of course, the book of Esther. Until recently one always had to add that there was no copy of Nehemiah either and to note that there is an absence of evidence from Qumran that Nehemiah was considered one book with Ezra, as it was later; in fact, there is practically no indication of the presence of either book at Qumran, whether of the text or influence from it.[3] A fragment with the text of Neh 3:14-15 has turned up, although it remains unpublished (possibly more than one fragment of the manuscript has survived). Some of the other books in the Hebrew Bible, it must be admitted, just barely make the list: a part of the text of Habakkuk, for instance, may appear on one small fragment (4QXII[g] frg. 102) where the editor, Russell Fuller, reads ישרה נפשו[ו]. He identifies the two words as coming from "Hab 2:4?" (the first three letters and the last are adorned

---

2. See B. Webster, "Chronological Index of the Texts from the Judaean Desert," in E. Tov, ed., *The Texts from the Judaean Desert: Indices and an Introduction to the* Discoveries in the Judaean Desert *Series* (DJD 39; Oxford: Clarendon, 2002), 351-446. He includes fourteen "biblical" scrolls in the Archaic period (250-150 B.C.E.), places 23 in the Late Herodian period (30-68 C.E.), and two in the "Late to Post-Herodian period (4Q2, 4Q21) (see pp. 371, 375, for example). All of the earliest scriptural copies are of pentateuchal books, other than 4QJer[a].

3. 4QEzra (4Q117) consists of three fragments preserving bits and pieces of Ezra 4:2-6, 9-11; 5:17-6:5 (see E. Ulrich. "4QEzra," in Ulrich et al., eds., *Qumran Cave 4: XI, Psalms to Chronicles* [DJD 16; Oxford: Clarendon, 2000], 291-93 and pl. 38). In an oddly anachronistic move, the text is labeled "4QEzra (= Ezra-Nehemiah)" in the list of Qumran mss. in DJD 39 (p. 48).

with supralinear circlets indicating a high degree of uncertainty in reading them).[4] Some others, like Chronicles, do not fare much better: 4QChr (4Q118) consists of one fragment with letters from two columns, with the text of the first column being unidentified and the second offering a few letters from four verses in 2 Chronicles (2 Chr 28:27–29:3).[5]

Almost all the copies are inscribed in various styles of the square (or Assyrian) script, but twelve manuscripts were written in paleo-Hebrew (with three unidentified ones — 4Q124-125; 11Q22) and at least five in Greek. The list below gives the numbers of identified copies for each book of the Hebrew Bible. The numbers in the list may not be exact, since there are at times problems in determining whether a fragment belongs to a particular manuscript or whether one is dealing with pieces from what was once an entire book, but they should be nearly correct. The totals represented as "19-20" or "8-9" copies for a book indicate some uncertainty about whether a few fragments come from one or two copies; the numbers in parentheses express the actual number of scrolls involved, in cases where more than one book was copied on a single scroll (they are counted once for each book, thus the larger totals for some books).[6]

Genesis	19-20	Minor Prophets	8-9
Exodus	17 (15)	Psalms	36
Leviticus	13 (12)	Job	4
Numbers	7 (5)	Proverbs	2
Deuteronomy	30	Ruth	4
Joshua	2	Song	4
Judges	3	Ecclesiastes	2
1-2 Samuel	4	Lamentations	4
1-2 Kings	3	Daniel	8
Isaiah	21	Ezra	1
Jeremiah	6	Nehemiah	1
Ezekiel	6	1-2 Chronicles	1

4. R. E. Fuller, "The Twelve," in E. Ulrich et al., eds., *Qumran Cave 4: X, The Prophets* (DJD 15; Oxford: Clarendon, 1997), 316.

5. See J. Trebolle Barrera, "4QChr," in E. Ulrich et al., eds., DJD 16:295-97.

6. E. Tov writes: "Although most of the scrolls contain only one biblical book, 5 Torah scrolls contain two consecutive books. . . . Likewise, the individual books of the Minor Prophets were considered as one book contained in one scroll"; *Textual Criticism of the Hebrew Bible* (2nd rev. ed.; Minneapolis: Fortress/Assen: Van Gorcum, 2001), 103-4.

The total for these figures, using the larger numbers in the uncertain cases, is 208; working with the smaller numbers in those instances, it is 201. If one adopts the larger number in each case and groups them by categories familiar from the later Hebrew Bible, there are 87 manuscripts containing pentateuchal texts, 54 with materal from the Prophets (Former Prophets, 12, and Latter Prophets, 42), and 67 with remains of the Writings. The books most frequently represented are: Psalms, Deuteronomy, Isaiah, Genesis, Exodus, Leviticus — a group among which pentateuchal books are strongly in evidence, with the other canonical divisions of the Hebrew Bible represented by one member each.

OTHER COPIES

The numbers are quite impressive, yet the ones listed are not the only witnesses to the scriptural texts found in the Qumran caves. As mentioned above, there are at least five copies of Greek translations of scriptural books: one of Exodus, two of Leviticus, one of Numbers, and one of Deuteronomy — all of them are pieces from Greek copies of pentateuchal books. Other small fragments may come from still more copies, though not enough text has survived to clinch the case (see 7Q3-5 and the discussion in Chapter 4 below). In addition, there are three manuscripts that have been identified as targums: one of Leviticus (4Q156) and two of Job (4Q157, 11Q10), the last of which (11Q10) is extensively preserved.

Besides these scriptural copies, there are other kinds of works that are valuable for a study of the scriptural text and its history. As is well known, the caves at Qumran have yielded a series of commentaries on prophetic works. The writers of these *pesharim* cite a passage from a scriptural book (occasionally books) and then explain the meaning of it. Having completed the commentary on that passage, writers of the continuous *pesharim* then move on to the next or another one found farther along in the book.[7] These citations from scriptural books and the many "biblical" quotations in other works (e.g., the *Damascus Document*) considerably augment the fund of information about the scriptural text in the Dead

---

7. The texts and translations with extensive commentary can be found in M. P. Horgan, *Pesharim: Qumran Interpretations of Biblical Books* (CBQMS 8; Washington: Catholic Biblical Association of America, 1979).

Sea Scrolls. It so happens that, while only one tiny piece possibly containing Habakkuk survives from the relevant part of a manuscript of the
Twelve Prophets, the text of the first two chapters of the book is extensively preserved in the commentary on it. There are also Tefillin (phylacteries) and Mezuzot, collections of scriptural texts placed in a small container and attached to one's arm (and head; see, for example, Exod 13:9)
or doorway (see Deut 6:9; 11:20). Since it is not always possible to distinguish the two types when only fragments are extant, the numbers may not
be exact. But 28 texts identified as Tefillin were found at Qumran (21 in
cave 4 — 4Q128-48; the others are 1Q13; 5Q8; 8Q3; XQ1-4)[8] and three at
other sites; there are eight Mezuzot from Qumran (4Q149-55; 8Q4)[9] and
one from Murabba'at.

TEXTS FROM OTHER JUDEAN DESERT SITES

Several additional places in the Judean Desert have yielded copies of scriptural books. Not nearly as many were found in them as at Qumran, but
their contributions are noteworthy nevertheless.

Masada (7): The finds at the famous site are securely dated in that they
cannot be later than 73 or 74 C.E., the year when the fortress was taken by
the Romans. The numbers are markedly lower than for the smaller
Qumran site, consistent with the fact that a different kind of community
used it.[10]

---

8. The rabbinic rules regarding Tefillin or Phylacteries prescribe that four passages be included: Exod 13:1-10; 13:11-16; Deut 6:4-9; and Deut 11:13-21. These passages
also appear on the Qumran examples, though some of them contain other or rather
expanded passages (e.g., the Ten Commandments). See L. H. Schiffman, "Phylacteries
and Mezuzot," in Schiffman and J. C. VanderKam, eds., *Encyclopedia of the Dead Sea
Scrolls* (2 vols.; New York: Oxford University Press, 2000), 2:675-77; D. Nakman,
"*Tefillin* and *Mezuzot* at Qumran," in M. Kister, ed., *The Qumran Scrolls and Their
World* (Between Bible and Mishnah; 2 vols.; Jerusalem: Yad Ben-Zvi, 2009), 1:143-55
(Hebrew).

9. Schiffman, "Phylacteries and Mezuzot," 2:675-77. The prescribed passages are
Deut 6:4-9 and 11:13-21, though the Qumran copies also have extra ones such as the Ten
Commandments.

10. The texts were published in S. Talmon, *Hebrew Fragments from Masada*
(Masada VI: Yigael Yadin Excavations 1963-1965: Final Reports; Jerusalem: Israel Exploration Society, Hebrew University of Jerusalem, 1999), 31-97.

Genesis	1
Leviticus	2
Deuteronomy	1
Ezekiel	1
Psalms	2
Murabba'at (7 [6])[11]	
Genesis	2
Exodus	1 (on the same manuscript as one of the Genesis copies)
Numbers	1
Deuteronomy	1
Isaiah	1
Minor Prophets	1 (a relatively well-preserved scroll)
Nahal Hever (3)[12]	
Numbers	1
Minor Prophets	1 (Greek, extensively preserved)[13]
Psalms	1
Nahal Hever/Se'elim (2)	
Numbers	1
Deuteronomy	1
Se'elim (1)[14]	
Numbers	1
Sdeir (1)[15]	
Genesis	1

There are also copies of Joshua (1) and Judges (1) from an unknown location. As at Qumran, so at the other sites the books attested are pentateuchal and prophetic works along with Psalms.

---

11. For the texts, see J. T. Milik in P. Benoit, Milik, and R. de Vaux, eds., *Les Grottes de Murabba'ât* (DJD 2; Oxford: Clarendon, 1961), 75-80 and 181-205.

12. The copies from Nahal Hever (other than the Minor Prophets scroll) and Nahal Hever/Se'elim were edited by P. Flint in J. H. Charlesworth et al., eds., J. VanderKam and M. Brady, consulting eds., *Miscellaneous Texts from the Judaean Desert* (DJD 38; Oxford: Clarendon, 2000), 133-66, 173-82.

13. The edition is E. Tov, ed., *The Greek Minor Prophets Scroll from Nahal Hever (8HevXIIgr)* (The Seiyâl Collection 1; DJD 8; Oxford: Clarendon, 1990).

14. See M. Morgenstern in DJD 38:209.

15. See C. Murphy in DJD 38:117-24.

NATURE OF THE TEXTS

The scrolls, despite the limits dictated by their fragmentary state of preservation, have made significant contributions to knowledge about the texts of scriptural books and their history.

General Comments

Before looking at specific examples, it is fitting to reflect on the sum total of the scriptural manuscript evidence.

First — and to state the obvious — the copies furnish the oldest original language evidence for the many passages they represent, centuries older than any other witness apart from some Greek *papyri* from the second and first century B.C.E. — Greek papyri that are contemporary with many of the scrolls. As the scrolls from Qumran were copied in the period between the third century B.C.E. and the first century C.E., they are several hundreds of years older than the most ancient Greek *codices* of the Bible (fourth century C.E.), and they, in many cases, antedate by a full millennium the earliest extant copies of the Masoretic Text (MT). In an age when all texts had to be handcopied, the earlier the evidence the less opportunity, one hopes, there was for scribal lapses and other common copying errors to occur. There is no guarantee that older is better, but the ancient copies offer unique comparative evidence, allowing one to test whether the more recent (MT, LXX, etc.) and the more ancient copies (the scrolls from the Qumran caves) are the same, almost the same, or quite different in their readings and to draw conclusions from the results (e.g., are the changes systematic or are they of other kinds).

While all of this is familiar enough, it bears repeating because, with the passage of time, it is too easy to forget what an extraordinary find the Qumran scrolls, including the scriptural ones, prove to be — discoveries in a place whose climate was thought to preclude preservation of ancient parchment and papyrus.

Second, the manuscripts from the Judean wilderness provide evidence that scriptural texts were transmitted with considerable care by Jewish copyists. The differences between the Judean Desert texts and MT are indeed numerous though frequently very slight, often ones that do not affect the meaning of the text for most purposes (e.g., spelling changes, omission or addition of a conjunction). Statements in rabbinic literature describe the meticulous procedures used later in copying scriptural texts; it seems great care was also taken at an earlier time, as the Judean Desert texts suggest. The scribes were not transmitting only one form of the texts; yet, from whatever scriptural model they were copying, they presumably did the work with care according to prevailing rules of the profession. An interesting question is exactly what the scribes responsible for the Qumran scrolls understood proper transmission of a text to involve. The question will be considered below.

Third, despite the more recent finds, only a very limited set of data has survived, and it yields a correspondingly limited perspective on the history and varieties of the scriptural texts. Nevertheless, the admittedly challenged perspective available today is a broader one than was accessible to all those talented text critics whose work preceded the Qumran and other Judean Desert finds. Before 1947, the textual evidence at their disposal was of relatively recent date: the manuscript trail for MT could be traced back no farther than ca. 900 C.E.,[16] and that for the Samaritan Pentateuch (SP) goes back to an even more recent date.[17] There are many Greek witnesses that are centuries older than the earliest copies of MT and SP,[18] yet, however valuable, they are translations, not copies in the original languages. Other than the second-first century Nash Papyrus,[19] there was little ancient Hebrew evidence on which to base one's study. Probes were made using scriptural citations in texts such as *Jubilees*, but the manuscript evidence for it is also relatively late. The Judean Desert discoveries, however fragmentary, are a wonderful supplement to the textual base and a very unexpected one. Among the greatest contributions of the new material is that in a number of cases there is now Hebrew manu-

---

16. The Cairo Codex, containing only the Prophets, dates from 895 C.E., while the Aleppo Codex, which once contained the entire Hebrew Bible but from which large parts are missing, comes from the first half of the tenth century. Codex Leningradensis, which underlies the latest editions of the Hebrew Bible, was copied in 1008 C.E. See, e.g., E. Würthwein, *The Text of the Old Testament* (2nd ed.; Grand Rapids: Eerdmans, 1995), 35-37.

17. The earliest copy may have been made in 1150 C.E.; Würthwein, *The Text of the Old Testament*, 47.

18. Some papyri fragments date from before the turn of the eras (e.g., John Rylands Library 458, from the second century). The oldest full copy, Vaticanus (B), was copied in the fourth century C.E.

19. The papyrus bears the text of the Ten Commandments, with elements from both Exodus 20 and Deuteronomy 5, and Deut 6:4-5; see Tov, *Textual Criticism of the Hebrew Bible*, 118.

script evidence for readings previously known only from the versions, especially LXX.

The Textual Picture

As the experts have noted, the Qumran texts permit one to see that at the time when they were penned (third century B.C.E.–first century C.E.) there was, from copy to copy, a degree of fluidity in the wording of scriptural texts — just exactly as one might have expected. There was not a single, completely uniform, accepted wording of a scriptural book such as Genesis or Isaiah — something that would have been virtually impossible when all copying was done by hand. This is not to say that there was free variation in the wording of texts. Rather, within fairly narrow limits (in most cases) there are noticeable differences from manuscript to manuscript. Some examples will illustrate differing measures of variation.

To present an overview of the range of evidence, the language employed by Eugene Ulrich for what he calls the "four principal categories of variation detectable through comparison of the Qumran manuscripts, MT, SP, and OG" will be useful.[20]

Orthography

Anyone who has read the scrolls found in the caves of Qumran is aware that the scribes made much more frequent use of consonants to mark the presence of certain vowels *(matres lectionis)* than one finds in MT. As someone said recently, they were rather more British than American in their spelling. Orthography is a category of textual variation that can easily be dismissed as devoid of significance — as documentation for a phase in Hebrew spelling and pronunciation, nothing more. But, by their very nature, *matres lectionis* represent a decision regarding the proper parsing of a form whenever the consonantal text is ambiguous or potentially ambiguous. At times the analysis is the one any Hebrew reader would have made, but at others deciding on the preferred reading and marking it by a fuller

---

20. E. Ulrich, "The Jewish Scriptures: Texts, Versions, Canons," in J. Collins and D. Harlow, eds., *The Eerdmans Dictionary of Early Judaism* (Grand Rapids: Eerdmans, 2010), 97-119, here 110. OG = Old Greek.

spelling offered more of a challenge. For example, in Isa 40:6 the consonantal text of MT has ואמר. The Masoretes understood the form to be וְאָמַר. The text of the verse so analyzed reads: "A voice says, 'Cry out!' *And he said*, 'What shall I cry?'" In 1QIsaᵃ the spelling of the word is: ואומרה. According to this reading the verse is worded: "A voice says, 'Cry out!' *And I said*, 'What shall I cry?'" The copyist/interpreter of MT saw the verse as a report about a conversation between the voice and a "he"; the spelling in the Isaiah scroll presents it as direct address and first person response. The reading of the Isaiah scroll is the one translated in LXX: καὶ εἶπα.

Individual Textual Variants

Many differences in readings between manuscripts concern small items that are not matters of orthography. These populate every manuscript and can arise for various reasons. Here are a few examples.

| Isa 6:3 | MT: | Holy, holy, holy |
| | 1QIsaᵃ | Holy, holy |

For whatever reason, the Qumran copy has only two instances of *holy* (this is not the only variant in Isa 6:3).[21] The absence of one element from the familiar threefold formula is supported by no other ancient copy of Isaiah.

| Gen 1:9 | MT/SP | Let the waters be gathered into one *place* (= מקום) |
| | 4QGenʰ¹ LXX | Let the waters be gathered into one *gathering* (= מקוה) |

In this instance, two Hebrew words looking almost alike were interchanged. The reading of MT/SP shows greater variation in word choice in the clause; the other reading involves using a noun associated with the same root as the verb (the root קוה) of the sentence.

| Isa 45:7 | MT: | I make weal [שלום] and create woe [רע] |
| | 1QIsaᵃ | I make good [טוב] and create woe [רע] |

21. See P. W. Flint and E. Ulrich, eds., *Qumran Cave 1: II, The Isaiah Scrolls* (2 vols.; DJD 32; Oxford: Clarendon, 2010), 2:125.

The cave 1 manuscript uses an antonym to contrast with רע, not the less directly opposed שלום.

Isa 40:12 MT:	measured the waters [מים]
1QIsaᵃ	measured the waters of the sea [מי ים]

The two readings differ only in the presence or absence of a second *yod*. Arguments could be mounted for the originality of either, though *sea* could be a more appropriate counterpart to the other elements of nature in the verse.[22]

Isolated Interpretive Insertions

Ulrich says of this category: "Learned scribes occasionally inserted into the text they were copying what they considered an appropriate piece of additional material."[23] In the Qumran period at least, scribes, while copying with diligence, still felt some freedom to take a more active role with regard to a scriptural text than simply transcribing it. One well-documented pattern in a series of scrolls is to blend or combine wording from parallel scriptural passages. For example, a person familiar with the Bible knows that the Ten Commandments are preserved in two places — Exodus 20 and Deuteronomy 5. In Exod 20:11 the reason for keeping sabbath is the model set by God in the first week of the world:

Exod 20:11 MT   For in six days the LORD made heaven and earth, the sea, and all that is in them, but rested the seventh day; therefore the LORD blessed the sabbath day and consecrated it.

Deut 5:15 motivates it with the Israelites' experience of slavery in Egypt and the Lord's deliverance of them from it:

Deut 5:15 MT   Remember that you were a slave in the land of Egypt, and the LORD your God brought you out

22. See the discussion by Z. Talshir, "Biblical Texts from the Judaean Desert," in Kister, ed., *The Qumran Scrolls and Their World*, 1:118-19 (Hebrew).

23. "The Jewish Scriptures," 111.

> from there with a mighty hand and an outstretched arm; therefore the LORD your God commanded you to keep the sabbath day.

Near the end of Deut 5:15, one of the Qumran copies (4QDeut[n]) has additional words compared to MT: ". . . to keep the sabbath day and to hallow it. For in six days the LORD made heaven and earth, the sea, and all that is in them and rested the seventh day; so the LORD blessed the sabbath day and hallowed it" (4:4-7). The words additional to the form in MT are from the parallel version in Exod 20:11. Combining material from parallel passages is a characteristic not only of some scriptural copies from Qumran but also of SP (and the 4QReworked Pentateuch manuscripts, the *Temple Scroll*, and other texts), although in Deut 5:15 SP does not add material from Exod 20:11.

Psalm 145: In MT, one verse is missing from the acrostic psalm: although each verse begins with a word starting with the successive letters of the Hebrew alphabet, there is none for the letter *nun*, which should have appeared between the *mem* sentence in v. 13 and the *samekh* sentence in v. 14. It is natural to think it was dropped from the text by scribal error, even if the mechanism for the omission is not obvious. At this place where MT lacks the *nun* verse, other witnesses have:

11QPs[a] LXX   Faithful is God [11QPs[a]]/the LORD [LXX] in all his words, and gracious in all his deeds.

The Hebrew word for "faithful" (נאמן) begins with *nun;* the two witnesses thus supply the missing verse. The *nun*-sentence was not secondarily stitched together from elsewhere in the Psalter as the expression figures only here. In this case one should remember that what looks to be a manifestly superior text is not necessarily the original reading, since the author of the poem could have been the one who carelessly omitted one of the necessary lines. In that case, someone would have come along later and made the face-saving addition.

New and Expanded Editions of Biblical Books

There are some cases where sizable and systematic variations separate the witnesses for scriptural books, including those from Qumran. Some examples include entire books; the best-known exhibit is Jeremiah.

The versions of the book of Jeremiah found in MT and in LXX are of much different lengths. MT Jeremiah is estimated to be some 13 percent longer than the Greek text; also, the two locate some units differently.[24] Among the fragmentary Hebrew copies of Jeremiah found at Qumran, two are similar to the longer readings of MT (4QJer[a,c]) and two align closely with the shorter readings of LXX (4QJer[b,d]). The shorter version is generally regarded as textually superior; support from the two Hebrew manuscripts (4QJer[b,d]) shows that the LXX translator(s) did not arbitrarily subtract large amounts of text from their Hebrew model but rather rendered a Hebrew copy with a much shorter text than the one now found in MT Jeremiah. Conversely, the other two copies show that the scribes in the tradition eventuating in MT also reproduced an early form of the text.

The only fragment surviving from 4QJer[b] happens to preserve a section that illustrates some shorter readings and a differing order of verses.

MT: Jer 10:3-11:

3For the customs of the peoples are false: a tree from the forest is cut down, and worked with an ax, by the hands of an artisan; 4people deck it with silver and gold; they fasten it with hammer and nails, so that it cannot move. 5Their idols are like scarecrows in a cucumber field, and they cannot speak; they have to be carried, for they cannot walk. Do not be afraid of them, for they cannot do evil, nor is it in them to do good.

6*There is none like you, O* LORD*; you are great, and your name is great in might.* 7*Who would not fear you, O King of the nations? For that is your due; among all the wise ones of the nations and in all their kingdoms there is none like you.* 8*They are both stupid and foolish; the instruction given by idols is no better than wood!*

9Beaten silver is brought from Tarshish, and gold from Uphaz. They are the work of the artisan and of the hands of the goldsmith; their clothing is blue and purple; they are all the product of skilled workers.

10*But the* LORD *is the true God; he is the living God and the ever-*

---

24. See Tov, *Textual Criticism of the Hebrew Bible,* 320-27. The largest difference in location involves the oracles against the nations that are chs. 46-51 in MT but are found after 25:13 in LXX. For a study of the MT and LXX forms of the book (written before most of the cave 4 Jeremiah copies appeared in print), see J. G. Janzen, *Studies in the Text of Jeremiah* (HSM 6; Cambridge, Mass.: Harvard University Press, 1973).

lasting King. At his wrath the earth quakes, and the nations cannot endure his indignation.

11Thus shall you say to them: The gods who did not make the heavens and the earth shall perish from the earth and from under the heavens.

The Greek version of the passage lacks vv. 6-8, 10 (the parts in italics above).

4QJer[b] preserves words from vv. 4, 9, 11 (with words from v. 5 restored in two places), in the Greek order: 4, 5a, 9, 5b. In the column, line 5 has words from v. 4 at the end, while line 6 has words from v. 9 at the end and line 7 has words from v. 11 at the end.

Line 5	and with g]old they fasten it with hammers	= v. 4
Line 6	]blue and purple	= v. 9
Line 7	]shall perish from the earth	= v. 11

The Hebrew fragment shows that the Greek translator(s) worked with a Hebrew text much shorter than the one in MT.

In general, one may say that manuscripts aligning frequently with the textual traditions embodied now in MT, LXX, and/or SP are found at Qumran, but these configurations do not exhaust the data or even represent it properly. As Emanuel Tov has written:

> If the tripartite division [that is, that there are texts aligning with MT or SP or LXX] is merely a matter of prejudice, attention should now be directed to the actual relation between the textual witnesses. The textual reality of the Qumran texts does not attest to three groups of textual witnesses, but rather to a textual multiplicity, relating to all of Palestine to such an extent that one can almost speak in terms of an unlimited number of texts.[25]

Some copies do not fall into any of the old, familiar categories — agreeing with either MT, SP, or LXX — and chart a different course textually. A copious number of textual options were available at the time, and indeed many of them are represented at the one site of Qumran. The data at hand

---

25. *Textual Criticism of the Hebrew Bible,* 161; he thinks, nevertheless, that a few groups of closely related texts can be detected (see, e.g., p. 163).

are limited, but there is no reason to surmise that Jewish experts were concerned about a measure of fluidity in the texts of scripural books until late in the first century C.E., when Josephus wrote a surprisingly strong statement about a fixed scriptural text (*Ag. Ap.* 1.38-42; see Chapter 3 below).

An End to Fluidity

Each of the texts found at the other sites, all of them a little later than the Qumran corpus, may fall into the pre-Masoretic category (though the books preserved at Masada are ones for which there were no variant literary editions),[26] perhaps suggesting that by the end of the first or beginning of the second century C.E. the textual plurality apparent in the Qumran scrolls had given way to a far greater uniformity. There may have been social and political reasons for this development, in that the people who happened to use and copy a certain type of text became the central or nearly the only element in society engaged in such activity after the destruction of the temple in 70 C.E. Tov comments: "It is not that M [= MT] triumphed over the other texts, but rather, that those who fostered it probably constituted the only organized group which survived the destruction of the Second Temple. Thus, after the first century CE a description of the transmission of the text of the Hebrew Bible amounts to an account of the history of M."[27]

CONCLUSIONS FROM THE EVIDENCE

After surveying the evidence, what conclusions may be drawn from it and which questions are suggested by it?

Several experts have crafted comprehensive theories to organize the data now accessible. It has been difficult for textual critics of the Hebrew Bible to move out from under the impress of the older three-text model — that provided by MT, SP, and LXX. Frank Moore Cross, following William Foxwell Albright, postulated three local varieties of Hebrew texts, each of which was represented by a familiar witness: SP was a prime witness to the

---

26. E. Ulrich, "Two Perspectives on Two Pentateuchal Manuscripts from Masada," in S. Paul et al., eds., *Emanuel: Studies in Hebrew Bible, Septuagint, and Dead Sea Scrolls in Honor of Emanuel Tov* (VTSup 94; Leiden: Brill, 2003), 461-64.

27. *Textual Criticism of the Hebrew Bible*, 195.

more expansive Palestinian form of the text for the books it includes, LXX to the Egyptian Hebrew text, and MT (apparently by default) to the Babylonian text.[28] By the time of the Qumran copies, these local texts were no longer isolated; all were found in the land of Israel — in fact, at the one small site of Qumran, so that each type could influence the others for good or ill.

Shemaryahu Talmon focused more on the role of different groups in the survival of the texts associated with them and the corresponding loss of many other kinds: Jews preserved MT, Samaritans continued to copy SP, and Christians transmitted LXX.[29] Emanuel Tov broadened the horizon somewhat, although he too has reckoned with the traditional witnesses in naming five categories of texts, though they are a strange combination in some respects. They are: Proto-Masoretic (or Proto-Rabbinic), in which category, on his reckoning, 47 percent of the copies from Qumran fall; Proto-Samaritan (6.5 percent); Close to the Hebrew Source of the LXX (3.3 percent); Non-Aligned texts (47 percent). He also speaks of a fifth category — texts copied in the Qumran practice (or spelling), though he does not give a percentage for them since they are included in the other four. An obvious criticism of Tov's percentages is that he has inflated the numbers for the MT-like category, placing in it any text that is equally close to MT and SP or LXX. Peter Flint calculates that "of the fifty-seven (47 percent) analyzable Qumran biblical scrolls that supposedly fall into this [proto-MT] category, only twenty-four . . . are strictly close to the traditional text, while the other thirty-three . . . are as close to the Masoretic Text and either the Samaritan Pentateuch or the Hebrew source of the Septuagint."[30] Ulrich has focused on the history of texts for

28. See, e.g., Cross's essay, "The Evolution of a Theory of Local Texts," in Cross and S. Talmon, eds., *Qumran and the History of the Biblical Text* (Cambridge, Mass.: Harvard University Press, 1975), 306-20.

29. For a summary of his approach, see Talmon's essay, "The Textual Study of the Bible — A New Outlook," in *Qumran and the History of the Biblical Text*, 321-400. In his lengthy study he proposed "that a major problem to be investigated with regard to the history of the Bible text is not so much the existence of a limited plurality of text-types, but rather the loss of other presumably more numerous textual traditions. Thus phrased, the issue of whether a single *Urtext* broke up into 'three distinct local families' in which subsequently and separately manuscript variants emerged, or whether conversely, primal traditions which varied among themselves to a limited degree progressively lost their lease on life and ultimately crystallized in a restricted number of *Gruppentexte* should be studied from a new angle" (327).

30. P. Flint, "The Biblical Scrolls and the Text of the Hebrew Bible/Old Testament," in J. VanderKam and Flint, *The Meaning of the Dead Sea Scrolls: Their Significance for*

individual books and thinks the periods in which they were composed and transmitted overlapped. In a number of cases, what he calls variant literary editions arose, with the newer sometimes but not always replacing the older.[31] One of the many strengths of his approach is that it is not as constrained as the others are by the older three-witness model.

NEW EVIDENCE AND THE TEXT-CRITICAL QUEST

Discovering what the biblical authors and editors actually wrote would seem to be a noble aim, one to which many have devoted great industry. It should be acknowledged, of course, that even the more recently accessible manuscript evidence is far removed in time from the earliest forms of the texts of scriptural books and sections, even if there is dispute aplenty about when the various compositions and sections of them were penned and arranged. If one follows those who think much of the Hebrew Bible reached its ultimate form in the Persian period, the Judean Desert manuscript finds take one back only to a point a few centuries later. That, of course, is much better than the situation confronting earlier scholars, but the chronological gap between the earliest written form(s) and the surviving manuscript evidence remains considerable. While that gap is a fact, it is also a fact that the student of the Hebrew Bible is, comparatively speaking, in a rather advantageous position. For example, the text of Plato's works, apart from some fragmentary second-third century C.E. papyri, is based on fifty-one manuscripts copied in the ninth century and later.[32]

To see how it is possible to do better than one could before although puzzles remain (with the Qumran evidence supplying some new ones), it is instructive to examine the passage that is perhaps the best-known textual variant in the Qumran scrolls — the longer reading preserved in

---

Understanding the Bible, Judaism, Jesus, and Christianity (San Francisco: HarperSan-Francisco, 2002), 146.

31. A number of Ulrich's essays on the subject appeared in his *The Dead Sea Scrolls and the Origins of the Bible* (SDSSRL; Grand Rapids: Eerdmans, 1999). For a recent statement of his theory, see "The Evolutionary Production and Transmission of the Scriptural Books," in S. Metso, H. Najman, and E. Schuller, eds., *The Dead Sea Scrolls: Transmission of Traditions and Production of Texts* (STDJ 92; Leiden: Brill, 2010), 209-25.

32. See G. Fine, ed., *The Oxford Handbook of Plato* (New York: Oxford University Press, 2008), 71; the oldest manuscript is dated to 895 C.E. (the very date of the oldest surviving witness of MT).

4QSam[a] at the transition from 1 Samuel 10 to 1 Samuel 11. Though it involves a longer stretch of text, it may be that a simple scribal error led to the omission of an entire paragraph that is found in 4QSam[a], a genuine copy of the books of Samuel. First the data will be presented followed by a look at plausible explanations for the available manuscript evidence.

For the passage in question, 1 Sam 10:27–11:1, there are four rather old configurations of the text that confront the reader and that must be considered in interpreting it. As those who have examined the passage have noted, the phrase at the end of the MT form of 1 Sam 10:27 — ויהי כמחריש — and the Hebrew expression presupposed by the LXX rendering of the beginning of 11:1 — ויהי כמו חדש — have sufficient look-alike qualities that, if they occurred in the same copy, could have caused textual mischief for a scribe who was not particularly alert. Here is how the witnesses handle the section (with the look-alike phrases in italics).

MT: 10:27 . . . They despised him [Saul] and brought him no present. *But he held his peace.* 11:1 Nahash the Ammonite went up. . . .

4QSam[a] (X frg. a 5-9): . . . They despised him and brought him no present. *blank*
[Now Na]hash, king of the Ammonites, had been grievously oppressing the Gadites and the Reubenites. He would gouge out the right [ey]e of e[ach] of them and would not grant [I]srael a [deliv]erer. No one was left of the Israelites ac[ross the Jordan who]se right eye Naha[sh, king of] the [A]mmonites, had not [go]uged out. B[u]t there were seven thousand men who [had escaped from] the Ammonites and had entered Jabesh-gilead.
About a month later, Nahash the Ammonite went up . . .[33]

LXX . . . They despised him and brought him no present. 11:1 *About a month later* Nahash the Ammonite went up. . . .

Josephus, *Ant.* 6.67-71: he seems to assume the ending of 10:27 as it is in 4QSam[a] and LXX (that is, without *But he held his peace*), followed by the statement *About a month later,* after which he offers the additional material in a form resembling but not identical to the

---

33. The translation of the section is from the NRSV; brackets have been inserted to show where there are gaps in the fragment.

extra paragraph in 4QSam[a]. He then resumes with 11:1 without repeating the introductory *About a month later.*

The textual situation may be clearer if the three key items are represented with letters, yielding the following diagram:

X = But he held his peace (ויהי כמחריש)
Y = the extra paragraph
Z = About a month later (ויהי כמו חדש)

The individual witnesses contain these elements:

MT: X
4QSam[a]: Y + Z
LXX: Z
Josephus: Z + Y

That is, no surviving text preserves all three items represented by the letters. Yet, if the look-alike readings X and Z and the additional paragraph were present in an earlier copy (one that is no longer extant) and X and Z were the triggers for the omissions that yielded the varied texts now available, one could say about the versions:

MT: the copyist whose work gave rise to the form of the text now represented in MT skipped from the end of X through Z, thus omitting Y and Z. This may not be a standard form of haplography, but it could have happened.
4QSam[a]: the copyist omitted X but transcribed Y and Z — a procedure that seems strange.
LXX: the copyist skipped X and Y and preserved only Z — a standard case of haplography.
Josephus: skipped X and placed Z before Y (that is, he changed the position of a date in the text, something that he does elsewhere).[34]

With identifiable mechanisms for haplography, it is reasonable to suppose, given the surviving readings, that omissions of different portions of text occurred. But this does not account for the form of the 4Q copy.

---

34. E. C. Ulrich, Jr., *The Qumran Text of Samuel and Josephus* (HSM 19; Missoula: Scholars, 1978), 168 (see 166-70 for his analysis of the text-critical issues).

Despite agreement between 4QSam[a] and Josephus in attesting additional material closely related in content and at the same spot, the two are not identical. The parallel section in Josephus is much longer and includes some items not present in the Qumran manuscript, such as the report about the military purpose served by King Nahash's grisly policy of gouging out the right eyes of Israelites across the Jordan. Yet, as Ulrich has shown, the elements found in the Qumran plus appear in Josephus's *Antiquities* and in the same order. There is one exception to the common order — Josephus places the "About a month later" statement before the plus, not after it as in 4QSam[a]. In the DJD edition of 4QSam[a], Cross wrote: "It is possible that the phrase ויהי כמו חדש occurred in a Hebrew text both there [i.e., where Josephus has it, before the plus] and in 11:1, thereby triggering the haplography of the whole paragraph. In any case, the ויהי כמחריש of M is best seen as a corruption of ויהי כמו חדש after the haplography."[35] If he is correct, MT would preserve only a misreading of one trigger for omission which it mistakenly attaches to the end of 10:27. None of the versions seems to offer the earliest form of the text, although, with the extant evidence, one can surmise how it may have read.

The most parsimonious explanation may be the one suggested by Cross: the "About a month later" phrase occurred on both sides of the plus. The text represented in LXX is easily explained as a result of haplography, from instance one to instance two of the phrase, with omission of the intervening material. The textual tradition now found in MT did the same but was further corrupted when ויהי כמו חדש was misread as/altered to ויהי כמחריש to fit the context. Josephus retained the first instance of the trigger phrase and the extra material, while he lacks the second instance of the phrase, possibly to avoid repetition of a date he had just mentioned. The most difficult textual witness to explain is 4QSam[a]. It lacks the first instance of the trigger but includes the extra material and the second instance.[36]

35. F. M. Cross, D. W. Parry, R. J. Saley, and E. Ulrich, eds., *Qumran Cave 4: XII, 1-2 Samuel* (DJD 17; Oxford: Clarendon, 2005), 66.

36. The passage as represented in the various witnesses has, of course, received extensive analysis, with various solutions proposed. See the lengthy bibliog. in DJD 17:1-2. A. Rofé has taken a different approach to the plus in 4QSam[a] and *Antiquities*: he judges it to be neither an original reading nor a textual variant but a midrash on points unclear in the passage and based on material located in other places in the scriptures. See, e.g., his essay, "The Acts of Nahash according to 4QSam[a]," *IEJ* 32 (1982): 129-33. Tov is among those who consider the longer form of the text in 4QSam[a] to be original; *Textual Criticism of the Hebrew Bible*, 342-44.

The Qumran copy itself shows a haplography within — but not the same as — the one under discussion. In it the words "About a month later Nahash the Ammonite went up and besieged Jabesh-" are written in a supralinear position, but by the scribe who recorded the text, not by another hand. The cause for omission of these words was the repeated name יבש.

Another kind of issue that has become more pressing with the availability of the scriptural copies from the Judean Desert is the distinction between textual and exegetical variants. The question arises especially in works that one would not classify as "biblical" manuscripts but in which scriptural texts are adduced in some form. It is a problem one encounters in dealing with the many citations and adaptations of scriptural texts in a work such as the book of *Jubilees*. The writer very frequently quotes material from Genesis or Exodus, at times whole lines, at other times just phrases.[37] The issue is whether differences in wording from, say, MT or LXX reflect readings of Genesis and Exodus manuscripts or whether they are due to the way in which the writer adapted the material to the new contexts in *Jubilees*. Which are textual variants in distinction from textual interpretations and modifications? A textual variant would be one that arises in the course of manuscript transmission; an interpretive variant would likely arise in a different way.

The issue becomes more complicated because, it seems, scribes felt it was within their rights to help the text along a little. Ulrich has defined what he calls "individual textual variants" (see the list above, where they are the second type) as ones differing from the parent text being copied and consisting of unintentional changes — "e.g., numerous types of errors, inadvertent substitution of *lectiones faciliores*, loss of letters, loss of one or more words through inattention or parablepsis" — and intentional ones — "clarifying insertions, scribal correction (whether correct or not), additional information, linguistic smoothing, euphemistic substitutions, literary flourishes, theological ideas."[38]

What Ulrich includes under his category "intentional variants" is an intriguing set of differences vis-à-vis the parent text — various kinds of changes such as "clarifying insertions." Some examples occur in the *Temple Scroll*. Aspects of the relationship between this lengthy composition and the

---

37. See J. C. VanderKam, *Textual and Historical Studies in the Book of Jubilees* (HSM 14; Missoula: Scholars, 1977), 103-205, for a listing and study of the material.

38. Ulrich, "The Jewish Scriptures," 111.

legal sections of the Pentateuch are well known: it often collects elements from all texts on a topic (e.g., a festival) and works them into the first mention of the subject in the scriptural text that is being treated.[39] But the relationship changes in the latter parts of the scroll — in the Deuteronomic Paraphrase, where Deuteronomy 12-23 serves as the base for cols. 53-58 and 60-62 and where the scroll adheres more closely to the base text. Regarding the *Temple Scroll* as a whole, Lawrence Schiffman has written: "It is clear that the author/redactor and his sources had before them *Vorlagen* of the canonical Torah, in its present shape, which demonstrated genuine textual variation when compared with the Masoretic Text (MT). To this textual base, the author(s) added their own interpretations and adaptations. One of the challenges of scholarship is to distinguish these layers."[40]

From the Deuteronomic Paraphrase Schiffman examined a series of readings in which its text agrees with LXX against MT and the reading has halakhic significance. These are good test cases for distinguishing textual from interpretive variants — for determining what the original wording of the text might have been.

Consider, for example, the variants in TS 54:19-55:1//Deut 13:7 (Eng. v. 6), where MT reads: "If anyone secretly entices you — even if it is your brother . . . or your mother's son. . . ." The enticement is to idolatry, and in this case, however close the relative or neighbor guilty of the offense may be, he is to be executed. Presumably those closest to the offending party are to be witnesses against him, something not allowed in other kinds of legal cases.

TS 54:19:	כי ישיתכה אחיכה בן אביכה או בן אמכה
MT Deut 13:7:	כי יסיתך אחיך בן אמך
LXX Deut 13:7:	ἐὰν δὲ παρακαλέσῃ σε ὁ ἀδελφός σου ἐκ πατρός σου ἢ ἐκ μητρός σου

An added bonus in this case is that 4QDeut[c] frgs. 22-23 line 1 reads the word אביך, suggesting it contained the longer reading, and SP also supports it. The longer reading specifies that both the brother who is the son of the mother and also the brother who is the son of the father are relatives

---

39. See, e.g., F. García Martínez, "Temple Scroll," in Schiffman and VanderKam, eds., *EDSS*, 2:927-33.

40. L. H. Schiffman, "The Septuagint and the Temple Scroll: Shared 'Halakhic' Variants," in G. J. Brooke and B. Lindars, eds., *Septuagint, Scrolls and Cognate Writings* (SBLSCS 33; Atlanta: Scholars, 1992), 278; repr. in *The Courtyards of the House of the Lord: Studies on the Temple Scroll* (STDJ 75; Leiden: Brill, 2008), 86.

to whom the law applies. Perhaps one would have inferred this from the shorter formulation, but the longer reading makes the point explicit.

In such an instance it is easy to formulate a case that either reading could be original. In favor of the shorter one in MT, one could maintain that the less specific reading is likely to be earlier and the longer one is an attempt to prevent misunderstandings. In favor of the longer reading one could argue that the shorter reading is haplographic: a scribe's eye jumped from the first instance of the word בן to the second and thus skipped over the intervening words. Both readings would qualify as textual variants because they appear in copies of Deuteronomy itself, not only in the *Temple Scroll*.[41] Schiffman does not decide which reading is original but simply notes that the compiler of the Deuteronomic Paraphrase in 11QT found the reading in his scriptural *Vorlage*. It may be that MT is defective in this place.

The ancient "biblical" scrolls (or, rather, in almost all cases, fragments) from the Qumran caves reveal much about the transmission of the scriptural texts in the later Second Temple period. For one, they place before the reader's eyes many examples of how Jewish scribes transmitted texts that later became constituents of the Hebrew Bible; they also document numerous minor differences between copies, the small sorts of variants that beset any work and that are of interest primarily to text critics. In some cases, however, there is evidence for larger variation between copies, as with the manuscripts of Jeremiah. No discussion in the scrolls themselves regarding variant wordings in different copies of scriptural books has been found, but the modern experts who work on these texts agree that the last centuries B.C.E. and the first century C.E. were times of considerable fluidity in the wording of scriptural texts.

An appropriate way in which to end the chapter is with a passage found in *Pesher Habakkuk*. The commentary on the prophetic book, like other texts in this category, quotes a passage and then offers an interpretation of it. Sometimes, in the comment, the expositor demonstrates that he is aware of a wording of the text at variance with the one he had just quoted. His practice was to use both readings, as though it was a bonus to have more text on which to comment. MT Hab 2:16 can be translated as:

You will be sated with contempt instead of glory.
Drink, you yourself, and be uncircumcised [והערל].

41. The status attributed to the *Temple Scroll* by those who copied and used it is a debated point. See García Martínez, "Temple Scroll," 930.

The text of Hab 2:16 quoted in *Pesher Habakkuk* before the interpretation reads:

> You will be sated with contempt instead of glory.
> Drink, you yourself, and stagger [והרעל]. (11:8-9)

Then, in the commentary to the passage the writer speaks about being uncircumcised (11:13), the reading found in MT, and later mentions the cup of the Lord's wrath — reflecting the reading in his own scriptural text.[42] In this case the expositor exploited the two readings; he did not lament their existence. Those who, like the commentator, could read works such as Habakkuk seem to have been comfortable with a level of textual variation in the sacred books, much as readers of the English Bible cope well with the numerous divergent translations available today.

There are many other issues that arise in connection with the so-called "biblical" scrolls from Qumran. To this point there has been no discussion of whether there was a canon of scripture, a Bible, at the time of the scrolls, and, if so, which works belonged in it. These and related matters are the subject of the third chapter. The second is devoted to scriptural interpretation in the scrolls.

---

42. W. H. Brownlee noted and discussed the two readings in *The Text of Habakkuk in the Ancient Commentary from Qumran* (JBLMS 11; Philadelphia: SBL, 1959), 76-78; on 118-23 he list this and four other examples of the phenomenon that he calls "dual readings."

CHAPTER 2

Commentary on Older Scriptures in the Scrolls

A s seen in the previous chapter, an examination of the scriptural texts among the Dead Sea Scrolls soon leads one to the border — a porous one — between textual variation and textual interpretation. When are they the differences that happen naturally in the process of handcopying and when are they the results of scribes' efforts to "improve" the text being copied? The present chapter will examine more explicit aspects of scriptural interpretation in the scrolls — cases in which the writers overtly explain the meaning of an older text or derive support from it. At the time when the communities associated with the scrolls were active, the books known today as the components of the Hebrew Bible/Protestant Old Testament were, with one exception (Daniel), already old. Despite their age, or perhaps partly because of it,[1] many of these books were thought by the writers to have extraordinary value for present concerns, a value so remarkable that they were believed to be authoritative in the contemporary situation — a fundamental assumption that bears repeating and whose importance can hardly be over-emphasized.

When one thinks of scriptural interpretation among the scrolls, the first type to spring to mind is probably *pesher* exposition. The texts called *pesharim* are explicit commentaries on older texts, in that they cite an ancient text and then offer explanations of it. The interpretation is at times

---

1. M. Haran makes the point at some length in the first volume of *The Biblical Collection: Its Consolidation to the End of the Second Temple Times and Changes of Form to the End of the Middle Ages* (3 vols.; Jerusalem: Bialik Institute and Magnes, 1996-2008) (Hebrew); see, e.g., 1:50-54.

physically separated from the text cited by a short blank space. Some aspects of these fascinating works are treated below, but at this point it should be remembered that scriptural commentary — commentary on older, authoritative works — is a far more widely-attested phenomenon in the Qumran texts than merely in the *pesharim*. The Qumran scrolls are a scripturally-saturated literature, whether through explicit citation, paraphrase, allusion, or commentary.[2] The writers possessed a thorough knowledge of the older texts and displayed an eagerness to use them in their own compositions in ways that served a variety of ends. Their knowledge of the older works is evident in their legal texts, rules, hymnic and liturgical works, wisdom compositions, narratives, rewritten scripture, and more.

Scriptural interpretation seems to have been a thriving cottage industry among the authors. Perhaps this was the case for elites in all the Jewish groups at the time (Josephus says as much for the Pharisees: they "are considered the most accurate interpreters of the laws"; *J.W.* 2.102 [LCL, trans. Thackeray]), but an abundance of actual examples fills the Qumran texts. The scrolls themselves demonstrate that scriptural interpretation was a constant exercise in the community. In a familiar passage, the *Rule of the Community* (the *Serekh*) prescribes: "And where the ten are, there shall never lack a man among them who shall study the Law continually, day and night, concerning the right conduct of a man with his companion. And the Congregation shall watch in community for a third of every night of the year, to read the Book and to study the Law and to bless together" (1QS 6:6-8).[3] Earlier in the same text there is a broader formulation in which the instructor of the community is charged with the responsibility of teaching members in such a way "that they may seek God with a whole heart and soul, and do what is good and right before Him as He commanded by the hand of Moses and all His servants the Prophets" (1QS 1:1-3).

Enthusiastic and persistent study of scriptures is evident in sectarian texts as well as in others that may reflect the views of the wider group of which the Qumran community was a part — the group called Essenes in Greek and Latin sources. Josephus says of the Essenes that they "apply themselves with extraordinary zeal to the study of the works of the an-

2. For general comments on interpretation, see M. Bernstein, "Interpretation of Scriptures," in *EDSS*, 1:376-83; J. G. Campbell, *The Exegetical Texts* (CQS 4; London: T. & T. Clark, 2004), esp. 20-32, 100-10.

3. Translations of the scrolls are from G. Vermes, *The Complete Dead Sea Scrolls in English* (New York: Penguin, 1997).

cients" (*J.W.* 2:136), although he adds in the passage that they choose especially ones useful to body and soul and mentions subjects such as "the healing of diseases, the roots offering protection and the properties of stone." Elsewhere he remarks that "[t]here are some among them who, trained as they are in the study of the holy books and the different sorts of purifications, and the sayings of the prophets, become expert in foreseeing the future: they are rarely deceived in their predictions" (*J.W.* 2.159). Philo augments the evidence by observing that the Essenes "work at ethics with extreme care, constantly utilizing the ancestral laws, laws which no human mind could have conceived without divine inspiration" (*Good Person* 80).[4] These passages emphasize interpretation of the law/laws and of the prophecies.

Philo adds in the same place:

> They continually instruct themselves in these laws, but especially every seventh day; for the seventh day is thought holy. On that day they abstain from other work and proceed to the holy places called synagogues, where they sit in appointed places, according to their age, the young men below the old, attentive and well-behaved. One of them then takes up the books and reads, and another from among the more learned steps forward and explains whatever is not easy to understand in these books. Most of the time, and in accordance with an ancient method of inquiry, instruction is given them by means of symbols. (*Good Person* 81-82)

Possibly some of the commentary literature originated in such settings.

Not only were the writers in this tradition heavily invested in scriptural interpretation; they were also skillful at it (in their historical context), as the surviving examples attest. Ancient scriptural interpretation often produced results that sound strange today, in the sense that they often clash with ones fashioned by modern experts. Presumably, modern scholarly interpretations would have sounded strange to ancient readers. But the earlier students of the text, besides enjoying a greater proximity to and feel for scriptural language, were adept practitioners of exegetical procedures that were acceptable to them and, in most cases, to their contemporaries. There is no need to attribute all of the exegetical insights embedded

---

4. The translations of Philo are from M. D. Goodman in G. Vermes and Goodman, eds., *The Essenes: According to the Classical Sources* (Sheffield: JSOT, 1989).

in the Qumran texts to the ingenuity of the scrolls communities; they stood in a centuries-long tradition of exposition and no doubt drew frequently upon it. The scrolls provide examples indicating the sorts of methods and techniques for interpretation that were used at the time and the fund of expository materials available — whatever form that deposit might have taken. They exhibit the efforts of learned, pious readers who were trying to cope with the issues with which the texts *and* their circumstances confronted them and to do so according to the hermeneutical principles that had been developed by their time and were appropriate for the task at hand.[5] No one seems to have thought of ideas such as sources within texts, various editions or redactions of them, and similar hypotheses. They solved problems within a different system than the ones employed by modern scholars of the Bible.

OLDER EXAMPLES OF INTERPRETATION

In the Hebrew Bible

There are fine examples of scriptural interpretation within the Hebrew Bible itself, and many of them are familiar. On a large scale, the books of Chronicles reinterpret Samuel-Kings (and more), while the various legal sections in the Pentateuch are often understood to be, at least in part, representations of older law codes (e.g., Deuteronomy for the Covenant Code [Exod 20:22–23:33]), and later sections of Isaiah contain reflections upon older ones. Famous examples of explicit scriptural citations and applications are the quotation from Mic 3:12 in Jer 26:18 (where the precedent in Micah for threatening destruction of the temple perhaps saves Jeremiah's life) and Daniel's use of Jeremiah's seventy-year prophecy in the ninth chapter of his book.

In the case of Daniel 9, one can observe an expositor who was working not too long before the Qumran period and operating in a way that would

---

5. J. L. Kugel writes of four assumptions adopted by ancient Jewish interpreters: (1) "the Bible is a fundamentally cryptic document"; (2) "Scripture constitutes one great Book of Instruction, and as such is a fundamentally *relevant* text"; (3) "Scripture is perfect and perfectly harmonious"; and (4) "all of Scripture is somehow divinely sanctioned, of divine provenance, or divinely inspired"; *Traditions of the Bible: A Guide to the Bible As It Was at the Start of the Common Era* (Cambridge, Mass.: Harvard University Press, 1998), 14-19.

have appealed to the exegetes whose work survives in the Qumran scrolls. There Daniel is pictured as struggling to understand a text (or texts) that troubled him: the seventy years predicted by the Lord through Jeremiah had passed without the improved situation he foresaw materializing. During the first year of Darius the Mede, who now ruled the realm of the Chaldeans, "I, Daniel, perceived in the books[6] the number of years that, according to the word of the LORD to the prophet Jeremiah, must be fulfilled for the devastation of Jerusalem, namely, seventy years" (Dan 9:2). There was much for him to ponder in the prophetic writings. Jeremiah had proclaimed, "[t]his whole land shall become a ruin and a waste, and these nations shall serve the king of Babylon seventy years. Then after seventy years are completed, I will punish the king of Babylon and that nation, the land of the Chaldeans, says the LORD, making the land an everlasting waste" (Jer 25:11-12). And in chapter 29 the prophet wrote to the first wave of exiles (those from the deportation of 598 B.C.E.) that they were to settle in the foreign land where they found themselves: "For thus says the LORD: Only when Babylon's seventy years are completed will I visit you and I will fulfill to you my promise and bring you back to this place" (29:10). With the Chaldeans now defeated and under the control of Darius, the time span Jeremiah envisaged for Jerusalem's devastation should have run its course and the exiles should have returned, but the eagerly anticipated event had not occurred.

For the present purposes, it is important to observe Daniel's reaction: he is troubled, but he does not conclude that Jeremiah must therefore have been wrong and that the copy of his prophecies should be trashed. He assumes the prophet was correct, as well he might since, according to the wording of the text, Jeremiah was quoting the Lord himself in his prediction. Nor does Daniel suggest that Jeremiah was, like his opponent Hananiah (see Jeremiah 28), a fraud merely claiming to speak in the deity's name. Daniel believes that he — Daniel — was the one who had the problem, that is, *he* had not yet grasped the true meaning of the authentic prophetic message.

---

6. J. A. Montgomery (*A Critical and Exegetical Commentary on the Book of Daniel* [ICC; Edinburgh: Clark, 1927], 360) maintained that the plural "books" designates "the Canon of the Prophets, which had already obtained authoritative value. The term is the one Biblical ref. to the Canon of the Prophets." J. J. Collins (*Daniel: A Commentary on the Book of Daniel* [Hermeneia; Minneapolis: Fortress, 1993], 348) agrees that the books of the prophets are meant, but properly adds that one should not speak of the prophetic collection as closed or canonized at this period.

The interpretive solution at which Daniel, under Gabriel's guidance, arrives is that Jeremiah's years are to be understood as weeks of years, each year meaning seven years. The notion of a week of years is employed in several works from approximately the time of the book of Daniel: the Apocalypse of Weeks (*1 En.* 93:1-10; 91:11-17), the book of *Jubilees,* and several Qumran texts.[7] One could easily dismiss Gabriel's verdict as a desperate solution of the sort adopted later by millenarian groups whose analysis of the course of history and the timing of the end proved inaccurate. But, to Gabriel's credit, he had scriptural support for his reading. By appealing to the concept of a week of years, he points the reader to Leviticus 25 (vv. 1-7; the phrase "weeks/sabbaths of years" occurs in v. 8) and the weighty chapter 26 that follows.[8] There the Lord threatens that if Israel does not obey him and observe his commandments, "I will set my face against you, and you shall be struck down by your enemies; your foes shall rule over you, and you shall flee though no one pursues you. And if in spite of this you will not obey me, I will continue to punish you sevenfold for your sins" (26:17-18; see also vv. 21, 24, 28; the result will be that the land will enjoy its Sabbath years, vv. 34-35). Daniel perceived that the divine response to Israel's disobedience was taking the form mentioned in Leviticus 26 — sevenfold punishment. If the original time of punishment was 70 years, the continued sin of Israel entailed that the sevenfold clause would take effect. Thus, the 70 years became seventy weeks of years or 490 years, just as Leviticus 26 said it would. Here a pentateuchal passage clarifies a prophetic puzzle.

Older Literature Outside the Hebrew Bible

Another source illustrating for the Qumran exegetes ways in which one could interpret earlier scriptures was older literature such as the booklets

---

7. For a brief survey of these texts, see J. C. VanderKam, *Calendars in the Dead Sea Scrolls: Measuring Time* (London: Routledge, 1998), 93-109; "Sabbatical Chronologies in the Dead Sea Scrolls and Related Literature," in T. H. Lim, ed., *The Dead Sea Scrolls in Their Historical Context* (Edinburgh: T. & T. Clark, 2000), 159-78. For a more detailed study, see J. S. Bergsma, *The Jubilee from Leviticus to Qumran: A History of Interpretation* (VTSup 115; Leiden: Brill, 2007), 233-94.

8. Experts have often noted that Gabriel's interpretation draws upon Leviticus 25–26. For some recent examples, see M. Fishbane, *Biblical Interpretation in Ancient Israel* (Oxford: Clarendon, 1985), 479-85 (where he also treats 2 Chr 36:19-21 and Isa 61:1); Collins, *Daniel,* 352-53; Bergsma, *The Jubilee from Leviticus to Qumran,* 214-25.

of *Enoch,* the *Aramaic Levi,* and the book of *Jubilees.* Numerous copies of these works were found in the caves around Khirbet Qumran,[9] and they seem to have enjoyed a certain popularity and even authority in the communities of the scrolls. They too, in their own ways, exemplify the robust occupation with more ancient literature that characterized Jewish writers in the period; they also illustrate exegetical procedures utilized later by the covenanters of the sectarian works found at Qumran.

The first part of the collection known today as *1 Enoch,* chapters 1-36 or the Book of the Watchers, furnishes the earliest examples of the ways in which some understood the challenging words in Gen 6:1-4 about the sons of God who married the daughters of men. The familiar variations on the angel story (understanding "sons of God" to mean "angels") found especially in *1 Enoch* 6–11 contain not only explanations of the Genesis passage but also ideas that address more profound problems such as the nature of evil and the divine justification for sending the flood.[10] This part of the book is rich with other interpretive passages such as the throne vision in chapter 14 or the picture of paradise in chapter 32, to name only two examples.[11]

Further instances surface in the Book of the Luminaries or the Astronomical Book (*1 Enoch* 72–82), a work represented at Qumran in four copies (4Q208-11). The composition can strike the reader as virtually devoid of contact with the Hebrew scriptures apart from its association with Enoch.[12] Yet, it is evident that Gen 1:14-19, the paragraph devoted to cre-

---

9. The copies of the different parts of *Enoch* are 4Q201-2, 204-12; the copies of *Aramaic Levi* are 1Q21, 4Q213, 213a, 213b, 214, 214a, 214b; and those of *Jubilees* are 1Q17-18, 2Q19-20; 3Q5; 4Q176 (frgs. 19-20), 216, 218-24, and 11Q12. For more on them, see Chapter 4 below.

10. There have been many studies of these chapters, with the most impressive one still being D. Dimant's dissertation, "The 'Fallen Angels' in the Dead Sea Scrolls and in the Apocryphal and Pseudepigraphic Books Related to Them" (Hebrew University, 1974) (Hebrew). For a summary, see J. C. VanderKam, *Enoch and the Growth of an Apocalyptic Tradition* (CBQMS 16; Washington: Catholic Biblical Association of America, 1984), 123-29; *Enoch: A Man for All Generations* (Columbia: University of South Carolina Press, 1995), 31-42. On the larger topic, cf. D. R. Jackson, *Enochic Judaism: Three Defining Paradigm Exemplars* (LSTS 49; London: T. & T. Clark, 2004).

11. Thorough discussions of these passages are available in G. W. E. Nickelsburg, *1 Enoch 1: A Commentary on the Book of 1 Enoch, Chapters 1–36; 81–108* (Hermeneia; Minneapolis: Fortress, 2001).

12. For the following section, see the fuller analysis in J. C. VanderKam, "Scripture in the Astronomical Book of Enoch," in E. G. Chazon, D. Satran, and R. A. Clements, eds., *Things Revealed: Studies in Early Jewish and Christian Literature in Honor of Michael E. Stone* (JSJSup 89; Leiden: Brill, 2004), 89-103.

ation of the sun, moon, and stars on the fourth day, has left its imprint on the Book of the Luminaries in several places. In Gen 1:16 the Priestly writer reports that "God made the two great lights — the greater light to rule the day and the lesser light to rule the night — and the stars." He never refers to the two great lights by name; their identity as sun and moon must be inferred from the domains they rule. *1 Enoch* 78:3 refers to "the two great luminaries," while 72:4, 35, 36 call the sun "the great luminary" and 73:1 describes the moon as "the smaller luminary."

Adopting the same phrases to describe the sun and moon is one modest indication that the writer of the Book of the Luminaries knew and borrowed from Gen 1:16, but there is additional evidence that he placed the section under contribution. In fact, one of his exegetical accomplishments is to offer a solution to a problem in Gen 1:16, a difficulty sensed and variously solved already in antiquity. In Gen 1:16 the writer says that both the sun and the moon are great/large lights, but later in the very same verse he calls the sun the greater and the moon the smaller light. A discerning reader might ask how the moon can be both great and small (see also *b. Ḥul.* 60b; *Gen. Rab.* 6.3; *Pirqe R. El.* 4; *Tg. Ps.-J.* Gen 1:16; *3 Bar.* 9:6-7). To solve the puzzle, the writer of the Enochic booklet appealed to Isa 30:26, a difficult verse that talks about the relation between sun and moon and may do so in connection with the week of creation. There, as the prophet speaks of future divine favors, he writes: "Moreover the light of the moon will be like the light of the sun, and the light of the sun will be sevenfold like the light of seven days, on the day when the LORD binds up the injuries of his people, and heals the wounds inflicted by his blow." The passage is adduced in several other ancient sources as providing a clue for solving the problem posed by Gen 1:16. That is, the verse from Isaiah equates the light of the sun and moon in some sense, but it adds that the sun's illumination will be sevenfold.

The Book of the Luminaries borrows some of these expressions to clarify the relations between the sun and moon.

72:37: "its [the sun's] light is seven times brighter than that of the moon"

73:3: "when its [the moon's] light is evenly distributed (over its surface), it is one-seventh the light of the sun."[13]

---

13. The translations are by J. C. VanderKam in G. W. E. Nickelsburg and VanderKam, *1 Enoch: A New Translation* (Minneapolis: Fortress, 2004).

In this book that contains the words of the seventh patriarch, all relations between sun and moon are expressed by factors of seven (see 73:5-8; 74:3; 78:6-8, 11; 4Q209 7 ii-iii; 4Q210 1 iii 6). The principle is valid for the brightness of both and for the times the moon is visible and the percentage of its surface that is illuminated. The fractions in the Aramaic fragments from Qumran cave 4 are sevenths and halves of sevenths, in the Ethiopic text sevenths and fourteenths.[14] Note the clear statement in 78:4: "In the disc of the sun there are seven parts of light added to it beyond what the moon has; a specific amount is placed (in the moon) until the seventh part of the sun passes over." Enoch, then, combines a passage from the Torah with one from the Prophets to answer an exegetical question. The solution offered is that where Genesis says the sun is the greater and the moon the lesser light, it is referring to their brightness; when Genesis says they are both great luminaries, it is talking about their size — a common inference in antiquity, since, to the naked eye, the two biggest lights in the sky appear similar in size.

The book of *Jubilees,* extremely well attested among the Qumran manuscripts (fourteen copies), is a long interpretation of Genesis 1– Exodus 24 that takes the form of rewriting or re-presenting the stories in them. It is now classified as a prime example of the category *Rewritten Bible or Rewritten Scripture,*[15] and as the writer re-presents Genesis-Exodus

---

14. The booklet, like other parts of *1 Enoch,* was translated from Aramaic into Greek and from Greek into Ethiopic. The Ethiopic version is the only one in which the complete text has survived.

15. G. Vermes coined the term *Rewritten Bible* as a generic classification for works such as *Jubilees; Scripture and Tradition in Judaism: Haggadic Studies* (2nd rev. ed.; StPB 4; Leiden: Brill, 1973; 1st ed. 1961). Part II of the book is entitled "Rewritten Bible" and deals with developments of the Abraham stories. Vermes writes after studying what the Book of Yashar says about the patriarch: "Finally, this examination of the Yashar story fully illustrates what is meant by the term 'rewritten Bible'. In order to anticipate questions, and to solve problems in advance, the midrashist inserts haggadic development into the biblical narrative — an exegetical process which is probably as ancient as scriptural interpretation itself. The Palestinian Targum and Jewish Antiquities, Ps.-Philo and Jubilees, and the recently discovered 'Genesis Apocryphon' . . . , each in their own way show how the Bible was rewritten about a millennium before the redaction of Sefer ha-Yashar" (95). For later works such as the Book of Yashar, "rewritten Bible" is appropriate; for earlier ones like *Jubilees,* composed at a time when there was no Bible in the sense of a closed canon, a more neutral expression such as "rewritten scripture" is appropriate. For the category and debate about it, see D. K. Falk, *The Parabiblical Texts: Strategies for Extending the Scriptures among the Dead Sea Scrolls* (CQS 8; LSTS 63; London: T. & T. Clark, 2007), 1-25.

he furnishes some wonderful examples of careful textual work. One large-scale instance is the chronology — a period of fifty Jubilees (each consisting of forty-nine years) that measures from creation until the entry into the land. The author knew from Leviticus 25 that in the Jubilee Year — the fiftieth year — each Hebrew slave was to be freed and each person was to regain possession of his ancestral property. The writer of *Jubilees* transposed the law of the Jubilee Year from an individual to a national level: early in the fiftieth Jubilee period of his chronology the Israelites were freed from Egyptian slavery (the year of the world 2410) and forty years later (2450) — still within the fiftieth Jubilee — were to enter the land long ago given to them but now improperly occupied by others, the land of Canaan.[16]

It appears that the author also engaged in some very minute exegesis. An example is his claim that the Sinai covenant was made in the third month, on the fifteenth day — his date for the Festival of Weeks, the festival that he associates with the making and renewal of the covenant. In fact, he dates scriptural covenants with Abra(ha)m (Genesis 15 and 17) to the same date, the middle of the third month (that the 15th is the middle of a 31-day month is in itself problematic and has caused some discussion).[17] It is reasonable to think that he read the puzzling statement in Exod 19:1 in such a way that it supported his point about the date for the festival. The scriptural text says literally: "In the third month after the Israelites had gone out of the land of Egypt, on that very day [ביום הזה], they came into the wilderness of Sinai." The expression "on that very day" might puzzle an attentive reader since the text (despite the NRSV translation: "On the third new moon") had not specified a particular day to this point. Some day in the third month is under consideration, but Exod 19:1 does not say which one and yet refers to it as "that very day." After the notice about the Israelites' arrival in the Sinai wilderness, one reads that the Lord ordered them to be prepared for the third day when he would appear — when the covenant would be made (see vv. 11, 15, 16). It seems that the author took the word "that" (הזה) and read it as a number, since letters also represented numbers. The numerical value of the two letters adds up to 12 (ז = 7, ה = 5), so he concluded that the Israelites entered the wilderness of Sinai and thus

---

16. J. C. VanderKam, "Studies in the Chronology of the Book of Jubilees," in *From Revelation to Canon: Studies in the Hebrew Bible and Second Temple Literature* (JSJSup 62; Leiden: Brill, 2000), 522-44.

17. L. Ravid, "The Book of Jubilees and Its Calendar — A Reexamination," *DSD* 10 (2003): 371-94.

came to the mountain on the *twelfth* day of the third month. Three days later (see Exod 19:11, 15, 16), that is, on the fifteenth (the Festival of Weeks), the Lord concluded the covenant with Israel. *Jubilees* itself was revealed beginning on 3/16, according to chapter 1.[18]

The author of *Jubilees* was heir to a complicated tradition regarding the patriarch Levi. The work called the *Aramaic Levi Document* (why the editors have placed the word *Document* in the title is difficult to understand), which is also well attested at Qumran (1Q21, 4Q213, 213a, 213b, 214, 214a, 214b)[19] and seems to have antedated *Jubilees*,[20] contains material that takes the modest, not to say negative, character Levi of Genesis and gives him a thorough makeover such that he becomes a fitting first high priest, one who received visions and a divine call to his office. *Jubilees* amplifies and reworks that tradition, which blends the Genesis references to Levi — including his and his brother Simeon's slaughter of the Shechemites in chapter 34 — with those from elsewhere, such as Mal 2:4-7, into an altogether positive portrait of the ancestor of the priests and Levites.[21] He also managed to glide over Jacob's words critical of Levi in Gen 49:5-7 (in fact, he largely omits Jacob's "blessing" of his sons).[22]

SCRIPTURAL INTERPRETATION IN THE SCROLLS

The people of Qumran and their Essene colleagues living in other places could, therefore, turn to the compositions now in the Hebrew Bible and to

---

18. For a more extended defense of this reading, see J. C. VanderKam, "Studies on the Prologue and *Jubilees* 1," in R. A. Argall, B. A. Bow, and R. A. Werline, eds., *For a Later Generation: The Transformation of Tradition in Israel, Early Judaism and Early Christianity* (Harrisburg: Trinity Press International, 2000), 266-79.

19. For the textual evidence from Qumran and elsewhere and discussions of it, see J. C. Greenfield, M. E. Stone, and E. Eshel, *The Aramaic Levi Document: Edition, Translation, Commentary* (SVTP 19; Leiden: Brill, 2004); and H. Drawnel, *An Aramaic Wisdom Text from Qumran: A New Interpretation of the Levi Document* (JSJSup 86; Leiden: Brill, 2004).

20. J. Kugel, however, maintains that *Jubilees* is the earlier text; "Levi's Elevation to the Priesthood in Second Temple Writings," *HTR* 86 (1993): 1-64.

21. For the Levi traditions, see R. A. Kugler, *From Patriarch to Priest: The Levi-Priestly Tradition from* Aramaic Levi *to* Testament of Levi (SBLEJL 9; Atlanta: Scholars, 1996).

22. See VanderKam, "*Jubilees'* Exegetical Creation of Levi the Priest," *RevQ* 17/65-68 (1996): 359-73.

other earlier literature such as the Enoch booklets, *Aramaic Levi*, and *Jubilees* as sources for and examples of how to read older, meaningful texts. All of these works are represented in their depository of scrolls. The covenanters added to the older models their own exegesis of many of these works.

Continuous *Pesharim*

In the sectarian literature, a prominent style of interpretation is *pesher* exegesis of the continuous kind.[23] This type of running commentary, at times verse-by-verse, was unknown in this form prior to the discovery of the *Commentary on Habakkuk* in cave 1. The word *pesher* is a scriptural term. One use of it is in Eccl 8:1: "Who is like the wise man? And who knows the *interpretation* of a thing?" The root is more widely attested in the Aramaic portions of the book of Daniel, where both the verb (5:12, 16) and noun (2:4-7; 4:3, 15, 16 [Eng. 6, 8, 19]; 5:12, 15, 16, 26; 7:16) are employed in contexts dealing with the interpretation of dreams, visions, and a puzzling inscription. The emphasis appears to lie on explicating something unclear.[24] There is a measure of overlap with the world of divination in this kind of exposition. It is as if the pesherist, like the diviner, is called upon to decode a mysterious communication from the divine realm — in this case an ancient scriptural text. There is a similar verb פתר in Hebrew, also meaning "to interpret," which figures a number of times in the Joseph stories, in verses where he decodes dreams (Gen 40:8, 16, 22; 41:8, 12, 13, 15; cf. the noun פתרון found in the Joseph stories).

There have been many attempts to describe what is involved in the Qumran works marked by successive, ordered instances of citation plus explanation. When the only example available was *Pesher Habakkuk*, Karl Elliger wrote the oft-cited formulation of the presuppositions underlying

23. For the distinction between continuous and thematic *pesharim*, see J. Carmignac, "Le Document de Qumrân sur Melkisédeq," *RevQ* 7/27 (1969-1971): 343-78. In addition to these two kinds of texts, there are also isolated examples of *pesher* in works that are otherwise not *pesharim*, such as the *Damascus Document*.

24. See the analysis of the terms in M. P. Horgan, *Pesharim: Qumran Interpretations of Biblical Books* (CBQMS 8; Washington: Catholic Biblical Association of America, 1979), 230-37; for the genre, see G. J. Brooke, "Qumran Pesher: Towards the Redefinition of a Genre," *RevQ* 10/40 (1981): 483-503; and T. H. Lim, *Pesharim* (CQS 3; London: Sheffield Academic, 2002), 44-53.

such exegesis: "1. Prophetische Verkündigung hat zum Inhalt das Ende, und 2. Die Gegenwart ist die Endzeit."[25] These traits are indeed in evidence in *Pesher Habakkuk,* where the interpreter consistently links the seventh-sixth centuries B.C.E. prophecies about the Chaldeans and Judeans to conditions and people of his time, a time when the divine judgment of the wicked and rescue of the righteous were anxiously anticipated. But lying behind even these presuppositions is the assumption that the ancient prophecy was valuable, true, worth studying, authoritative, authentic. In addition, the interpreter assumes that he has the correct reading, perhaps one traceable to the Teacher of Righteousness himself, if that is the meaning of the familiar words with which 1QpHab 7:4-5 interprets the end of Hab 2:2 ("so that with ease someone can read it"): "interpreted this concerns the Teacher of Righteousness, to whom God made known all the mysteries of the words of His servants the Prophets." If so, the *pesharim* are instances of inspired text joined with revealed interpretation — a formidable combination indeed. The method of *pesher* interpretation fits comfortably in a theology asserting that God had determined what would happen from the beginning; there was no problem, then, with his knowing events a few centuries before they were to occur and encoding them in prophetic oracles. The expositors also believed that God had embedded in the prophetic scriptures information about highly significant events — ones having to do with the decisive turning point in history, that is, the latter days, which happened to be their days. One had to know how to spot the clues to unlock their mysteries.[26]

Pesher exegesis as exemplified in the Qumran scrolls can impress one as arbitrary, but — whatever the inferences drawn by practitioners of it — there is no doubt the expositor(s) examined the details of the base text. So, for example, it is clear that where the author of *Pesher Habakkuk* finds the Wicked Priest adumbrated in the prophetic text he has paid close attention to the tenses of the verbs the prophet used in connection with the evil person. An event expressed with a past tense form in Habakkuk he can relate to the attested actions of the Wicked Priest; the ones in a future formulation he predicts will befall the Wicked Priest. The same is true for other characters and events. In the text cited above regarding the Teacher of

---

25. K. Elliger, *Studien zum Habakuk-Kommentar vom Toten Meer* (BHT 15; Tübingen: Mohr, 1953), 150: "1. Prophetic proclamation has as its content the end; and 2. The present is the end time."

26. See H. Ringgren, *The Faith of Qumran: Theology of the Dead Sea Scrolls* (Philadelphia: Fortress, 1963), 60-63.

Righteousness, the prophecy reads an imperfect verb pointing to a present or future activity (ירוץ).[27]

Other Forms of Interpretation

Beyond the type of explicitly marked interpretation found in the continuous *pesharim,* the scriptural explanations attested in the scrolls could take varied forms. As a number of modern commentators have noted, there is evidence that the Qumran expositors engaged in what could be called simple-sense exegesis. An example occurs in *Commentary on Genesis A* (4Q252) col. 4, where one finds the sort of information one would expect in an entry in a Bible dictionary. When dealing with Gen 36:12 — which says that a certain Timnah was the concubine of Eliphaz, Esau's son, and that she became the mother of Amalek — the expositor adds about Amalek: "whom Saul smo[te] as He said to Moses, in the last days *you will wipe out the memory of Amalek from under the heaven* (Deut. xxv,19)." The writer adduces other scriptural passages about Amalek — ones from 1 Samuel and one from Deuteronomy pointing to the destruction of the nation descended from him, a destruction that Saul carried out. He merely alludes to the Samuel passages (14:48; 15:3, 7) but quotes the one from Deuteronomy, which he duly introduces with a formula "as He said to Moses" (כאשר דבר למושה). The text accumulates and associates scriptural passages concerning Amalek but also furnishes an instance of prediction followed by fulfillment. It is interesting that it adds the phrase "in the last days," which is not part of the citation from Deuteronomy. It seems to point here to the future farther removed (cf. Exod 17:14, where there is talk of the Lord wiping out the memory of Amalek).[28]

Though one could characterize the example in part as simple-sense exegesis (this = that), it illustrates on a modest scale what happens more often in scriptural interpretation in the scrolls. The procedure of gathering

27. Cf. J. C. VanderKam, "The Wicked Priest Revisited," in D. C. Harlow et al., *The "Other" in Second Temple Judaism: Essays in Honor of John J. Collins* (Grand Rapids: Eerdmans, 2011), 350-67.

28. The official publication is by G. Brooke, "252. 4QCommentary on Genesis A," in Brooke et al., eds., J. C. VanderKam, consulting ed., *Qumran Cave 4: XVII, Parabiblical Texts, Part 3* (DJD 22; Oxford: Clarendon, 1996), 185-207, with pls. 12-13. On the interpretation in 4Q252, see also M. J. Bernstein, "4Q252: From Re-Written Bible to Biblical Commentary," *JJS* 45 (1994): 1-27.

pertinent passages from different locations in the scriptures is attested in larger and smaller ways in various texts, and the eschatological slant is endemic in the scrolls — as Elliger determined regarding *Pesher Habakkuk*.

The largest examples of collecting related scriptural passages in one place come from the *Temple Scroll* (11Q19-20; 4Q524?) and the 4QReworked Pentateuch texts (4Q364-67). Both furnish frequent instances in which the compiler rephrases a law that appears in several scriptural codes but with differing details and formulations; he takes the several texts and blends their details into one consistent statement that is located at the point where the subject first appears. These cases are more complicated, however, since there is debate about how to classify the *Temple Scroll* and especially 4QReworked Pentateuch — are they themselves scriptural or are they not scriptural but rather interpretations of scripture and thus of a lower level of authority. The issue will be treated in Chapter 3 below.

One of the manuscripts previously classified as a copy of *Reworked Pentateuch* is 4Q158. For various reasons it should be separated from the others (4Q364-67). It appears to be an interpretive text of a different character (4Q158 is now labeled 4QBiblical Paraphrase), not the kind present in the *Reworked Pentateuch* copies, 4Q364-67.[29] In it there are some instances of associating narrative sections of scripture. For example, 4Q158 frgs. 1-2 reproduce the story from Genesis 32 regarding Jacob's wrestling with the mysterious "man" at Peniel. In this case, though all the lines are fragmentary, the preserved parts have distinctive words from the passage (e.g., "wrestled," the question — "what is your name," "Penuel," "upon the two sockets of the hip"). The recounting is extensive, stretching from line 1 to line 13 so that there is no mistaking what the context is. Yet suddenly, somewhere near the end of line 13 the context changes (the end of the line has not survived), because at the beginning of line 14 the Lord is speaking to Aaron, giving him a command to meet Moses — the command found in Exod 4:27: "The LORD said to Aaron, 'Go into the wilderness to meet Moses.'" The text then becomes more fragmentary to the end of the preserved section (line 19), with some indication that words from Exod 3:12 were also used. John Strugnell suggested long ago that the writer was associating two stories about potentially hostile mysterious beings — Jacob's experience at the

---

29. For a study of the interpretation in the work, see M. Segal, "Biblical Exegesis in 4Q158: Techniques and Genre," *Text* 19 (1998): 45-62; and the more comprehensive study of M. M. Zahn, *Rethinking Rewritten Scripture: Composition and Exegesis in the 4QReworked Pentateuch Manuscripts* (STDJ 95; Leiden: Brill, 2011).

place that received the name Peniel from the incident and Moses' encounter with the Lord in Exod 4:24-26 (the verses directly before the Lord's order to Aaron [reflected in line 14]).[30] His hypothesis may be correct (no one has offered a better solution), but, if so, there would have been space for nothing more that a quick reference to the Exodus 4 incident in this column; mention of it would likely have preceded the extant bits of text on frgs. 1-2 that contain the Genesis 32 story. The implication is that the text would have used Exodus as its base and would have given the reader a flashback to a passage somewhat like it in Genesis. By chance, the largest preserved part is from the flashback, not from the larger context in which it figured.

In another place in 4Q158 the writer associates two scriptural passages, but in a somewhat different way, and in doing so he illustrates that the struggle to solve scriptural problems was alive and well among the authors/compilers of the Qumran texts. The problem posed by the texts is this: in Deut 18:15-16 one reads: "The LORD your God will raise up for you a prophet like me from among your own people; you shall heed such a prophet. This is what you requested of the LORD your God at Horeb on the day of the assembly when you said, 'If I hear the voice of the LORD my God any more, or ever again see this great fire, I will die.'" Though Moses here claims that the people made a request and comment at Horeb (= Mount Sinai) regarding raising up a prophet and the very practical need for mediation, no such request figures in the Exodus Sinai pericope as worded in MT. The people did, of course, ask Moses to approach the deity because they were afraid (Exod 20:18-19), but they said nothing about raising up a prophet.

In face of the unsupported claim in Deuteronomy, interpreters took steps to remove the difficulty. In 4Q158 frg. 6 the text of Exod 20:19-21 appears in the form it takes in SP; that is, material from Deutronomy 5 and 18 is worked into the text of Exodus. The passage Deut 5:24-27 is inserted into Exod 20:19 (4QpaleoExod^m does the same);[31] 4Q158 frg. 6 then reproduces the end of v. 19 and vv. 20-21. At this point the Samaritan version of Exodus and 4Q158 6 4-10 cite Deut 5:28-29 followed by Deut 18:18-22. To see how the text looks, it will be helpful to set SP Exod 20:18-22 (the only fully preserved form of the expanded version) next to the same verses in MT.

30. J. Strugnell, "Notes en marge du volume V des 'Discoveries in the Judaean Desert of Jordan,'" *RevQ* 7/26 (1970): 169.

31. For the text, see E. Ulrich, *The Biblical Qumran Scrolls: Transcriptions and Textual Variants* (VTSup 134; Leiden: Brill, 2010), 79; and M. Abegg, P. Flint, and E. Ulrich, *The Dead Sea Scrolls Bible* (San Francisco: HarperSanFranciso, 1999), 55.

Versions of Exodus 20:18-22

Samaritan Pentateuch	Masoretic Text
[Exod 20:18] When all the people witnessed the thunder and lightning, the sound of the trumpet, and the mountain smoking, they were afraid and trembled and stood at a distance, [Exod 20:19a] and said to Moses,	[Exod 20:18] When all the people witnessed the thunder and lightning, the sound of the trumpet, and the mountain smoking, they were afraid and trembled and stood at a distance, [Exod 20:19] and said to Moses,
[Deut 5:24] "Look, the Lord our God has shown us his glory and greatness, and we have heard his voice out of the fire. Today we have seen that God may speak to someone and the person may still live. [Deut 5:25] So now why should we die? For this great fire will consume us; if we hear the voice of the Lord our God any longer, we shall die. [Deut 5:26] For who is there of all flesh that has heard the voice of the living God speaking out of fire, as we have, and remained alive? [Deut 5:27] Go near, you yourself, and hear all that the Lord our God will say. Then tell us everything that the Lord our God tells you, and we will listen and do it.	"You speak to us, and we will listen;
[Exod 20:19b] But do not let God speak to us, or we will die."	but do not let God speak to us, or we will die."
[Exod 20:20] Moses said to the people, "Do not be afraid; for God has come only to test you and to put the fear of him upon you so that you do not sin." [Exod 20:21] Then the people stood at a distance, while Moses drew near to the thick darkness where God was. [Exod 20:22a] The Lord said to Moses:	[Exod 20:20] Moses said to the people, "Do not be afraid; for God has come only to test you and to put the fear of him upon you so that you do not sin." [Exod 20:21] Then the people stood at a distance, while Moses drew near to the thick darkness where God was. [Exod 20:22a] The Lord said to Moses:
[Deut 5:28] "I have heard the words of this people, which they have spoken	

41

to you; they are right in all that they
have spoken. [Deut 5:29] If only they
had such a mind as this, to fear me
and to keep all my commandments
always, so that it might go well with
them and with their children forever!

[Deut 18:18] I will raise up for them a
prophet like you from among their
own people; I will put my words in
his mouth. He will speak to them everything that I command. [Deut 18:19]
Anyone who does not heed his words
that he shall speak in my name, I my-
self will hold accountable. [Deut
18:20] But any prophet who presumes
to speak in my name a word that I
have not commanded him to speak or
who speaks in the name of other gods
— that prophet shall die. [Deut 18:21]
You may say to yourself, 'How can we
recognize a word that the Lord has
not spoken?' [Deut 18:22] If a prophet
speaks in the name of the Lord but
the thing does not take place or prove
true, it is a word that the Lord has not
spoken. The prophet has spoken it
presumptuously; do not be frightened
by it.

[Deut 5:30] Go say to them, 'Return
to your tents.'

[Deut 5:31] But you, stand here by me,
and I will tell you all the commandments, the statutes and the ordi-
nances, that you shall teach them, so
that they may do them in the land
that I am giving them to possess."

[Exod 20:22] The Lord said to
Moses . . .

{[Exod 20:22] The Lord said to
Moses . . . [see above]}

The order in the versions (the latter two are very fragmentary and do
not preserve the entire passage) is:

Samaritan Exodus	4Q158	4QpaleoExod^m
Exod 20:18-19a	Exod 20:18-[19a]	
Deut 5:24-27		Deut 5:24-27
Exod 20:19b-22a	Exod 20:19b-21	Exod 20:19b
Deut 5:28-29	Deut 5:28-29	
Deut 18:18-22	Deut 18:18-22	
Deut 5:30-31		
Exod 20:22b		

By interweaving related verses from Deuteronomy 5 and 18 into Exodus 20, the expanded version provides a basis for the claim made in Deut 18:16: at Horeb the people asked for a prophet like Moses. It appears that in lines 5-6 of 4Q158 frg. 6 the writer makes an attempt to smooth the transition from Deut 5:29 to Deut 18:18 by adding: ". . . the sound of my words. Say to them" before the beginning of 18:18: "A Prophet [like you. . . ." An interesting feature of the example is that the procedure of 4Q158, which is not a copy of Exodus, is almost exactly paralleled in copies of Exodus — the one in SP and 4QpaleoExod^m where it survives.

There are also more modest examples of the phenomenon of collecting related (or so they seemed to the interpreter) scriptural passages in one place — exercises in association that could serve varied purposes. 4Q265 is an intriguing but sadly fragmentary text. It uses some sectarian language (it was once called *Serekh Damascus*), as in its list of penalties that resembles the ones in the rule texts, and it treats other subjects, a number of them having to do with the Sabbath. After the sections regarding the seventh day, the text turns to the garden of Eden story and draws into connection with it the legislation now located in Lev 12:2-5.

And in the firs[t] week [Adam was created and his wife; he spent forty days before] he was brought to the garden of Eden. And a bone [from his bones and flesh of his flesh was the woman. A week] she spent before she was brought to him in the [second week. On the eightieth day she was brought to the Garden of Eden. For] holy is the Garden of Eden, and every fresh shoot that is in it is holy. Therefo[re he said, *If a woman conceives and bears a male child,*] *then she shall be unclean for seven days; as at the time of her menstruation, she shall be unclean* (Lev. xii,2). *Then* [*she shall continue for*] *thi*[*rty-three days in the blood*] *of her purifying* (Lev. xii,4). *But if she bears a female child,* [*then she shall be unclean two weeks as in her*

menstruation. And she shall contin]ue in the blood of her purifying
[for sixty-six days (Lev. xii,5). She shall not touch any holy thing, nor
come into the Sanctuary until the days of her purification are com-
pleted] (Lev. xii,4).[32]

The exegesis offered here and paralleled in *Jub.* 3:8-14 deals with several issues. One seems to have been Leviticus's baffling commands about
different periods of impurity following the birth of a male or female baby.
Why should there be such a difference and why these numbers of days?
Genesis 2 makes clear that the man was formed before the Lord made the
garden into which he placed him (2:7-8; cf. 3:23). Subsequently, after naming the animals and finding no suitable mate, he was put into a deep sleep
and the woman was formed from a rib the Lord removed from him (2:21-
23). So, the man was made outside the garden and presentation of the
woman to him occurred later. Moreover, a number of clues suggested that
Eden was a sanctuary — an inference widely drawn in ancient texts: the
cherub that guarded the way to Eden is reminiscent of the cherubim in the
temple, the river Gihon (one of the four rivers of Eden) reminded one of
the Gihon near the Temple Mount, the skins that the Lord God used to
make clothing for the pair uses the word for priestly garments (כתנת עור),
the verbs for tilling and keeping the garden are also used for temple service; furthermore, it was the place where God was present and met people
just as he did in the sanctuary. In addition, Ezekiel 28, which mentions the
garden, offered clues associating Eden and the sanctuary, including a list of
precious stones that has detailed overlaps with those in the high priest's
breastplate. Since the woman in Leviticus 12 was not to enter the sanctuary
for certain periods of time after the births of children and since Eden was a
sanctuary, the passages seemed to have a connection.[33] That the male and

32. The translation is a form of G. Vermes's rendering, modified according to the
readings and restorations proposed by E. Qimron, "Improving the Editions of the
Dead Sea Scrolls," *Meghillot* 1 (2003): 135-37 (Hebrew). The official edition is by J. M.
Baumgarten, "Miscellaneous Rules," in Baumgarten et al., eds., *Qumran Cave 4: XXV,
Halakhic Texts* (DJD 35; Oxford: Clarendon, 1999), 57-78, with pls. 5-8. See also his essay,
"Purification after Childbirth and the Sacred Garden in 4Q265 and Jubilees," in G. J.
Brooke and F. García Martínez, eds., *New Qumran Texts and Studies: Proceedings of the
First Meeting of the International Organization for Qumran Studies, Paris 1992* (STDJ 15;
Leiden: Brill, 1994), 3-10.

33. See, e.g., J. C. VanderKam, "Adam's Incense Offering (Jubilees 3:27)," *Meghillot*
5-6 (2007): *141-56, for a survey of the evidence; and Kugel, *Traditions of the Bible*, 108-
10.

female babies are termed זכר and נקבה in Leviticus 12 could have made a reader think of the first pair (see Gen 1:27) and Eden together, since the first two chapters of Genesis were a continuous story for ancient expositors, not parts of separate accounts of origins as modern scholars have analyzed them.

As a result, the author felt justified in applying the information from Leviticus 12 to his interpretation of Genesis 1-3 and vice versa. Because of its poor state of preservation, the specifics of how the writer of 4Q265 presented some of the data remain uncertain, but he clearly deals with times before the man and the woman were brought into the garden and associates the periods in Leviticus 12 with them. *Jubilees* shows how this was carried out in detail, with the man entering the garden forty days after his creation and the woman eighty days after she was formed. *Jubilees* further accounted for the information from Leviticus 12 by noting that the man and woman were created in the first week (Gen 1:26-28 says they were made on the same day) but the woman, who was at first only the man's rib, was shown to him at the end of the second. On the author's view, this is why Leviticus 12 mentions an initial seven-day period of uncleanness for the mother of a male child and fourteen for the one who gives birth to a female. Notice too that in 4Q265 every green shoot in Eden is holy, just as Leviticus 12 prohibited the new mother from touching anything holy. It so happens that both 4Q265 and *Jubilees* deal with this material after they present sections about the Sabbath.[34]

Turning to the category of thematic *pesharim* (i.e., *pesharim* on a topic, not on a single, continuous stretch of scriptural text), the remarkable text called 11QMelchizedek comes immediately to mind. Melchizedek was the priest-king of Salem who met Abram as the latter was returning from defeating a coalition of kings and rescuing his nephew Lot along with other captives: "And King Melchizedek of Salem brought out bread and wine; he was priest of God Most High. He blessed him and said, 'Blessed be Abram by God Most High, maker of heaven and earth; and blessed be God Most High, who has delivered your enemies into your hand!' And {Abram} gave him one-tenth of everything" (Gen 14:18-20). This terse account leaves the reader almost begging for more information, especially in light of Ps 110:4, the only other reference to him in the Hebrew Bible: "The

---

34. See A. Shemesh, "4Q265 and the Authoritative Status of Jubilees at Qumran," in G. Boccaccini and I. Ibba, eds., *Enoch and the Mosaic Torah: The Evidence of Jubilees* (Grand Rapids: Eerdmans, 2009), 247-60.

LORD has sworn and will not change his mind, 'You are a priest forever according to the order of Melchizedek.'" The New Testament book of Hebrews is a familiar witness to the sorts of ideas that grew up around this enigmatic character.

11QMelchizedek paints a portrait of him seemingly differing from the ones in the scriptural texts.[35] In fact, it seems as if the Melchizedek of 11QMelchizedek has nothing to do with the one in the Hebrew Bible or the book of Hebrews. The surviving parts of the cave 11 scroll begin with citations of scriptural passages regarding the Jubilee and Sabbatical Year (Lev 25:13; Deut 15:2), and all of this material is connected with the release of captives. On the Day of Atonement at the end of the tenth Jubilee, the sons of light and the men of Melchizedek's lot will receive atonement. Melchizedek will judge and will be involved in punishing those belonging to Belial. Melchizedek, the reader learns, is the one called "God" in Ps 82:1 ("*God* has taken his place in the divine council; in the midst of the gods he holds judgment") and the individual to whom reference is made in Ps 7:8-9. The portrait of a heavenly, eschatological Melchizedek is achieved through an interweaving of material from varied texts in the scriptures. What does this character have to do with the Melchizedek of the Bible?

It turns out that Melchizedek in 11QMelchizedek has much to do with the scriptural verses about him. In Genesis 14 two topics of interest in the context of the Melchizedek pericope are the release of captives taken by the invading kings (Lot was one of those captured) and the restoration of property to its rightful owners. According to scriptural legislation, both of these actions were to happen in the Year of the Jubilee; in addition, Deuteronomy 15 (quoted in the text) stipulates that in the seventh year debts were to be remitted and Hebrew slaves released (15:12-15). Another scriptural passage relating to this topic is also quoted in 11QMelchizedek: Isa 61:1-2 calls for release of the captives in the year of the Lord's favor (notice that the Qumran text amazingly speaks of the year of Melchizedek's favor rather than of the Lord's favor). So the topics mentioned in Genesis 14 are in fact ones taken up in the text from cave 11, but they are transposed to an eschatological key.

It was also possible, using the passage in Psalm 110, to understand

---

35. There is a large bibliography on the text. Here it will suffice to mention: P. J. Kobelski, *Melchizedek and Melchireša'* (CBQMS 10; Washington: Catholic Biblical Association of America, 1981); and E. F. Mason, *'You Are a Priest Forever': Second Temple Jewish Messianism and the Priestly Christology of the Epistle to the Hebrews* (STDJ 74; Leiden: Brill, 2008), esp. 168-90.

Melchizedek as a heavenly figure, just as the writer understood him to be in Psalms 7 and 82. He may have read Ps 110:4 as saying: "You are a priest forever, by my word, Melchizedek." That is, verse 4 could be construed as continuing the direct address in the first verses of the psalm. If so, the interpretation casts the words of the psalm in a different light. They are usually taken as part of a royal psalm promising the king victory over his foes.[36] The author of 11QMelchizedek, if he thought verse 4 was directly addressed to Melchizedek and not to a king who was a priest like Melchizedek, might have thought the rest of the psalm was spoken to him as well. Hence, the first verses presented Melchizedek as sitting at God's right hand until he made his enemies his footstool and executed justice among the nations.[37]

CONCLUSION

There is no way of knowing how much literature other than what was found in the caves was accessible to the scrolls communities, but their situation was presumably far different than the one existing at the present time. Modern people are surrounded by endless numbers of books and other publications (something about which Qohelet warned), and no one is able to keep up with all the secondary literature, even in a seemingly restricted field like the Dead Sea Scrolls. The sundry works represented in the scrolls provide documentation that the scriptural books were available to the communities and were the objects of intense scrutiny. Perhaps their members were able to concentrate on them with fewer distractions than modern people have (though they kept their day jobs), and concentrate they did — whether for their own edification or refuting their opponents. They regarded those ancient books as authoritative, but in ways that not all the faithful since their time have adopted. Millions of others — Jews and Christians — have esteemed the scriptures as authoritative, even canonical, but not all later believers have thought, as the people of the scrolls did, that the scriptures contained encoded messages which, if they could only

36. H.-J. Kraus, *Psalms 60–150* (CC; Minneapolis: Augsburg, 1989), 346-47.
37. See VanderKam, "Sabbatical Chronologies," 169-76, and the literature cited there. D. Flusser was the one who suggested that the author of 11QMelchizedek had read Psalm 110 as direct address to Melchizedek; "Melchizedek and the Son of Man," in *Judaism and the Origins of Christianity* (Jerusalem: Magnes, 1988), 189; repr. from *Christian News from Israel* 17 (1966): 23-29.

decipher them, would address their own times and not only ancient ones. Their assumptions about the scriptural text strike many today as strange, even bizarre, but these ancient Jews assiduously studied and interpreted the texts they knew so well and did so within their own hermeneutical system. The scriptures were the authorities, and they spoke to their deepest concerns — such as helping them to see their place in God's plan, directing their conduct, offering them comfort, and supplying them with fuel for condemning their enemies. They in turn honored those scriptures by devoting their best efforts to clarifying and applying them.

Use of the word "scriptures" in connection with the Qumran library leads, however, into some problems that will be the topic of the next chapter. Which were the authoritative works for the writers of the texts found in the Qumran caves, and how can one tell?

CHAPTER 3

Authoritative Literature According to the Scrolls

To grapple with the topic for this chapter, the information in the Dead Sea Scrolls will play the primary role, but it will be helpful to adduce related data from another important Jewish source for late Second Temple times — the New Testament. The significance of the scrolls for the study of the New Testament will be the subject of the sixth and seventh chapters. For the present purposes, New Testament statements about authoritative literature will be examined as comparative evidence. This may appear a dubious procedure, as one may claim that the various parts of the New Testament do not disclose so much about the Hebrew scriptures as they do about the Greek translations of them; but as a matter of fact, a number of New Testament passages reflect the very practices with regard to scriptural works documented by the scrolls removed from the caves around Khirbet Qumran.

Although it would be simple to say that the subject of this chapter is *canon,* it is well known that it is problematic to use the word for the time being studied.[1] According to Jonathan Z. Smith, "[c]anon is a subtype of the genre *list*,"[2] and it occupies a crucial place in religious systems. "That is to say, bracketing any presuppositions as to its character as revelation (and from this question the historian of religion must abstain), the radical and

---

1. For the first part of the chapter, see J. C. VanderKam, "Revealed Literature in the Second Temple Period," in *From Revelation to Canon: Studies in the Hebrew Bible and Second Temple Literature* (JSJSup 62; Leiden: Brill, 2000), 1-3.

2. J. Z. Smith, "Sacred Persistence: Toward a Redescription of Canon," in *Imagining Religion: From Babylon to Jonestown* (Chicago Studies in the History of Judaism; Chicago: University of Chicago Press, 1982), 44.

arbitrary reduction represented by the notion of canon and the ingenuity represented by the rule-governed exegetical enterprise of applying the canon to every dimension of human life is that most characteristic, persistent, and obsessive religious activity."[3] Eugene Ulrich distinguishes three elements in the concept of *canon:* a book, not its textual form; reflective judgment (examining what has been the case and ratifying it); and a closed list of the books.[4] Experts often note that, in Jewish or Christian writings of the Second Temple period, there is no word for "canon" in the later technical sense of a set list of authoritative writings. This term for a list of normative books is of later Christian coinage: ". . . the first application of the noun to the collection of holy scriptures appears in the last part of the fourth century and continued in common use from the time of Jerome."[5] Since the specialized use of the term may have originated among patristic writers, it is, of course, not helpful as a point of entry into the issue with which the present chapter is concerned. There was, apparently, no such entity at the time of the communities associated with the Dead Sea Scrolls.

If one succeeds in avoiding the word "canon," there is another pitfall worth sidestepping — an evolutionary one. The Jewish canon of scripture existed at least by some point in the rabbinic period, and in fact all one needs to do these days is open a copy of the Masoretic Text to see how it looks. It is a fixed list of books divided into three units: first the *Torah* (the five books of the law of Moses), second the *Nevi'im* (the prophetic books), and third the *Ketuvim* (the Writings). That is a fact, but it would be inappropriate to begin a study of earlier times with the idea that there was, from an early period, a linear development toward a threefold canon and that examining the sources has as its goal to identify those glimmerings of the future tripartite canon. It may be strange to point this out as a pitfall, as it may seem obvious, but in reading the technical literature on the subject one gets the impression that such an assumption is alive and well in the field. Who knows what shape the Hebrew Bible would have taken if the communities of the scrolls rather than rabbinic groups had carried the day and survived into the Middle Ages?

Although one must avoid the *word* "canon" with its specific connotation (a closed list of books) when discussing the Second Temple period, it

3. Smith, "Sacred Persistence," 43.

4. E. C. Ulrich, "The Notion and Definition of Canon," in L. M. McDonald and J. A. Sanders, eds., *The Canon Debate* (Peabody: Hendrickson, 2002), 30-33.

5. B. S. Childs, *Introduction to the Old Testament as Scripture* (Philadelphia: Fortress, 1979), 50.

is nevertheless clear enough that a *concept* of authoritative writings was afloat. Thus one should assemble the pertinent information in the early Jewish texts to explore what is involved in the concept. The concept of authoritative writings as used here includes at least two elements: (1) esteemed written works that (2) functioned authoritatively for a community or communities. Gerald Bruns argues that *power* lies at the heart of what is meant by canon; his point is pertinent to our subject, even though the word "canon" is being avoided:

> The distinction between canonical and non-canonical is thus not just a distinction between authentic and inauthentic texts — that is, it is not reducible to the usual oppositions between the inspired and the mundane, the true and the apocryphal, the sacred and the profane, and so on. On the contrary, it is a distinction between texts that are forceful in a given situation and those which are not. From a hermeneutical standpoint, in which the relation of a text to a situation is always of primary interest, the theme of canonization is *power.*[6]

As an example, Bruns cites Josiah's enforcement of the book of the Torah found in the temple during his eighteenth year as king of Judah (2 Kings 22–23).[7] That book operated powerfully, authoritatively for the king, the priest Hilkiah, the prophetess Hulda, and for the nation, and it effected a reform. A canon is a norm that obligates a community; authoritative literature performs the same function. But before it can carry out this role, a community must in some way acknowledge its authority. Books, whatever claims they make for themselves, are powerless unless groups of people recognize or acknowledge their authority. In the Second Temple period some books performed or operated in this fashion, but there was not, as nearly as one can tell, an exclusive list of books — these and only these — for the Jewish people or even for smaller communities such as the one using the site of Qumran and others sharing their point of view. Yet, some element of exclusion must have been involved, as not all writings would have been regarded as authoritative and would have functioned with power. For example, the books 1-2 Maccabees were probably not deemed authoritative by the people of the

---

6. G. L. Bruns, "Canon and Power in the Hebrew Scriptures," in R. von Hallberg, ed., *Canons* (Chicago: University of Chicago Press, 1984), 67.

7. Bruns, "Canon and Power in the Hebrew Scriptures," 68-71.

scrolls, as no copy of either was found in the caves, and the Hasmoneans, the heroes of the two books, were opponents of the communities.

A few other preliminaries: Anyone familiar with the field of canon history knows there was formerly a dominant theory that posited a three-step development of the threefold Hebrew canon of scripture.[8] According to it, the Torah was recognized and closed at the time of Ezra (fifth century B.C.E.), the Prophets by about 200 B.C.E. (since, for example, Daniel could no longer get in), and the Writings at the Council of Jamnia in ca. 90 C.E. The theory has taken a pummeling from a number of experts and from various angles. Its adherents assumed much and drew far-reaching conclusions from very modest amounts of evidence. Those who have attacked it, however, have had little choice but to draw on the same limited set of data, although the Judean Desert literature has enlarged that fund noticeably.[9] Those are the texts with which the present chapter is largely concerned.

Another point worth highlighting is that, while the Second Temple sources frequently use terms that have a specific meaning when employed in connection with the rabbinic canon of scripture, one should not assume that in the Second Temple texts they have the same value. For example, the word "Prophets" does not necessarily cover only the prophetic literature now in the Hebrew Bible; there is reason for caution even about the word "Torah" because of the complications the so-called *Reworked Pentateuch* texts have introduced into the discussion (see Chapter 2 above). When a text such as the *Rule of the Community* refers to "the law and the prophets," can the modern reader assume to know exactly which books the terms embraced? At any rate, the texts should be studied carefully before making a decision about which compositions these seemingly clear terms include. It will also be worthwhile to look carefully at instances where ancient books serve as authorities and, if possible, check whether there are different uses for them and levels of authority attributed to them.

THE IMPORTANCE OF SCRIPTURE

Both the Dead Sea Scrolls and the New Testament books contain works penned by people who, in their thinking and writing, attributed great im-

---

8. H. E. Ryle, *The Canon of the Old Testament* (2nd ed.; London: Macmillan, 1909), gave a standard formulation of the hypothesis.

9. For a brief summary, see VanderKam, "Revealed Literature in the Second Temple Period," 11-16.

portance to the compositions they called "scripture(s)" or "what is writ-ten." The writers of the scrolls and those who composed the New Testa-ment books often quoted the legal or prophetic works, and members of the scrolls communities even composed commentaries on prophetic texts. In those commentaries they supply the earliest ancestors of the running commentaries on scripture that have been so popular over the centuries and remain so today (see Chapter 2 above). Authors in both communities used a scripturally-informed language, even when they were not quoting or directly commenting on it. They seem to have known the scriptures thoroughly and reflected that familiarity in everything they wrote.

Think, for instance, of Paul's famous argument that one becomes right with God through faith in the divine promise fulfilled in Christ (Galatians 2–4).[10] The apostle appeals to a number of scriptural passages there, in-cluding most famously Gen 15:6 and Hab 2:4. Or consider his elaborate struggle with the place of Israel in God's plan as it comes to expression in Romans 9–11. There he repeatedly calls on scriptural sections in formulat-ing his complicated argument.[11] Examples of this phenomenon could be multiplied.

For the purposes of this chapter, it is more instructive to adduce some places where Jesus used the scriptures in discussion with Jewish conversa-tion partners who strongly disagreed with him. One should be careful about drawing conclusions from the passages because the Gospels were written much later and for their authors' own goals, yet, whatever time they reflect, they illustrate assumptions about and procedures with the scriptures. It is evident from the ways in which the encounters are re-corded that both Jesus and his opponents knew and relied upon the scrip-tures as determinative in disputes. A helpful example occurs in Matt 19:3-9 (par. Mark 10:2-12), a discussion between some Pharisees and Jesus regard-ing a practical yet complicated issue — divorce. The Pharisees open with a general question: "Is it lawful for a man to divorce his wife for any cause?" (v. 3). Jesus's initial response is to cite Gen 1:27, that God, in creating hu-mankind on the sixth day, "made them male and female"; he then adds Gen 2:24, which speaks about a man leaving his father and mother, joining his wife, and the two of them becoming one flesh (vv. 4-5). The Pharisees

10. For a comparison between Paul's interpretations in this part of Galatians and exegesis in the Qumran texts, see T. H. Lim, *Holy Scripture in the Qumran Commen-taries and Pauline Letters* (Oxford: Clarendon, 1997), 50-65.

11. See J. R. Wagner, *Heralds of the Good News: Isaiah and Paul 'In Concert' in the Letter to the Romans* (NovTSup 101; Leiden: Brill, 2002).

do not disagree (naturally, they accepted the authority of Genesis and knew these passages) but counter with Deut 24:1 (regarding a man's right to compose a "certificate of divorce" that he gives to the wife who displeases him and sends her away), which they summarize but do not quote. In response to the verses Matthew's Jesus had cited, they wonder why Moses nevertheless required only that a certificate of dismissal be given when divorcing a woman. "He said to them, 'It was because you were so hardhearted that Moses allowed you to divorce your wives, but from the beginning it was not so. And I say to you, whoever divorces his wife, except for unchastity, and marries another commits adultery'" (vv. 8-9; see the sequel in Deut 24:2-4, where the latter subject arises).

There is much to weigh in this passage, but the point relevant here is that both the Pharisees and Jesus assume the question they are discussing is to be answered from the scriptures — something so obvious that no one in the scene comments on it or raises a question about it. The books to which they appeal are in the Torah — Genesis and Deuteronomy — and both sides accept the authority of those books and are able to produce relevant data from them as needed. One could almost construe the scene as an instance of pitting scripture against scripture, but the interweaving of the verbs "command" and "permit" suggests that something different is happening. The Jesus of the passage is drawing a distinction between the divine will (Gen 2:24) and an allowance for human frailty (Deut 24:1).[12] No one questions the authority of the two texts, and no one objects that Matthew's Jesus does not quote the text exactly. In fact, in quoting Gen 2:24 Matthew does not give it quite verbatim as it is in the editions of the Greek Genesis but leaves out a couple of pronouns, uses a slightly different verbal form for "join," and changes the syntax of the last part of the citation. Whether this is how he said it historically (not in Greek but in a Semitic version) or if the wording is due to the Gospel writer, it is presented as close enough for the purposes of the argument.

---

12. C. E. B. Cranfield, *The Gospel according to Saint Mark* (CGTC; Cambridge: Cambridge University Press, 1963), 319. "It is an appeal to origins and reflects a theology and ideology: God's original purpose has priority"; W. Loader, *Jesus' Attitude towards the Law: A Study of the Gospels* (Grand Rapids: Eerdmans, 2002), 89 (here he is commenting on the Markan form of the story; see 225 for his study of the Matthean version).

WAS THERE A COLLECTION OF AUTHORITATIVE SCROLLS IN THE SECOND TEMPLE PERIOD?

In this encounter and others, the two sides share much (agreement on authoritative texts and detailed knowledge about them), and the common ground they occupy allows the discussion to proceed. Among the questions the scene raises is how one knew at that time which works could serve as the authoritative bases for such a discussion and disagreement. By the first century c.e., all the books that are now in the Hebrew Bible/Old Testament were already very old, in most cases many centuries old. In the Dead Sea Scrolls there are copies of nearly all the books that later became part of the Hebrew Bible (see Chapter 1 above). All of the books are represented except one — Esther — and most of them are represented on multiple copies in the Qumran caves. The earliest manuscript of any work is not likely to be present among them; they are much later copies of more ancient compositions. So, the books had existed for a long time by the first century — a conclusion familiar from various kinds of data — and all of them were potentially available to readers. But the issue under discussion is: had those works been gathered into a single collection, one whose authority the various Jewish groups and the Jewish people in general recognized, even if it was not strictly exclusive in the sense of a canon? Was there at least a core group of books on which all could agree — a limited set of books that was a functional collection of authoritative texts? The answer appears to be "yes": there was agreement among the Jewish groups about a substantial number of ancient works, though probably not about all the compositions that later became the components of the Hebrew Bible.[13]

It is useful to keep in mind the simple fact that in the Second Temple period the various works like Genesis and Hosea were written on scrolls, and a scribe could include only so much text on one scroll. An ancient collection of scriptures would have taken the form of a set of individual scrolls; the books of the Law and Prophets would not have been copied on a single, long scroll, and certainly not in a codex — something that would come into use only much later. The practical point should be remembered in trying to imagine how people encountered the scriptures in antiquity:

13. See, e.g., VanderKam, "Revealed Literature in the Second Temple Period," 20-30. This conclusion conflicts with the thesis of R. Beckwith, who maintains that the Jewish canon had assumed final form already in the 160s b.c.e.; *The Old Testament Canon of the New Testament Church and Its Background in Early Judaism* (Grand Rapids: Eerdmans, 1985).

the scriptural works filled several scrolls, and to locate a passage one had to identify the right scroll before unrolling it to the relevant place.[14] So, the question is not whether there was one scroll or codex containing a whole set of individual compositions; rather, it is: was there a set of writings, a particular group of scrolls, that all or almost all Jews acknowledged as scripture (leaving aside the issue of how many of these scrolls any one community may have possessed)? The evidence from the era of early Judaism relating to the problem should be scrutinized, evidence that the Dead Sea Scrolls have massively augmented.

Several times in the New Testament the expression "the scripture [ἡ γραφή]" occurs in contexts that are relevant for the topic under consideration.[15] In Gal 4:30 (Galatians was written no later than the 50s),[16] Paul introduces a citation from Gen 21:10 with the words: "But what does the scripture say?" Here he uses the singular ἡ γραφή. He does the same for a quotation from Gen 12:3 in Gal 3:8 (see also 3:22; cf. Rom 4:3). In Rom 9:17 he employs the singular to preface the words of Exod 9:16, and in 10:11 he uses it in reference to Isa 28:16 (see 11:2).[17] Thus Paul, in the mid-first century C.E., uses "the scripture" (note the definite article) to include pentateuchal and prophetic works. It seems as if the word is a collective term denoting a known body of literature.

There are other examples of this usage elsewhere in the New Testament, but they occur in books that date from a time closer to the end of the first century. One such reference is especially interesting. In John 10:34-35, Jesus is arguing with the Jews as he and they are celebrating Hanukkah.[18]

14. See K. van der Toorn, *Scribal Culture and the Making of the Hebrew Bible* (Cambridge, Mass.: Harvard University Press, 2007), 9-26.

15. On the usage by the various New Testament writers, see G. Schrenk, "γράφω," *TDNT* 1 (1964): 749-55.

16. H. Koester places the writing of Galatians between 52 and 55 C.E.; *Introduction to the New Testament* (2 vols.; Hermeneia: Minneapolis: Fortress and Berlin: de Gruyter, 1982), 2:104.

17. For the term in Romans, see J. A. Fitzmyer, *Romans* (AB 33; New York: Doubleday, 1993), 373. He says the usage derives from passages such as 1 Chr 15:15 (LXX).

18. The fact that the discussion takes place on Hanukkah makes the issue of a human claiming to be god a timely one, as it was the defeat of Antiochus IV, who claimed divinity for himself, that the holiday celebrated; see J. C. VanderKam, "John 10 and the Feast of the Dedication," in H. W. Attridge, J. J. Collins, and T. H. Tobin, eds., *Of Scribes and Scrolls: Studies on the Hebrew Bible, Intertestamental Judaism, and Christian Origins* (College Theology Society Resources in Religion 5; Lanham: University Press of America, 1990), 203-14.

When they wish to stone him for what they understand to be blasphemous words from him ("The Father and I are one," v. 30), he says: "Is it not written in your law, 'I said, you are gods'? If those to whom the word of God came were called 'gods' — and the scripture [ἡ γραφή] cannot be annulled. . . ." It is striking that Jesus is quoted as saying Ps 82:6 was in the law (although such usage is attested elsewhere), but the following comment that the scripture cannot be broken or annulled seems to intend a larger corpus than just the psalm and to attribute an extraordinarily high status to whatever was covered by the term.[19]

The Hebrew equivalent of ἡ γραφή should be הכתוב. There is no instance in the Qumran scrolls in which הכתוב designates a collection of scrolls or scriptures. There are a number of Tannaitic examples in which הכתוב appears to signify something like "this is what the scriptural passage really means." Regarding *Torah* and *Hakatuv* in the Rabbi Ishmael midrashim, Azzan Yadin writes: ". . . it would appear that the two personifications of Scripture replicate the relationship between Scripture and its interpretation. TORAH — the past — , already spoken, authoritative voice of Scripture — is a metonymy for revelation, and HA-KATUV — the dynamic interpreter and teacher of halakhah — a metonymy for midrash. TORAH is Sinai, and HA-KATUV is the *bet midrash*."[20] The term is also attested in *b. Ḥag.* 18a, where Rabbi Aqiva adduces Lev 23:37 (the festivals are to be celebrated "each on its proper day") and asks: "Concerning what day does Scripture speak?"[21] At a much earlier time one reads in Neh 8:15 the expression ככתוב in reference to how to celebrate the Festival of Booths. There it appears to be a shorthand way of saying something like "as it is written in the book of Moses," but the absolute usage (the form is pointed with a definite article: "like/according to *the* scripture") is found in the verse. The term may be a general one for authoritative literature. Yet, other than the passages referenced in the context, there is no indication of what the term included.

There is a disappointingly small amount of information available

---

19. Cf. the comments of R. E. Brown, *The Gospel According to John* (2 vols.; AB 29-29A; Garden City: Doubleday, 1966-1970), 1:403, 408-11. For the wider usage of "law" to refer to the scriptures, Brown mentions John 12:34 and 1 Cor 14:21, though he also notes the rabbinic view that the setting for Psalm 82 was Sinai (410).

20. A. Yadin, *Scripture as Logos: Rabbi Ishmael and the Origins of Midrash* (Philadelphia: University of Pennsylvania Press, 2004), 32.

21. The translation is from J. Neusner, *The Babylonian Talmud: A Translation and Commentary* (22 vols.; Peabody: Hendrickson, 2005), 7:76 (the pages are those only of the translation of *Ḥagigah*).

about the process through which a canon of scripture became generally recognized in Judaism; as a result, basic questions — such as, what significance did the act of writing works down have (each of the words examined here has something to do with writing: "scripture," "what is written") — remain unanswered. The earliest explicit statement that the Jewish people had what appears to be a canon comes from the Jewish historian Josephus, who wrote most of his works in the 90s C.E. In a famous and oft-cited passage in *Against Apion,* he contrasts Jewish historical works with the many inconsistent ones the Greeks admired:

> Our books, those which are justly accredited [τὰ δικαίως πεπιστευμένα], are but two and twenty, and contain the record of all time.
>
> Of these, five are the books of Moses, comprising the laws and the traditional history from the birth of man down to the death of the lawgiver. This period falls only a little short of three thousand years. From the death of Moses until Artaxerxes, who succeeded Xerxes as king of Persia, the prophets subsequent to Moses wrote the history of the events of their own times in thirteen books. The remaining four books contain hymns to God and precepts for the conduct of human life.
>
> From Artaxerxes to our own time the complete history has been written, but has not been deemed worthy of equal credit with the earlier records, because of the failure of the exact succession of the prophets.
>
> We have given practical proof of our reverence for our own Scriptures [τοῖς ἰδίοις γράμμασι]. For, although such long ages have now passed, no one has ventured either to add, or to remove, or to alter a syllable; and it is an instinct with every Jew, from the day of his birth, to regard them as the decrees of God [θεοῦ δόγματα], to abide by them, and, if need be, cheerfully to die for them. (1.38-42 [LCL, trans. Thackeray])

There are a number of noteworthy statements in this section of the historian's defense of Judaism and the ones that precede it as he contrasts its records with the products of Greek historians.[22] The Greeks, he claims

---

22. See the insightful comments on the passage by J. Barton, *Oracles of God: Perceptions of Ancient Prophecy in Israel after the Exile* (London: Darton, Longman, and

(whether he was being fair to the Greeks here is not relevant to the present discussion), failed to keep public records, and their historians were more interested in displaying their literary brilliance than in presenting the truth. The Jews, he says, like the Egyptians, Babylonians, and Phoenicians, kept appropriate records and entrusted them to reliable people (the priests, whose ancestry is pure — something that can be documented); furthermore, their writers were inspired prophets. Josephus emphasizes that the ones enumerated are authoritative, inspired works ("justly accredited," "the decrees of God"), that there is a specific number of them (twenty-two), that they are different in character from the ones written later (when the exact succession of the prophets ended, that is, they are distinguished by belonging to an earlier period and only that one; also they are prophetic), and that every Jew accepts this. These elements are essential components in the concept of a canon of scripture, a Bible. It is difficult to determine whether Josephus exaggerated when he said all Jews agreed about this point, and his assertion about neither adding nor removing a syllable cannot literally be reconciled with the evidence from Josephus himself and other sources,[23] but he was a priest and very well informed regarding matters of religious significance.

It should also be noticed that Josephus's statement divides the twenty-two sacred books into three categories, two of them distinguished by the historical period covered: five books of the law of Moses, thirteen books of prophets after Moses, and four books of "hymns to God and precepts for the conduct of human life." The identity of the five books of Moses is not in dispute (he gives a chronological definition of the period covered [corresponding to Genesis 1–Deuteronomy 34]), and presumably many of the prophetic books are identifiable as well, although the number of them is not exactly

---

Todd, 1986), 58-60. Yet his further claim that Josephus does not speak absolutely of a closed canon is difficult to accept. Barton writes: "In maintaining the small compass of Jewish Scripture he does not, as a matter of fact, say that *no other book could conceivably be found* that would meet the criterion of prophetic authorship, only that no more than twenty-two have until now been found to do so" (59). Josephus's point is that this is precisely the case: there are only twenty-two. Barton considers Josephus's position unusual for his time.

23. For the expression as a stock way of saying one had been true to the sources, see H. W. Attridge, *The Interpretation of Biblical History in the* Antiquitates Judaicae *of Flavius Josephus* (HDR 7; Missoula: Scholars, 1976), 57-60; and S. Z. Leiman, "Josephus and the Canon of the Bible," in L. H. Feldman and G. Hata, eds., *Josephus, the Bible, and History* (Leiden: Brill, 1989), 52-53.

that of later collections ("prophetic" includes history books, as he says; they too are defined by the historical age covered).[24] Yet certainty about exactly which books Josephus would have included in his second and third categories is lacking, though some good guesses can be made. But the essential point is that one well-informed Jewish writer claims that by the 90s c.e. there was a specific, defined list of books that were uniquely authoritative for all Jewish people. That is, there was, according to Josephus, a Jewish canon at that time, a prophetic list with a specific number of works in it.

SCRIPTURAL PRACTICE

What does the evidence allow one to say about the period of the scrolls (before 70 c.e.) and the time of Jesus? Some scholars have argued that well before the first century c.e. Jewish leaders had made decisions about a canon — which books were inspired, authoritative, and which were not.[25] The thesis does not appear to be true in full,[26] but the evidence does imply that there was a significant area of agreement among Jewish groups regarding which ancient writings were authoritative, just as the New Testament passages studied above imply. Also, the scrolls writers, in reference to the scriptures, use the same vocabulary and practices as one finds in the New Testament (see below). The point is worth stressing: rather different groups

24. S. Mason has written a very helpful study of what Josephus does and does not say in the passage ("Josephus and His Twenty-Two Book Canon," in McDonald and Sanders, *The Canon Debate*, 110-27), but, while it is in a sense true, as he says, that his "most consistent ordering criterion is that of genre" (127), Josephus does speak explicitly of the historical periods covered as a basic distinction between the first two categories (the books of Moses, as Josephus writes, include not only law but history until the death of the law-giver). Hence, as the category of history cuts across his first and second group of books, genre is not a fully consistent way of ordering the books.

25. S. Z. Leiman, *The Canonization of Hebrew Scripture: The Talmudic and Midrashic Evidence* (Transactions of the Connecticut Academy of Arts and Sciences 47; Hamden: Archon, 1976), 26-37. Leiman grants that his thesis (the Law was canonical by the time of Ezra, the Prophets by ca. 500-400 B.C.E., and the writings by ca. 160 B.C.E.) is valid only for the mainline Jewish community. Groups like those associated with the scrolls developed canonical notions in an independent way. Beckwith *(The Old Testament Canon of the New Testament Church)* thinks not only that the canon was closed around the time Leiman places it (ca. 160 B.C.E.) but that all Jewish groups agreed about the canon.

26. For a critique of the views advanced by Leiman and Beckwith, see VanderKam, "Revealed Literature in the Second Temple Period," 17-29.

operated with the scriptures in very similar ways and with similar language. The evidence pertaining to the questions of authoritative status in the two bodies of literature — the scrolls and the New Testament — is presented in the following paragraphs in this order: statements about groups of authoritative works; statements that specific works were authoritative.

Statements about Groups of Authoritative Works

There are a number of passages in which writers refer to groups of books as authorities and do so using familiar names for those collections of scrolls. The most common expression is, of course, "the law and the prophets" and variations on that phrase.[27] Other evidence allows one to say that the people of the scrolls not only knew but also highly esteemed a large number of the books that would later form the Hebrew Bible, and that it is likely that these two key terms included many of the works designated by the terms "law" and "prophets" in the later Hebrew canon. 1QS 1:1-3 says of the *maskil* that he is to teach the community members to "seek God with a whole heart and soul, and to do what is good and right before Him, as He commanded by the hand of Moses and all His servants the prophets." Here God's authority is said to stand behind the words of Moses ("as He commanded by the hand of Moses") and the prophets ("all His servants the prophets"), although the passage does not spell out exactly in which works those prophetic words are to be found. The lines indicate that the life of community members was to be governed by these scriptures that possess divine force.[28] Or, 1QS 8:15-16 interprets the "way" or "path" of Isa 40:3 in this fashion: "This (path) is the study of the Law which He commanded by the hand of Moses, that they may do according to all that has been revealed from age to age, and as the Prophets have revealed by His

27. Barton (ch. 2, "'The Law and the Prophets,'" in *Oracles of God,* 35-95) concludes that only the Torah was and had been for a long time scripture in a full sense: "all other holy books, of whatever precise kind, were equal in being of secondary rank by comparison with the Torah" (93). He thinks the word "prophets" is used of a wide range of "second-order literature," with no noteworthy differences in rank among them, works that did not constitute a distinct section of a canon. For some reasons to question his view, see p. 126, n. 17.

28. See J. Licht, *The Rule Scroll: A Scroll from the Wilderness of Judaea 1QS • 1QSa • 1QSb: Text, Introduction and Commentary* (Jerusalem: Bialik, 1965), 59 (Hebrew). As he says, the two categories encompass the whole of scripture.

Holy Spirit."[29] For the writer, again the law (commanded by God through Moses) and the prophets (who speak by his Holy Spirit) are revealed and are the norm for the behavior of each person in the community. The terms "law" and "prophets" required no further clarification; the audience of the text, members of the specific group, presumably knew which scrolls the writer had in mind; whether others, say Pharisees, would have understood the labels to comprise exactly the same works the sources do not say.

The same terms figure in New Testament books. A famous example comes from the Sermon on the Mount, where Matthew quotes Jesus as teaching: "Do not think that I have come to abolish the law or the prophets; I have come not to abolish but to fulfill. For truly I tell you, until heaven and earth pass away, not one letter, not one stroke of a letter, will pass from the law until all is accomplished" (Matt 5:17-18).[30] Matthew's Jesus rejects nothing from the law and prophets; he fulfills them, having interpreted them in the correct way (see the examples in vv. 21-48). The exceptionally strong statement about the smallest detail of the law, even a part of a letter, leaves little doubt about the status it enjoyed and how secure the text seems to have been. Or, in answer to the question of a Sadducean teacher about which of the commandments in the law is the greatest, Matthew's Jesus quotes the two foundational ones from Deut 6:5 and Lev 19:18 and adds: "On these two commandments hang all the law and the prophets" (22:40). The last phrase is a comprehensive designation[31] — and it is noteworthy that Jesus is presented as mentioning the prophets to the Sadducees (since some claim, incorrectly, the Sadducees accepted the authority of the law alone). Another passage that shows the comprehensive significance of all this for the gospel message comes at the end of Acts, where Paul is speaking to Jews in Rome: "From morning until evening he explained the matter to them, testifying to the kingdom of God and trying to convince them about

29. It is widely believed that the term being explained is "way" or "path," though some have read the passage differently (see, e.g., D. Dimant, "Not Exile in the Desert but Exile in Spirit: The Pesher of Isa. 40:3 in the *Rule of the Community* and the History of the Qumran Community," in *Connected Vessels: The Dead Sea Scrolls and the Literature of the Second Temple Period* [Jerusalem: Bialik, 2010], 40-53 [Hebrew]; she also summarizes the views of other scholars). Whether one understands "way/path" to be explained or the entire quotation from Isaiah, the point about the law and the prophets is unaffected.

30. On the passage, see Loader, *Jesus' Attitude towards the Law*, 165-72, where he summarizes a range of interpretations of it.

31. On the statements in the Gospels, see C. A. Evans, "The Scriptures of Jesus and His Earliest Followers," in *The Canon Debate*, 186-90.

Jesus both from the law of Moses and from the prophets" (Acts 28:23; see also Rom 3:21). Here too the writer does not bother to explain to the reader which books he meant; he could assume they knew what fell under the rubrics "law" and "prophets." And the message had to be documented from them to be convincing for the debate to proceed.[32]

In addition to the familiar categories "law" and "prophets," one passage in the New Testament articulates what may be another inclusive designation for sacred writings. After Jesus rose from the dead, he appeared to his startled disciples and showed them by eating some fish that he remained a being of flesh and bone. "Then he said to them, 'These are my words that I spoke to you while I was still with you — that everything written about me in the law of Moses, the prophets, and the psalms must be fulfilled.' Then he opened their minds to understand the scriptures, and he said to them, 'Thus it is written . . .'" (Luke 24:44-46a; see v. 27). Luke 24:44 is often quoted as a case in which the Jewish scriptures fall into three categories, not just law and prophets but something else as well. Here "the psalms" may mean the book of that name or possibly, it is often suggested, an entire division of the scriptures of which it is the first book — in many traditional copies of the Hebrew Bible Psalms is the first book in the Writings, the third category (there is no explicit evidence for such usage in the Second Temple period, however).[33] It is instructive that in the very next verse Luke's Jesus uses the words "the scriptures [τὰς γραφάς]," the definite plural form of the word met above, as a way to refer to the entire col-

---

32. Acts 26:22 quotes Paul as saying to King Agrippa: "and so I stand here, testifying to both small and great, saying nothing but what the prophets and Moses said would take place," thus reversing the normal order. See also Matt 11:13. For a passage implying that "law and prophets" is a comprehensive designation for the scriptures, see Luke 24:27: "Then beginning with Moses and all the prophets, he interpreted to them the things about himself in all the scriptures." On the verse, see J. A. Fitzmyer, *The Gospel according to Luke X–XXIV* (AB 28A; Garden City: Doubleday, 1985), 1566-67.

33. Beckwith, in line with his theory about the very early development of a canon, writes: "This saying suggests that 'the Law of Moses', 'the Prophets' and '(the) Psalms' are now established names for the three parts of the canon"; *The Old Testament Canon of the New Testament Church*, 111. Against the idea that only the book of Psalms is meant by the third term, he objects that "the omission of the rest of the Hagiographa would be surprising in view of Jesus's regular use of the Book of Daniel in the gospels" (111-12). What he does not show is an example in which "psalms" means the books of the third division in the later Hebrew Bible. Also, it does not follow that if Psalms does not stand for the writings the author would be omitting the rest of the writings. They could be included under "prophets."

lection of sacred scrolls. He also uses a citation formula "Thus it is written" to appeal to the scriptures. It may be that "prophets" and "psalms" are both terms for prophetic literature: "However, because of the close association of the Psalter to the Prophets, as seen in the Dead Sea Scrolls, and because in the New Testament David is viewed as a prophet (cf. Acts 1:16; 2:30; 4:25) and the Psalms as prophecy (cf. Acts 1:20), 'the prophets and the psalms' should probably be taken together. That is, the things written about Jesus are found in the Law and the Prophets (including the Psalms), not in the Law, the Prophets, and the Writings."[34]

Luke is not the only ancient writer to employ three terms (even if they refer to only two categories) to designate the scriptures. In the Prologue to the Greek translation of the Wisdom of Sirach, the translator (the author's grandson) three times speaks of the law, the prophets, and the others or other books. Philo could also be cited as mentioning more categories than just the law and prophets (*Contempl. Life* 3.25).[35] Is there a similar usage of three (or more) terms for the sacred books in the Dead Sea Scrolls?

The editors of 4QMMT or the *Halakhic Letter* (4Q394-99) have claimed that it makes a major contribution to discussions of authoritative literature at Qumran. Although most of the work concerns itself with a series of legal disputes between the authors and others (a most valuable section), toward the end, in a peaceful message to the recipients, the writers address more theological or theoretical matters. Within this section they report, as the editors reconstruct the text: "And] we have [written] to you so that you may study (carefully) the book of Moses and the books of the Prophets and (the writings of) David [and the events of] ages past" (C 9-11).[36] This combination would have been the first and only reference in

34. Evans, "The Scriptures of Jesus and His Earliest Followers," 190-91; "The Dead Sea Scrolls and the Canon of Scripture in the Time of Jesus," in P. Flint, ed., *The Bible at Qumran: Text, Shape, Interpretation* (SDSSRL; Grand Rapids: Eerdmans, 2001), 76-79.

35. McDonald has compiled a convenient list of sources considered relevant to the question of canon, "Appendix A: Primary Sources for the Study of the Old Testament/Hebrew Bible Canon," in *The Canon Debate*, 580-82. The precise significance of the passages in the Greek Sirach and Philo for canonical development is disputed. For the passages, see VanderKam, "Revealed Literature in the Second Temple Period," 4-7.

36. E. Qimron and J. Strugnell, eds., *Qumran Cave 4: V, Miqṣat Ma'aśe ha-Torah* (DJD 10; Oxford: Clarendon, 1994), 59. They comment in the note to this passage that "David" "probably refers not only to the Psalms of David, but rather to the Hagiographa. This is a significant piece of evidence for the history of the tripartite division of the Canon" (59; see also p. 112, where they seem a little more hesitant about the meaning of "David").

64

Qumran literature to something resembling the three terms for sacred books attested in the Prologue to the Greek Sirach and Luke; in fact, one could argue, as several have, that it may attest a fourth category as well — "the events of ages past," though almost all of that phrase is reconstructed by the editors.

Ulrich has shown that much of the proposed text rests on the questionable placement of a fragment and on readings of letters that are unlikely to be correct. The section in question is preserved in 4Q397, and the editors reconstructed the text from letters and words on several fragments. There are two large pieces: frg. 18, which preserves the right-hand side of a column, with thirteen lines partially attested; and frg. 16, which contains parts of eleven lines that can reasonably be associated with most of the ones in frg. 18. Even if the fragments belong together, the amount of space separating them is not certain (there are no ends of lines on frg. 16). A translation of the extant, continuous text on frg. 18 for the expression being analyzed reads: "we . . . to you that you understand in the book of Mo. . . ." There is overlapping material in 4Q398 14-17 i: the fragment offers a first plural suffix but places a final *mem* after it; it also has the letters]*pr m* . . . The editors take the letters to be from the words "the book of Moses [*spr mwšh*]" On 4Q397 frg. 16 it is possible to read: *n*]*by'ym wbd* . . . ("[p]rophets and in d . . .")*.* The uncertain letters (represented by dots) are the ones they read as the last letters in "David."

Completely separate from the two large fragments, 4Q397 frgs. 18 and 16, is frg. 17, a small piece with only the letters *bspr* ("in the book," with tiny remnants of one letter from the line above and the line below). The editors placed the small fragment between the two larger ones, at line 10. The obvious question is whether it belongs there, and there seems to be no way of deciding, other than that the word *spr* is used in the context.[37]

Several of the letters in question are uncertainly or incorrectly read, as indicated by dots and circlets in the edition. In fact, in the editors' word *mwšh* ("Moses") Ulrich considers the *mem* as correctly read (it is clear) but questions the next letter (the *vav* of the edition) and whether a *shin* would have been the following letter due to space considerations. He thinks a word such as "midrash" is as likely. He also questions the readings of letters in the word *ktb*, the two surviving letters of *spr*, and the last three in the name "Mosheh" in 4Q398. So, it is far from certain and indeed unlikely that 4QMMT refers to a three-part collection of au-

37. See DJD 10, pl. 6.

65

thoritative writings. The textual evidence is far too shaky for any such conclusion.[38]

So, there are many instances of the presumably comprehensive phrase "the law and the prophets" in the New Testament and at Qumran, and a threefold expression occurs one time in the New Testament (where it is of uncertain meaning) but apparently never at Qumran. It would be welcome news to know which works were included under cover terms like "law" and "prophets." In the absence of a list supplying such data, is it possible to isolate criteria that, if met, would yield a degree of confidence that a particular book was regarded by the scrolls communities as among the law and the prophets, that is, as authoritative? At times one gets the impression that ancient writers, far from supplying information to answer modern scholars' questions, were skilled at not doing so. Yet, there are some useful principles for isolating specific authoritative books. In most cases the results are not surprising, but in some they may be. For the Dead Sea Scrolls, one can ask:[39]

1. Is the work attested in several or many copies? The condition is not sufficient for identifying authoritative works when used alone, but it would indicate a work was present and presumably used. A large number of copies would suggest it was probably used often; a small number could imply it was not.
2. Does the work function authoritatively? That is,
   a. Are citations from the book introduced by attributing their contents to God?
   b. Are citations from the book introduced by recognized citation formulas for authoritative works?
   c. Does the work have a commentary written on it (possibly this applies only to works regarded as prophetic)?

The first of the criteria listed is merely a basic condition, but if a work is not attested at all it is unlikely to have been important for the people behind the scrolls. The books that, by this criterion, would be the most obvious candidates for importance are Psalms (36), Deuteronomy (30), Isaiah (21), Genesis (19-20), Exodus (17 or 15), Leviticus (13 or 12), Daniel (8), and

---

38. E. C. Ulrich, "The Non-attestation of a Tripartite Canon in 4QMMT," *CBQ* 65 (2003): 202-14.

39. See, for instance, J. C. VanderKam, "Authoritative Literature in the Dead Sea Scrolls," *DSD* 5 (1998): 382-402.

perhaps the Twelve Prophets (8-9). Since there are reasons why copies would be in the caves other than as a reflection of their importance to the people using the site, not too much significance should be attached to these numbers; but it would be difficult to argue that Chronicles, Esther, Ezra, and Nehemiah were significant at Qumran because there are very few copies of them and no other indication they were influential. Moreover, some works that did not become parts of the Hebrew Bible are attested in more copies than many of these books that did become constituents of it: *Jubilees* (14), *Enoch* (11, but for different parts), the Book of Giants (9 or 10), and the *Serekh* (perhaps 11).

Statements That Specific Works Were from God and Thus Authoritative

The high status of a series of individual books is attested in the Qumran scrolls by this criterion. That is to say, beyond general statements about law and prophets like the ones noted above, there is a series of cases in various texts that document the authoritative status of specific books by declaring that the material in them comes from God. There are at least thirteen instances in which this happens (eight of them happen to be from the *Damascus Document,* a composition filled with scriptural citations and allusions).[40] For example, in CD 4:13-14 the writer conveys the revealed character of words in Isaiah by writing "just as God said by Isaiah the prophet, the son of Amoz, saying" before he quotes Isa 24:17.[41] In the same text, the writer had earlier introduced Ezek 44:15 with the words: "As God promised them by Ezekiel the prophet, saying" (CD 3:20-4:2). There are similar statements not only for words of Israel's prophets but also for books in the Pentateuch (e.g., CD 9:7-8; 4Q252 4:2-3; 1QM 11:5-7). This raises the question whether there exists such an introduction of a citation from a work that falls outside what would later be the specifically-defined canonical categories Law and Prophets. The answer is, yes.

One of the examples from the list in the article cited in note 39 above comes from the text that the editor has entitled David's Compositions, located at the beginning of the 27th column of the first *Psalms* scroll from

---

40. VanderKam, "Authoritative Literature in the Dead Sea Scrolls," 391-92.

41. Vermes's translation misses the direct mention of God, so "God" has been introduced into his rendering.

cave 11 (11QPs^a).[42] 11QPs^a, now joined in part by the fragmentary 11QPs^b and 4QPs^e, offers a collection of psalms, most of which are found in the Psalter as represented in MT. Those psalms come from books 4 and 5 of the Psalter (Psalms 90–150), but, besides offering smaller variants in the readings of individual psalms, the scroll presents what is often, in comparison with the traditional Hebrew text, a different arrangement of poems and nine additional units: Psalms 151, 154–55; a Plea for Deliverance; a poem also known from Sir 51:13-20b, 30; an Apostrophe to Zion; a Hymn to the Creator; 2 Sam 23:7; and the prose passage David's Compositions.

The text reports:

David son of Jesse was wise and brilliant like the light of the sun; (he was) a scribe, intelligent and perfect in all his ways before God and men.

YHWH gave him an intelligent and brilliant spirit, and he wrote 3,600 psalms and 364 songs to sing before the altar for the daily perpetual sacrifice, for all the days of the year; and 52 songs for the Sabbath offerings; and 30 songs for the New Moons,[43] for Feast-days and for the Day of Atonement.

In all, the songs which he uttered were 446, and 4 songs to make music on behalf of those stricken (by evil spirits).

In all, they were 4,050.

All these he uttered through prophecy which was given him from before the Most High.

It is not difficult to see why this fully preserved passage has intrigued so many. For the present set of questions, however, the number of David's compositions is important — 4,050, a number comfortably above the 150 psalms in the traditional book of Psalms. Where are the other 3,900? Perhaps the number is merely a literary embellishment, meant to give David more publications than his son Solomon's 4,005 (see 1 Kgs 4:32), as commentators often suggest. But all his poetic efforts, wherever they are, were, according to David's Compositions, written through divine inspiration, through the gift of prophecy from God himself. His poetry must, there-

---

42. J. A. Sanders, ed., *The Psalms Scroll of Qumrân Cave 11 (11QPs^a)* (DJD 4; Oxford: Clarendon, 1965). For David's Compositions, see 91-93 and pl. 16.

43. This can hardly be the correct translation in a text that attests the 364-day calendar; the meaning is "firsts of the month."

fore, be authoritative or scriptural. The writer of the text and his group considered as inspired more than just the 150 Psalms now in MT.[44]

Quotations from a Book Introduced with Citation Formulas

The citation formula that Jesus uses, "Thus it is written" in Luke 24:46a, is one that, with closely allied expressions, is familiar both from elsewhere in the New Testament and from the scrolls (and other Jewish literature).[45] In Acts 15, at the Jerusalem council, James gives the definitive solution to the problem that had occasioned the meeting (which of the laws of Moses non-Jewish Christians were to obey). He refers to what Simon had already said and remarks: "This agrees with the words of the prophets, as it is written . . ." (15:15-18). He then cites Amos 9:11-12. If one compares the wording of the citation with the Greek text of Amos, one sees the quotation is not verbatim, but this is of no consequence in the story.

In the scrolls there are similar examples, with citations from scriptural works introduced by formulas like "as it is written," "thus it is written." 1QS 5, in a context legislating that members of the group separate from perverse people, says: "No member of the Community shall follow them in matters of doctrine or justice, or eat or drink anything of theirs, or take anything from them except for a price; as it is written [כי כן כתוב], *'Keep away from the man in whose nostrils is breath, for wherein is he counted?'*" (5:15-17, the citation is from Isa 2:22). In col. 8 of the same text, where again there is talk about existing apart from others, it reads: "they shall separate from the habitation of unjust men and shall go into the wilderness to prepare there the way of Him; as it is written [כאשר כתוב], *Prepare in the wilderness the way of . . . , make straight in the desert a path for our God* (Isa. xl,3)" (8:13-14).

Of the more frequently employed citation formulas in the scrolls

---

44. J. C. VanderKam, "Studies on 'David's Compositions' (11QPs^a 27:2-11)," in B. A. Levine et al., eds., *Frank Moore Cross Volume* (Eretz Israel 26; Jerusalem: Israel Exploration Society, 1999), 212*-20*.

45. See, e.g., J. Fitzmyer, "The Use of Explicit Old Testament Quotations in Qumran Literature and in the New Testament," *NTS* 7 (1960-61): 297-333; repr. in *The Semitic Background of the New Testament* (BRS; Grand Rapids: Eerdmans and Livonia: Dove, 1997), 3-58. M. J. Bernstein, "Introductory Formulas for Citation and Re-citation of Biblical Verses in the Qumran Pesharim," *DSD* 1 (1994): 30-70. C. D. Elledge has compiled a full list of citation formulas and places where they are employed, in "Exegetical Styles at Qumran: A Cumulative Index and Commentary," *RevQ* 21/82 (2003): 165-91.

(ones known from elsewhere in most cases to identify authoritative literature) — ones involving the words כתוב or אמר — there are 21 instances of the former and 17 of the latter that preface citations from the following books: Exodus (1), Leviticus (4), Numbers (3), Deuteronomy (5), 2 Samuel (1), Isaiah (9), Jeremiah (1), Ezekiel (4), Hosea (3), Amos (2), Micah (1), Zechariah (2), Malachi (1), Psalms (2), Proverbs (1), and Daniel (2). Also, *Jubilees* may be the book so referenced in 4Q228 1 i 9 (cf. CD 16:2-4) and a Levi text in CD 4:15.[46]

A Commentary

The books that were subjected to commentary in *pesher* form are: Isaiah (6), Hosea (2), Micah (2), Habakkuk (1), Nahum (1), Zephaniah (2), and Psalms (3).[47] In a sense, at least parts of other books receive extended commentary in various forms, including Genesis (e.g., 4Q252), Jeremiah, and Ezekiel (for the two prophetic works, see 4Q383-90).

Indeed, one can make a case that there were not only some psalms but also several books not included in the Hebrew Bible or Old Testament that the people of the scrolls considered authoritative. It may not be a large group of compositions, or rather, there is insufficient evidence to assert it was a sizable set, but there are some especially good candidates. Among them are the writings of *Enoch* and *Jubilees*. How many other Jewish people and groups attributed scriptural authority to these books remains unknown. What can be said is that at least one New Testament writer attributed a very high status to an Enochic writing. As is well known, the author of Jude quotes from *1 En.* 1:9: "It was also about these that Enoch, in the seventh generation from Adam, prophesied [προεφήτευσεν], saying, 'See, the Lord is coming with ten thousands of his holy ones, to execute judgment on all, and to convict everyone of all the deeds of ungodliness that they have committed in such an ungodly way, and of all the harsh things that ungodly sinners have spoken against him'" (vv. 14-15). Many copies of the books of *Enoch* have been found among the Dead Sea Scrolls (11), and the passage is attested among them.[48] It seems that the scrolls communi-

---

46. See VanderKam, "Authoritative Literature in the Dead Sea Scrolls," 391-96.

47. The numbers in parentheses indicate how many copies of the *pesher* were found in the caves.

48. See VanderKam, "Revealed Literature in the Second Temple Period," 23-29; "Authoritative Literature in the Dead Sea Scrolls," 396-402.

ties believed that God continued to reveal himself in their time — for example, he told the Teacher of Righteousness the meaning of the ancient prophecies — and therefore more books could be added to the earlier scriptures. The first Christians obviously believed the same thing and added an entire testament to the Jewish scriptures. In this sense, neither community limited the category of authoritative works to the ones that later were deemed parts of the Hebrew Bible, and perhaps they and possibly other Jewish groups disagreed about whether some works now in the Hebrew Bible belonged there.

The discussion above leads to these conclusions:

1. The scriptures were tremendously important to the people of the scrolls, Jesus, and his followers, and all of them acknowledged the authority of what they called "scripture," "what is written."
2. All could refer to the books they considered authoritative as "law" and "prophets." They may have differed in some cases about which books were scriptural, but they agreed about many of them, as the texts illustrate. There was a sizable group of authoritative books, but not all Jews may have agreed on every work in that category, though there is too little evidence for deciding.
3. The books that meet the criteria listed above are, among the scrolls, the ones with the clearest status as authorities.

The scrolls and the New Testament books allow one to appreciate the ways in which Jewish people operated with the scriptures and to see that indeed there were authoritative texts to which anyone could turn for decisive evidence on a variety of questions. Even very diverse groups shared much in this regard, although the data at hand do not permit one to define fully which books would have fallen into the authoritative categories for each group of Jews. The law and prophets are frequently cited as known corpora, but exactly which books the second term included is not entirely clear, and perhaps there would be some surprises in what the first term included as well.[49]

---

49. See, e.g., the comments about the Reworked Pentateuch texts (4Q364-67) in J. C. VanderKam, "Questions of Canon Viewed through the Dead Sea Scrolls," in McDonald and Sanders, *The Canon Debate*, 91-109.

CHAPTER 4

New Copies of Old Texts

Among the texts discovered in the Qumran caves are copies of many works that had been known before the scrolls were found. The most famous examples are the many copies of books that are now in the Hebrew Bible. More than two hundred of the nine hundred copies of works identified in the eleven caves fall into this category, and all of the books that were later collected into the Hebrew Bible are represented on at least one copy — with the exception of the book of Esther. Although almost all of the "biblical" scrolls are very fragmentarily preserved, those copies, by far the oldest surviving manuscripts of scriptural works, have introduced a new age in the textual criticism of the Hebrew Bible and have had a marked influence on modern translations of the scriptures (see Chapter 1 above).

The scriptural manuscripts are not the only Qumran texts that furnish the earliest copies of previously known works. A set of other writings, many of which today are classified as "apocryphal" and "pseudepigraphal," also belong under this rubric. The relevant compositions have been surveyed in several studies,[1] and the textual contributions of the new copies have been

---

1. See J. C. VanderKam, "The Scrolls, the Apocrypha, and the Pseudepigrapha," *HS* 34 (1993): 35-47; "The Apocrypha and Pseudepigrapha at Qumran," in J. H. Charlesworth, ed., *The Bible and the Dead Sea Scrolls*, vol. 2: *The Dead Sea Scrolls and the Qumran Community* (Waco: Baylor University Press, 2006), 469-91; M. E. Stone, "The Dead Sea Scrolls and the Pseudepigrapha," *DSD* 3 (1996): 270-95; and P. W. Flint, "'Apocrypha,' Other Previously Known Writings, and 'Pseudepigrapha' in the Dead Sea Scrolls," in Flint and J. C. VanderKam, eds., *The Dead Sea Scrolls after Fifty Years: A Comprehensive Assessment* (2 vols.; Leiden, 1998-99), 2:24-66; "Noncanonical Writings in the Dead Sea Scrolls: Apocrypha, Other Previously Known Writings, Pseudepigra-

explained in some detail in preliminary and official publications. Authors of the surveys have noted that the categories "apocrypha" and "pseudepigrapha" are often neither precise nor appropriate and that the terms express a degree of prejudice. Apocrypha in its narrower sense is a Protestant word for books in Catholic Bibles that are not in Protestant ones, and pseudepigrapha, more of a catch-all title than a helpful designation, implies a degree of falsehood for these works that may not be fitting. There is a limited measure of usefulness in continuing to employ terms that are sanctioned by a long scholarly tradition, but they raise so many problems that they will be avoided where possible in this chapter. Rather, the following pages will focus on those works outside the Hebrew Bible that were known before the Qumran discoveries and for which the Qumran caves have yielded the earliest copies. Omitted from the survey is the *Damascus Document*. It was available, of course, before the Qumran discoveries because of the two copies identified in the Cairo Geniza collection. Fragments from ten manuscripts of the work have been identified among the scrolls (eight from cave 4 [4Q266-73], one from cave 5 [5Q12], and one from cave 6 [6Q15]), and they have made possible some important advances in the analysis of the *Damascus Document* and its original structure.[2] It is omitted here because the focus in this chapter is upon the traditional literature inherited by the communities of the scrolls, not on sectarian compositions.

THE TEXTS

The extrabiblical compositions known before 1947 and for which the scrolls provide the earliest copies will be examined in the order in which they appear in Emanuel Tov's official inventory list of the Qumran texts.[3]

Jubilees

Before the Qumran finds, *Jubilees* could be studied in a full Ethiopic version that became available to Western scholars in the mid-nineteenth cen-

---

pha," in *The Bible at Qumran: Text, Shape, and Interpretation* (SDSSRL; Grand Rapids: Eerdmans, 2001), 80-126.

2. See J. M. Baumgarten, ed., *Qumran Cave 4: XIII, The Damascus Document (4Q266-273)* (DJD 18; Oxford: Clarendon, 1996).

3. E. Tov, *Revised Lists of the Texts from the Judaean Desert* (Leiden: Brill, 2010).

tury, when the first copy was brought from Ethiopia to Europe by a missionary. Experts had long been aware that a book entitled *Jubilees* or the *Little Genesis* once existed because there were excerpts from it in Greek and Latin sources and also some hints that it was a Hebrew composition. The Hebrew original, however, seemed not to have survived. In some of the earliest publications about Qumran cave 1, experts reported that Hebrew fragments of *Jubilees* had been found. To date, the following manuscripts of the book have been identified and published.

Manuscript	Contents	Date
1Q17[4]	27:19-20	Early Herodian
1Q18	35:8-10	Late Hasmonean
2Q19	23:7-8	Herodian
2Q20	46:1-3	Herodian
3Q5	23:6-7, 12-13	Herodian
4Q176 19-20	23:21-23, 30-31	Herodian
4Q216	Prologue, 1:1-2, 4-7, 7-15, 26-28; 2:1-4, 7-12, 13-24	Hasmonean (ca. 125 and 75-50)
4Q217 (?)	1:29 (?)	Late Hasmonean
4Q218	2:26-27	Herodian
4Q219	21:1-2, 7-10, 12-16, 18–22:1	Early Herodian
4Q220	21:5-10	Herodian
4Q221	21:22-24; 22:22; 23:10-12; 33:12-15; 37:11-15; 38:6-8; 39:4-9	Early Herodian

4. Both 1Q17 and 1Q18 were published by J. T. Milik, "Livre des Jubilés," in D. Barthélemy and Milik, eds., *Qumran Cave I* (DJD 1; Oxford: Clarendon, 1955), 82-84. In that publication 1Q17 is identified as containing parts of *Jub* 27:19-21, but in fact nothing of v. 21 is preserved. 2Q19-20 were edited by M. Baillet in Baillet, J. T. Milik, and R. de Vaux, eds., *Les 'Petites Grottes' de Qumrân* (DJD 3; Oxford: Clarendon, 1962), 77-79. He also published 3Q5 in the same volume (96-98), although at the time he did not recognize it as a copy of *Jubilees*. Later he and others identified it correctly; see, e.g., Baillet, "Remarques sur le manuscrit du Livre des Jubilés de la grotte 3 de Qumran," *RevQ* 5/19 (1964-66): 423-33. 4Q176 frgs. 19-21 were published as part of the text *Tanḥumim* by J. M. Allegro, ed., *Qumran Cave 4: I (4Q158-4Q186)* (DJD 5; Oxford: Clarendon, 1968), 60-67; but M. Kister ("Newly-Identified Fragments of the Book of Jubilees: Jub 23:21-23, 30-31," *RevQ* 12/48 [1987]: 529-36) made the correct identification. The official edition of the remaining cave 4 fragments is J. C. VanderKam and J. T. Milik, "Jubilees," in H. Attridge et al., eds., VanderKam, consulting ed., *Qumran Cave 4: VIII, Parabiblical Texts, Part I* (DJD 13; Oxford: Clarendon, 1994), 1-140. The cave 11 material can be consulted in F. García Martínez, E. J. C. Tigchelaar, and A. S. van der Woude, eds., *Qumran Cave 11: II, 11Q2-18, 11Q20-31* (DJD 23; Oxford: Clarendon, 1998), 207-20.

Manuscript	Contents	Date
4Q222	25:9-12; 27:6-7	Late Hasmonean
4Q223-24	32:18-21; 34:4-5; 35:7-21; 36:7-23; 37:17–38:13; 39:9–40:7 (and 41:8-9?)	Late Hasmonean
11Q12	4:6-11, 13-14, 16-17 (or 11-12), 17-18, 29-30, 31; 5:1-2; 12:15-17, 28-29	Herodian

While these numerous fragmentary copies do not provide a large amount of the text of *Jubilees* (parts of 214 [possibly 217] verses from a total of 1307 in the book), important conclusions may be drawn from them.

The oldest copy, 4Q216, is an interesting one for several reasons. As can be seen from the list of passages preserved in it, it contains material from the beginning of the book. It shows that the introductory sentences of *Jubilees,* which are labeled a Prologue by modern scholars, were part of the text at a very early point. Also, the preserved fragments from 4Q216 demonstrate that the manuscript was accorded some care. The first fragments, ones that were from the initial columns of the manuscript, are copied in a later Hasmonean hand, while the fragments that belong in the next columns are written in an earlier hand, one that can be dated to ca. 125 B.C.E. The sections written in the two scribal hands belong to the same manuscript because one fragment contains a part of a column inscribed in the later hand which is still sewn to a piece from the following column that is penned in the earlier one. Had the two parts become separated, it would have been assumed that they came from different copies of *Jubilees.* The likely explanation for the presence of two scribal styles in one manuscript is that the outside sheet of the complete scroll became damaged in some way. Hence it was removed, its text was recopied, and the new sheet was sewn onto the older part. In other words, the manuscript was considered worth repairing.

4Q216 also serves as an important piece of evidence in the debate about the date of *Jubilees.* The earlier hand strongly favors the view that *Jubilees* could not have been written at so late a time as scholars had traditionally dated it. R. H. Charles, for example, maintained that *Jubilees* was composed around 110 B.C.E.[5] But if a copy is available from 125 (or 100, to be conservative), it is most unlikely that the book was written then. The

---

5. R. H. Charles, *The Book of Jubilees, or the Little Genesis* (London: Black, 1902), lviii-lxvi (where he established outside limits of 135 B.C.E. and 96 B.C.E.). In *APOT* 2:6 he wrote that it was composed between 109 and 105 B.C.E.

earliest manuscript from Qumran is, however, consistent with the views of several scholars who now place the book at earlier times in the second century B.C.E., whether in the immediate pre-Maccabean period or slightly later.[6]

The paleographical dates of the manuscripts indicate that *Jubilees* continued to be copied throughout the period when the Qumran site was occupied. While the earliest among them, 4Q216, was written in ca. 125 B.C.E., the latest among them, 11Q12, was prepared in the late Herodian period (ca. 50 C.E.).[7] Indeed, a reasonably strong case can be made that *Jubilees* was regarded as an authoritative work at Qumran, even if one cannot say precisely what level of authority it had. The simple fact that it is represented on so many copies — 14, or, if one follows J. T. Milik's view regarding 4Q217, 15 — says something about the value it was thought to possess. Among the "biblical" works at Qumran, only Psalms (36 copies), Deuteronomy (30), Isaiah (21), Genesis (19-20), and Exodus (17 or 15) are represented on more copies. No other work outside the "biblical" scrolls from the Qumran collection matches the number of copies of *Jubilees* (even the *Serekh* is available in just 12 copies).

Jubilees joins a number of other works discovered at Qumran that deal with the Genesis-Exodus story, and it is a major member of the series of writings connected with the name of Moses. It has proved to be an exegetical treasure trove, illustrating how one learned writer in the second century understood passages in the first two books of the Bible.[8]

One question raised in connection with *Jubilees* has been: Did the author understand his book as a replacement for Genesis 1–Exodus 20? After all, he largely reproduces the narrative and adds his own views about what is important and about the implications of the earlier composition. It seems unlikely that the writer, or at least the people of the scrolls, believed

6. The earlier date is defended by J. A. Goldstein, "The Date of the Book of Jubilees," *PAAJR* 50 (1983): 63-86; M. A. Knibb, "Jubilees and the Origins of the Qumran Community" (inaugural lecture in the Department of Biblical Studies, King's College, London, 17 January 1989); G. W. E. Nickelsburg, *Jewish Literature Between the Bible and the Mishnah* (2nd ed.; Minneapolis: Fortress, 2005), 73-74. A date of ca. 160-150 may be more likely (see J. C. VanderKam, *Textual and Historical Studies in the Book of Jubilees* [HSM 14; Missoula: Scholars, 1977], 214-85); *The Book of Jubilees* (GAP; Sheffield: Sheffield Academic, 2001), 17-21.

7. DJD 23:208.

8. See the materials accumulated in J. L. Kugel, *Traditions of the Bible: A Guide to the Bible As It Was at the Start of the Common Era* (Cambridge, Mass.: Harvard University Press, 1998).

Jubilees rendered Genesis-Exodus obsolete. So, for example, he refers to Genesis as the first Torah (*Jub.* 6:22; cf. 30:12) — hardly a title that expresses a negative verdict on it, and he notes that it too was revealed by the same angel of the presence who discloses *Jubilees* to Moses. It seems more in tune with the evidence to say that the writer of *Jubilees* saw his work as a supplement to the pentateuchal narratives or as a guide to reading them properly. The fact that in the scrolls communities, where *Jubilees* was thought to be of considerable value, there were about as many copies of Exodus as of *Jubilees* (a few more of Genesis) suggests that, for these people at least, both works were important and both were used.[9] Genesis was the subject of commentaries and rewritings, while *Jubilees* was deemed an authority (CD 16:2-4; perhaps 4Q228) and possibly served as an inspiration for the set of texts labeled "pseudo-Jubilees" (4Q225-27).

Aramaic Levi

Aramaic Levi is an intriguing if frustrating work. It is in all likelihood a very early text — but the text itself is the problem, primarily because of the turns that its transmission took. There is no complete copy of it available for study today. That there was such a work was known before 1947 from the fact that bits and pieces of it were preserved in different places; they became available to scholars only in the half-century or so before the first Qumran finds. It was not until 1896 that the first Aramaic parts (two and one-half leaves from one codex) were located among the thousands of texts in the Cairo Geniza, and in 1907 Charles announced the existence of three additions in the Mount Athos (Koutloumous) Greek manuscript of the *Testaments of the Twelve Patriarchs:* a prayer placed within *T. Levi* 2:3, a sentence after 5:2, and a longer section after 18:2. It so happens that the beginning and end of the extra text after 18:2 overlap with the Geniza material. These textual witnesses were thought to be sources from which the author of the later Greek *Testament of Levi* drew in composing his work.[10]

9. J. C. VanderKam, "Moses Trumping Moses: Making the Book of *Jubilees*," in S. Metso, H. Najman, and E. Schuller, eds., *The Dead Sea Scrolls: Transmission of Traditions and Production of Texts* (STDJ 92; Leiden: Brill, 2010), 25-44.

10. For the history of recovering the text of the book, see R. A. Kugler, *From Patriarch to Priest: The Levi Priestly Tradition from* Aramaic Levi *to* Testament of Levi (SBLEJL 9; Atlanta: Scholars, 1996), 25-27; J. Greenfield, M. Stone, and E. Eshel, *The Aramaic Levi Document: Edition, Translation, Commentary* (SVTP 19; Leiden: Brill, 2004),

Among the Qumran manuscripts, some fragments definitely contain parts of the text of this work, while others have been suggested as possible witnesses to it. Certainty is impossible due to the lack of a complete text and thus of adequate knowledge regarding its full contents. The following are the Qumran witnesses to the text:

1Q21: In DJD 1, Milik collected under the misleading title "Testament de Lévi" some 60 fragments, all of which are small. He considered the identification of fragments 1-6 "pratiquement certaine" and that of the others less so. He noted that fragments 3-4 could be situated in the Aramaic "Testament" of Levi known from the Cairo Geniza, and he also indicated that there were rather extended fragments of this same work among the cave 4 texts.[11]

4Q213-14: These are the numbers originally assigned to the cave 4 materials to which Milik was referring. The earlier forms of Tov's inventory note just these two copies of the relevant work in Qumran cave 4, yet in the official edition of the texts the editors, M. E. Stone and J. C. Greenfield, argued that each of the sets of fragments designated by these numbers contained within them fragments from three different manuscripts, distinguishable from one another by their scripts.[12] Thus, one now sees in the latest form of the list, not two, but six manuscripts:

4Q213 4QLevi[a] ar	Late Hasmonean (mid-first B.C.E.)[13]
4Q213a 4QLevi[b] ar	Late Hasmonean[14]
4Q213b 4QLevi[c] ar	Late Hasmonean[15]
4Q214 4QLevi[d] ar	Late Hasmonean

1-6; and H. Drawnel, *An Aramaic Wisdom Text from Qumran: A New Interpretation of the Levi Document* (JSJSup 86; Leiden: Brill, 2004), 14-32.

11. DJD 1:87-91.

12. M. E. Stone and J. C. Greenfield, "Aramaic Levi Document," in G. J. Brooke et al., eds., J. C. VanderKam, consulting ed., *Qumran Cave 4: XVII, Parabiblical Texts, Part 3* (DJD 22; Oxford: Clarendon, 1996), 1-72.

13. Stone and Greenfield, DJD 22:3.

14. Stone and Greenfield, DJD 22:26. There the editors quote F. M. Cross as saying that the script is late Hasmonean, resembling that of 4QKings[a] (dated to the mid-first century B.C.E. by J. Trebolle Barrera in E. Ulrich, F. M. Cross et al., eds., *Qumran Cave 4: IX, Deuteronomy, Joshua, Judges, Kings* [DJD 14; Oxford: Clarendon, 1995], 172).

15. Stone (DJD 22:37) refers to Cross's view that this manuscript may have been written by the scribe of 4Q213a (as Milik had thought); Stone, however, concluded that the script was only "of the same Hasmonaean type."

4Q214a 4QLevi^e ar	Late Hasmonean/Early Herodian
4Q214b 4QLevi^f ar	Hasmonean[16]

Judging from these paleographical dates as assigned in the official editions, all of the copies were made in the first century B.C.E. (the Hasmonean period in paleographical terms is understood to be from 150 B.C.E. to 30 B.C.E.) and are thus not among the earliest manuscripts at Qumran. However, the editors' dating arouses questions in light of the Accelerator Mass Spectrometry experiments performed on 4Q213. When the scientists conducted the test, the division of 4Q213 into three manuscripts had not yet been made, but it appears from the description that the test was carried out on what Stone and Greenfield isolated as 4Q213 (that is, not 213a and 213b). This follows from the fact that the Museum Inventory number for the manuscript is given as 817 (see Tov's list), the one now numbered 4Q213. According to the results of the AMS testing, the dates between which the manuscript falls are 191-155 B.C.E. or 146-120 B.C.E.[17] Using a later (from 1997) system for figuring dates, Greg Doudna recalculated and wrote that "Zurich's [the place of the laboratory where the test was done] date for 4QLevi^a ar was BP [= Before Present, that is, before 1950] 2125 ± 24, which calibrates to 197-105 BCE at the one-sigma range (two-sigma: 344-324 BCE or 253-203 BCE)."[18] As a result, it seems quite likely that this manuscript is older than Stone and Greenfield suggested, more in line with Milik's original dating of it to the second century.[19]

4Q540-41: These numbers had been labeled AhA (bis) = TLevi c? ar

---

16. The dates for the script(s) of the last three entries are given in DJD 22:44 (Cross thinks the script of 4Q214b looks like the hand of what the editors label 213a), 54 (it resembles that of 214b), 62.

17. G. Bonani et al., "Radiocarbon Dating of the Dead Sea Scrolls," *Atiqot* 20 (1991): 30 (Table 1, item no. 5).

18. G. L. Doudna, "Dating the Scrolls on the Basis of Radiocarbon Analysis," in Flint and VanderKam, eds., *The Dead Sea Scrolls after Fifty Years*, 1:445. "The interval of ± one *sigma* (1σ) means the laboratory reports with 68% confidence that the true date is somewhere within the reported date interval. An interval of ± two *sigma* (2σ) is wider, and expresses 95% confidence that the true date is within that range" (435-36). See also his Table A (468).

19. J. T. Milik, *The Books of Enoch: Aramaic Fragments of Qumrân Cave 4* (Oxford: Clarendon, 1976), 23; see also his earlier publication, "Le Testament de Lévi en araméen: Fragment de la grotte 4 de Qumrân," *RB* 62 (1955): 398-406. Stone and Greenfield retain their original dating in *The Aramaic Levi Document*, 4, but Drawnel notes the AMS evidence and accepts Milik's verdict; *An Aramaic Wisdom Text from Qumran*, 24.

and AhA = TLevi d? ar in Tov's lists on the basis of Émile Puech's preliminary publications of them.[20] More recently their names have been changed
to apocrLevi[a] ar and apocrLevi[b]? ar, reflecting the fact that now Puech
(their editor) does not consider them fragments from copies of *Aramaic
Levi*. They are also not included as witnesses to the text in the editions of
Stone-Greenfield and Henryk Drawnel.

4Q548: The fragments of this number are now considered parts of a
sixth copy of *Visions of Amram*, another Aramaic work with priestly affinities. Milik suggested that they may be related to *Aramaic Levi*, but it seems
not to be a copy of the work.[21]

There is no objective evidence for this claim, but *Aramaic Levi* could
well have been written in the third century B.C.E.[22] If so, it was, with the
books of *Enoch*, an early Aramaic work that was brought to Qumran, and
it seems to represent a prior stage in a tradition in which the scrolls communities saw themselves standing. It also shows a number of parallels with
Jubilees' treatment of Levi. For example, both sources evaluate most posi-
tively Levi's role in the slaughter of the men of Shechem, after the young
prince Shechem had raped their sister and the residents of Shechem had
proposed intermarriage between them and the clan of Jacob (Genesis 34).
Levi's part in that event, criticized in Genesis, earns him an eternal priesthood in *Aramaic Levi* and in *Jubilees*. In this tradition the priesthood is
traced back, not to the tribe of Levi, but to the person of Levi, as suggested
already in Mal 2:4-7. In *Aramaic Levi*, the third son of Jacob and Leah is ap-
pointed a priest in his lifetime, receives cultic instructions as well as a vision of the heavens, and carries out priestly duties. The composition seems
to have come from sacerdotal circles advocating their own positions regarding the priesthood and expressing them through stories about the
founder of the guild. For the author the priesthood

> is to be an office occupied by individuals who passionately protect
> communal and cultic purity and ferociously attack the sources of

---

20. É. Puech, "Fragments d'un apocryphe de Lévi et le personnage eschatologique:
4QTestLevi[c-d](?) et 4QAJa," in J. Trebolle Barrera and L. Vegas Montaner, eds., *The Madrid Qumran Congress* (2 vols.; Leiden: Brill and Madrid: Editorial Complutense, 1992),
2:449-501. The abbreviation AhA is for Aharonique.

21. See the discussion in Kugler, *From Patriarch to Priest*, 51-52.

22. Greenfield and Stone suggest the third or early second century B.C.E.; *The Aramaic Levi Document*, 19-22. Drawnel sides with Milik in speaking of the end of the
fourth or early third century B.C.E.; *An Aramaic Wisdom Text from Qumran*, 63-75.

evil; they are to live by norms that transcend those prescribed by the Torah; and they are to be known for their wisdom. The tapestry woven from the narrative flow and the themes of the document also suggest that there are priests who do not meet these requirements among Levi's descendants, clergy who are unconcerned about purity, rules of conduct, and wisdom. Aramaic Levi is perhaps a rejection of the latter kind of priest, and a plea for acceptance of the former type.[23]

The Book of Giants

There was evidence for the existence of a work entitled the Book of Giants (the giants in question are the children of the angels and daughters of men) before the Qumran discoveries, but again neither a text in its original language nor any witnesses to the entire composition survived. As a matter of fact, the first parts of the text became known only a few years before the initial Qumran discoveries were made. Ancient sources reported that Mani, the founder of Manicheism, had composed a "Book of Giants," but its contents remained largely a mystery. The name appears in a number of Manichean lists of the canonical books (preserved in Coptic and Chinese), and it was mentioned in other texts whose authors, whether Christian or Muslim, were critical of the Manicheans.[24] However, in 1943 W. B. Henning published fragments from the book preserved in Turfan in the Tarim Basin in Central Asia.[25] Milik later proposed that some Qumran fragments that seemed to belong within an Enochic tradition but did not contain texts known from *1 Enoch* were in fact from the original Jewish Aramaic work behind Mani's Book of Giants. In support of his view he supplied several fragments of the text, reread some Qumran pieces that had been published but not properly identified as coming from this work, and added a defense of his explanation regarding the nature of the composition.[26] His general conclusions about this matter have been confirmed in later, more extended studies. The fragments from Qumran reveal that the

23. Kugler, *From Patriarch to Priest*, 223.

24. See J. C. Reeves, *Jewish Lore in Manichaean Cosmogony: Studies in the* Book of Giants *Traditions* (HUCM 14; Cincinnati: Hebrew Union College Press, 1992), 9-49, for a detailed survey of the evidence.

25. W. B. Henning, "The Book of Giants," *BSO(A)S* 11 (1943-46): 52-74.

26. Milik, *The Books of Enoch*, 298-339.

gigantic sons of the angelic Watcher Shemihazah were named Hahyah and 'Ohyah; another giant bore the name Mahaway. Surprisingly, the fragments also mention Gilgamesh and Hobabish, the former a familiar name and the latter apparently a reflex of the monster Humbaba known from the Epic of Gilgamesh. These characters of Mesopotamian mythology became giants in the Book of Giants.

A rather large number of fragments from the Qumran caves do or may offer parts of the Book of Giants, although the evidence is so fragmentary that even the order of the contents is not always clear.[27] In Tov's list, these manuscripts are identified as copies of the Book of Giants:

> 1Q23 EnGiants[a] ar
> 1Q24 EnGiants[b]? ar
> 2Q26 EnGiants ar
> 4Q203 EnGiants[a] ar
> 4Q206 EnGiants[f] (frags. 2-3)
> 4Q530 EnGiants[b] ar
> 4Q531 EnGiants[c] ar
> 4Q532 EnGiants[d] ar
> 4Q533 EnGiants[e] ar (Eschatological Vision? ar)
> 6Q8 papEnGiants ar

In his study, Loren Stuckenbruck numbers those listed above among the copies of the Book of Giants, with the exception of 4Q533; he adds 4Q556, which is called Prophecy[a] ar by Tov. Stuckenbruck also gives a series of texts which he labels "Manuscripts Whose Identification with the Book of Giants Is Unlikely," that is, manuscripts that at least one scholar has identified as belonging to the Book of Giants but which probably are not witnesses of the text: 1Q19, 4Q533-37, 6Q14. Even among the ones he accepts he distinguishes different degrees of certainty that they belong: 1Q23, 6Q8, 4Q203, 4Q530-31 ("virtually certain"); 2Q26, 4Q532 ("probable"); 1Q24, 4Q556, 4Q206 2-3 ("plausible").[28] Stuckenbruck suggests the following sequence for the parts of the work on the basis of the texts most

---

27. L. T. Stuckenbruck (*The Book of Giants from Qumran: Texts, Translation, and Commentary* [TSAJ 63; Tübingen: Mohr Siebeck, 1997], 13-16) provides a "Synoptic Comparison of Three Reconstructions" (those of K. Beyer, J. C. Reeves, and F. García Martínez).

28. Stuckenbruck, *The Book of Giants from Qumran*, 41.

securely assigned to it in combination with the Manichean fragments of the Book of Giants:

1. Narrative Account of the Fall of the Watchers, Birth of the Giants, and the Giants' Misdemeanors on the Earth
2. Report of These Events to Enoch
3. Enoch's Petitionary Prayer
4. Conversations Among the Giants Concerning Their Deeds
5. First Pair of Dream-Visions
6. [Mahaway's First Encounter With Enoch]; [Mahaway Returns with Two Tablets]; [The First Tablet from Enoch to the Watchers and Giants Is Read]; 'Ohyah Is Incredulous about the Message from Mahaway
7. A Watcher Tells of His Powerlessness Against God's Angelic Forces; 'Ohyah and Gilgamesh Express Conflicting Interpretations of Their Dreams
8. [Initial Punishment of 'Azazel]; Giants Anticipate Their Judgment
9. Initial Punishment of Giants
10. The Second Tablet
11. Gilgamesh Remains Hopeful
12. Second Pair of Dream-Visions
13. Mahaway's Second Encounter With Enoch; Enoch's Interpretation of the Dreams
14. An Announcement (by Enoch?) of Post-Diluvian Bliss[29]

If all of the fragmentary texts listed above are indeed copies of the Book of Giants, it was very well represented in the Qumran library — more so than most "biblical" books. The composition builds upon the familiar Enochic story about the angels who descended from heaven and mated with women; the offspring of these marriages were giants, and these giants were responsible for the frightful increase of evil that caused the Lord to send the flood. The book belongs in a tradition that attempted to justify God's seemingly extreme act of sending the flood and did so by elaborating on the enigmatic yet suggestive words in Gen 6:1-4. Stuckenbruck summarizes the Book of Giants as follows:

---

29. Stuckenbruck, *The Book of Giants from Qumran*, 21-24. Brackets surrounding a heading indicate that there is no textual evidence from the Qumran copies documenting the section.

... BG retains elements from *1 Enoch* 6–11 (the fallen angel myth) and 12–16 (Enoch's communication with the fallen angels) and, in so doing, has integrated these themes while placing the focus on how the sons of the Watchers learn that they will be punished. If it can be said that *1 Enoch* 6–11 constitutes a kind of "expository narrative" of the myth in Gen 6:1-4, BG presupposes such an exegetical expansion and shifts the spotlight. This adjustment occurs not only laterally, but also with respect to intensity. The story of the giants' exploits, dreams, and plight seems to have been more detailed than the accounts concerning the Watchers or giants in either the *Book of Watchers* or *Jubilees*.[30]

The Book of Giants supplies further confirmation of how important Gen 6:1-4, as understood in *1 Enoch* 6–16, was to this tradition, and the number of copies at Qumran suggests that it was considered more than simply an entertaining diversion. In fact, Milik has maintained that it constituted a part of the Qumranic form of an Enochic pentateuch. He had noted that the composition entitled the Similitudes of Enoch (*1 Enoch* 37–71) was not represented on the Qumran fragments; also, he believed that parts of the Book of Giants did feature on two copies of the Enoch books: 4QEnoch[c] and 4QEnoch[e].[31] In his opinion, it was only later, when the Manichees adopted the Book of Giants, that it was replaced by the Similitudes (*1 Enoch* 37–71). His hypothesis has not carried the day, and it is not certain that the fragments of the Book of Giants actually belonged to the same manuscript as the copies of the Enoch books, although they may (see Stuckenbruck's evaluations above).

The history of the Book of Giants shows another avenue by which the communities of the scrolls exercised influence beyond their narrower confines. It seems that the Jewish-Christian baptismal sect, the Elchesaites, in which Mani was raised[32] embraced the Aramaic Book of Giants and that Mani used it as the basis for his book by the same name.

---

30. Stuckenbruck, *The Book of Giants from Qumran*, 28.

31. Milik, *The Books of Enoch*, e.g., 6.

32. "Elchasai, the founder of your Law" is mentioned in the Cologne Mani Codex 94.10-12; R. Cameron and A. J. Dewey, trans., *The Cologne Mani Codex (P. Colon. inv. nr. 4780)* (SBLTT 15; Missoula: Scholars, 1979), 76-77. See also 96.19; 97.12.

The Wisdom of Ben Sira (Sirach)

The Wisdom of Ben Sira, which is found in Greek codices of the Bible and became part of the wider canon in the Western and Eastern churches, was known to have been written in Hebrew. The earliest evidence for the original language comes from the invaluable preface to the Greek translation written by the translator himself, who happened to be the grandson of the author. About the book in their hands, he confided to his readers:

> You are invited therefore to read it with goodwill and attention, and to be indulgent in cases where, despite our diligent labor in translating, we may seem to have rendered some phrases imperfectly. For what was originally expressed in Hebrew does not have exactly the same sense when translated into another language. Not only this book, but even the Law itself, the Prophecies, and the rest of the books differ not a little when read in the original.

While full texts of the book were available in several ancient translations (e.g., Greek, Syriac, Latin), the Hebrew of Ben Sira was thought to have been lost. It is quoted a number of times in Jewish sources, but no Hebrew copies of the book itself were preserved. The textual situation began to change at the end of the nineteenth century, when fragmentary copies of Ben Sira in Hebrew were located in the Cairo Geniza. In 1896 Solomon Schechter identified a sheet from a manuscript as belonging to the Wisdom of Ben Sira. By 1900 a total of four copies (labeled A-D) of the Hebrew text had been isolated among the many remains of manuscripts in the Geniza. All were medieval copies, ranging in date from the tenth to the twelfth century c.e. In 1931 a fifth copy was identified (E), and later a few additional parts of B and C were published. After several more decades a sixth Geniza copy was made available (in 1974 or 1982 — there seems to be a dispute about who first identified it).[33] However, since all of these were late copies, some could still maintain that there were no ancient witnesses to the Hebrew text of Ben Sira — that the medieval Hebrew copies reflected a retranslation based on a later version such as the Syriac, not the original Hebrew text itself.

By that time, however, the situation had again started to change dramat-

---

33. For a history of the discoveries, see P. W. Skehan and A. A. Di Lella, *The Wisdom of Ben Sira* (AB 39; New York: Doubleday, 1987), 51-53.

ically with the Judean Desert discoveries of the 1950s and 1960s. Qumran cave 2 contained some very small fragments, 2Q18, which the editor, Maurice Baillet, identified as coming from Sir 6:14-15 (?, perhaps from 1:19-20) and 6:20-31. The first fragment preserves five letters, one on the first line of a small piece, and four on the second (three of which are marked as uncertainly read). The second fragment offers only the last letters on eight out of twelve consecutive lines (the ends of the other four are blank); they could be identified because this passage is found in ms. A from the Geniza. The samples of the text are small, but the editor properly noted their importance.[34] Because of the similar stichometric arrangement, Baillet entertained the idea that the Cairo manuscripts were copied from Qumran exemplars.

The fragile but valuable evidence from cave 2 was soon supplemented from an unexpected source. The famous Psalms manuscript from cave 11 (11QPs[a]) offered, among its several fascinating surprises, a copy of Sir 51:13-20b, 30b on cols. 21:11-17 and 22:1. One can see on plate 13 that the poem, an acrostic, begins at the right margin in line 11 (the end of the preceding line was left blank, following the last word of Ps 138:1-8). The first seven lines appear at the bottom of the preserved part of the column, but a goodly section must also have figured in the lost lower portion of the parchment. On col. 22 (plate 14) the last two words of the composition are written at the beginning of the first line, a blank space is left, and later in the same line the next poem, the Apostrophe to Zion, begins. James Sanders, the editor, wrote:

> The Q [= Qumran] text leaves little doubt about its authenticity. It is clearly a valid first-century copy of the original composition, and not a reconstruction from the versions. There are only three words in the text which present serious difficulties and they are far from insurmountable. . . . It is regrettable, of course, that not more of the text is preserved, and it is unfortunate that a few words at the bottom of Col. xxi are less than certain. But where the text is clear it seems highly reliable.[35]

34. Baillet in DJD 3:75: "Not only do they in fact document the ancient existence of a Hebrew text of Sirach, but this text is so much like that from the Geniza that it allowed the certain identification of a very small fragment. Moreover, the material disposition, as far as one can determine, seems to be the same as in ms. B" (my translation). He dated the fragments to the second half of the first century B.C.E. His edition can be found on pp. 75-77.

35. J. A. Sanders, ed., *The Psalms Scroll of Qumrân Cave 11 (11QPs^a)* (DJD 4; Oxford: Clarendon, 1965), 79.

The cave 11 copy shows the Greek order for verses 13-18 to be correct, not the order in the Geniza copies. Yet the Hebrew text from Qumran differs considerably from the Greek as well.

The canonical issues that have been spawned by the cave 11 Psalms manuscript naturally involve this acrostic poem known from Sirach 51. Does the presence of the poem in the manuscript mean that the compiler included it among David's compositions and as part of an authoritative book of Psalms? Did some in the land of Israel consider the poem to be Davidic, while in Alexandria it was regarded as part of the Wisdom of Ben Sira? Or was it a part of the original text of Ben Sira? The grandson-translator, who, one might expect, would know the truth about the matter, included it with his grandfather's other writings (unless it was added). Sanders observed: ". . . it is now quite clear that the canticle is totally independent of Sirach. If Jesus, son of Sira, of Jerusalem, had penned the canticle it would hardly have been found in 11QPs[a], which claims Davidic authorship."[36] Sanders concluded that the poem, with its encouragement to gain and espouse wisdom, better fits the context in Sirach than in a Davidic psalter, but "at Qumran it was clearly thought to be one of the 450 songs (xxvii 10) which David composed."[37] It is curious that at so late a date as the first half of the first century c.e., when 11QPs[a] was copied,[38] the Davidic attribution could still be maintained; by this time the Greek translation of the Wisdom of Ben Sira had existed for perhaps one hundred fifty years or more.

The Qumran finds relating to the original Hebrew text of the Wisdom of Ben Sira did not exhaust the treasures hidden in the Judean Desert. During the excavations at Masada, a fairly extensive section of a Hebrew scroll with text from Ben Sira was located on April 8, 1964. It was found "folded and crushed, near the northern wall of casemate 1109, lying close to the floor and under the debris covering this and other casemates."[39] The preserved parts contained major portions of 39:27-44:17 (material paralleled by ms. B from the Geniza). A total of twenty-six fragments fit into

---

36. Sanders, DJD 4:83.

37. Sanders, DJD 4:85. P. C. Beentjes (*The Book of Ben Sira in Hebrew: A Text Edition of All Extant Hebrew Manuscripts and a Synopsis of All Parallel Hebrew Ben Sira Texts* [VTSup 68; Leiden: Brill, 1997], 177-78) places the version of the acrostic in Geniza ms. B and the text of the cave 11 scroll in parallel columns so that the reader can easily compare them.

38. Sanders, DJD 4:6-9.

39. Y. Yadin, *The Ben Sira Scroll from Masada* (Jerusalem: Israel Exploration Society and Shrine of the Book, 1965), 1-2.

seven columns of text. The scribe wrote the lines in stichometric form, as in copies B, E, and F from the Geniza and the larger of the two pieces from cave 2. The handwriting — middle or late Hasmonean in date — suggests that the manuscript was copied in the first half of the first century B.C.E.[40]

Yigael Yadin, who first made the fragmentary material available, wrote about the significance of the scroll:

> Let it be pointed out at the very outset of this survey that the version of Ben Sira discovered at Masada — which is the most ancient of all extant MSS. (whether of the Hebrew original or in translation) — unmistakably confirms the main conclusions reached by a considerable number of scholars, that the MSS. discovered in the Cairo Genizah basically represent the original Hebrew version. At the same time, the Masada scroll confirms the findings of those scholars who maintained that the Genizah versions abound in corruptions partly due to copyists' errors and partly representing later developments, though still comparatively early, of the original version. Though the immediate importance of the discovery derives from the light it sheds on this basic problem, its chief contribution — for those who never cast doubt on the authenticity of the Genizah MSS. — lies precisely in the way it enables us, for the first time, to clarify the relationship of the various Genizah MSS. both to each other, and to the original consulted by the Greek and Syriac translators.[41]

Since ms. B from the Geniza contains the same stretch of text, the two can be compared. Yadin did so in his initial publication and concluded that, though they contain many variants, "the Scroll text is basically identical with that of the Genizah MSS.[42] Also, the Hebrew text from which the grandson translated the work into Greek is "the *closest* to that of the Scroll," and the scroll from Masada is the closest of all our witnesses to the original text.[43] It is a pity that the Masada fragments do not extend as far as chapter 51 so that one could ascertain whether that chapter appeared in the Hebrew original.

40. Yadin, *The Ben Sira Scroll from Masada*, 6.
41. Yadin, *The Ben Sira Scroll from Masada*, 1.
42. Yadin, *The Ben Sira Scroll from Masada*, 10.
43. Yadin, *The Ben Sira Scroll from Masada*, 11.

The result of all these discoveries is that about 68 percent of the Hebrew text of Ben Sira is now available.[44] The fact that there are witnesses from Qumran and Masada raises questions about why this book (or parts of it) would be found in such locations, because there seems to be nothing in the theology or philosophy of Ben Sira that would be especially appealing to the Essenes or the Sicarii. What can be said, however, is that the book was part of the older literary heritage of Judaism and thus could be expected to appear in many places and to command high respect for its authority. There is no evidence from Qumran or Masada regarding the status of the book, and it is not quoted in other texts found at either site. Only the placement of the poem known from Sirach 51 in the Psalms scrolls from cave 11 implies anything about the status of a *part* of the text.

Tobit

The book of Tobit is an appealing narrative work found in Greek copies of the scriptures but not in the Hebrew Bible. Like the Wisdom of Ben Sira, it was available in Greek copies and translations from it, but experts believed the Greek text rested on a Semitic original that had perished. In this case the fourth Qumran cave has yielded several copies of the book in two languages — Aramaic and Hebrew.

Five copies of Tobit from cave 4 have been identified and published:

4Q196 = 4QpapTobit[a] ar	late Hasmonean (ca. 50 B.C.E.)
4Q 197 = 4QTobit[b] ar	early Herodian (ca. 25 B.C.E.–25 C.E.)
4Q198 = 4QTobit[c] ar	late Hasmonean/early Herodian (ca. 50 B.C.E.)
4Q 199 = 4QTobit[d] ar	Hasmonean (ca. 100 B.C.E.)
4Q200 = 4QTobit[e]	early Herodian (ca. 30 B.C.E.–20 C.E.)[45]

44. This is the estimate of Skehan and Di Lella, *The Wisdom of Ben Sira,* 53. The percentage should now be raised because two additional leaves from ms. C have been identified and published: S. Elizur, "Two New Leaves of the Hebrew Version of Ben Sira," *DSD* 17 (2010): 13-29.

45. The texts were first treated by Milik and later published officially by J. A. Fitzmyer, "Tobit," in M. Broshi et al., eds., J. C. VanderKam, consulting ed., *Qumran Cave 4: XIV, Parabiblical Texts, Part 2* (DJD 19; Oxford: Clarendon, 1995), 1-76. The dates above for the scribal hands are the ones assigned by Fitzmyer.

4Q478 had been represented in older lists of Qumran texts as a possible sixth copy of Tobit, but it is now designated 4Q478 papFragment Mentioning Festivals. The small fragment preserves a few letters or words on five lines and is written in Hebrew; but it appears to contain none of the text of Tobit.[46]

Parts of all fourteen chapters of the book are present on one or more copies, with the first copy (4Q196) containing the largest amount of text (parts of chs. 1–7, 12–14); some 103 of Tobit's 245 verses are reflected on the Qumran fragments.[47] As Joseph Fitzmyer shows, "the Aramaic and Hebrew form of the Tobit story found at Qumran agrees in general with the long recension of the book found in the fourth-century Greek text of codex Sinaiticus."[48] However, he also cautions that the Aramaic Tobit from Qumran was not the text base from which the long recension was made.[49]

While the Qumran fragments have made a large contribution to understanding the textual history of the book by showing the general superiority of the longer recension, they raise the question of Tobit's original language. It seems a reasonable inference to say that the predominance of Aramaic copies at Qumran would point to it as the original language; also, an Aramaic copy is the oldest among the five (copy d). However, Klaus Beyer and Michael Wise have noted some features in the sparse remaining parts of the Hebrew copy that do not look very much like translation Hebrew (although it could be asked whether the modern scholar has the evidence to know what translation Hebrew of the time would look like). An example they note is the use of the infinitive absolute, something rare in Hebrew of this period.[50] Yet why this should be viewed as a sign of composition in Hebrew is not clear. Is there reason to think the construction would not be employed in translation Hebrew? As Fitzmyer concludes, one

46. See E. Larson and L. Schiffman, "478. 4QpapFragment Mentioning Festivals," in DJD 22:295-96.

47. J. A. Fitzmyer, "The Aramaic and Hebrew Fragments of Tobit from Qumran Cave 4," *CBQ* 57 (1995): 658.

48. DJD 19:2. J. T. Milik had earlier noted this point; *Ten Years of Discovery in the Wilderness of Judea* (SBT 26; London: SCM, 1959), 31-32. In his essay, Fitzmyer added that the Qumran texts are at times fuller than the representatives of the long recension (esp. Sinaiticus and the Old Latin) but at other times are shorter; "The Aramaic and Hebrew Fragments," 663.

49. DJD 19:4.

50. K. Beyer, *Die aramäischen Texte vom Toten Meer* (Göttingen: Vandenhoeck & Ruprecht, 1984), 298-300; *Die aramäischen Texte vom Toten Meer: Ergänzungsband* (Göttingen: Vandenhoeck & Ruprecht, 1994), 134-37; and M. O. Wise, "A Note on 4Q196 (papTob ar^a) and Tobit i 22," *VT* 43 (1993): 566-69.

cannot prove the point, but Aramaic does seem the more likely choice for the original language.[51]

Presumably the piety commended in the book of Tobit — the righteous acts carried out under trying conditions — would have been an attractive feature of the book. At the end there is an apocalyptic section (14:3-11) that could have been appealing to the people of the scrolls. In addition, the book supplies one of the few references to the Festival of Weeks (Pentecost in 2:1) in texts from the early second temple; that festival is fundamentally important in the scrolls.

Enoch

Perhaps no other book outside those in the later Jewish canon of scripture has generated so much scholarly interest as *1 Enoch* following discovery of the cave 4 copies of booklets in it. Eleven manuscripts — all written in Aramaic — have been identified as containing material found in four Enochic booklets:

4Q201 En^a ar (200-150 B.C.E.)	BW[52]
4Q202 En^b ar (ca. 150 B.C.E.)	BW
4Q204 En^c ar (ca. 30-1 B.C.E.)	BW [BG?] BD EE
4Q205 En^d ar (ca. 30-1 B.C.E.)	BW BD
4Q206 En^e ar (ca. 100-50 B.C.E.)	BW BD
4Q207 En^f ar (ca. 150-125 B.C.E.)	BD
4Q208 Enastr^a ar (ca. 200 B.C.E.)	AB
4Q209 Enastr^b ar (ca. early years C.E.)	AB
4Q210 Enastr^c ar (ca. 50 B.C.E.)	AB
4Q211 Enastr^d ar (ca. 50-1 B.C.E.)	AB
4Q212 En^g ar (ca. 50 B.C.E.)	EE

Milik argued that the writings of Enoch suffered a decline in popularity during the Qumran period. He based that conclusion on the fact that, of the

51. Fitzmyer, "The Aramaic and Hebrew Fragments," 670.

52. BW = the Book of the Watchers (*1 Enoch* 1-36); BD = the Book of Dreams (*1 Enoch* 83-90); EE = the Epistle of Enoch (*1 Enoch* 91-107); BG = the Book of Giants; and AB = the Astronomical Book (*1 Enoch* 72-82). The dates for the manuscripts are from Milik, *The Books of Enoch*, 5, 7. The booklets included on the copies are from his chart on p. 6.

eleven manuscripts, only one, 4QEnastr[b], was copied in the first century C.E.[53] However, it is not clear that his inference follows from the evidence at hand. The several copies from the late first century B.C.E. may have entailed that there was no need to make new ones in the early first century C.E.; and 4QEnastr[b] shows that at least one Enochic work (the most technical and tedious among them) was transcribed in the first century C.E.

Since the Aramaic copies of the Enoch booklets have been surveyed and studied in depth a number of times and their implications for the history of the text and the early dates for some of these booklets have been noted,[54] these subjects will not be repeated here. Rather, a more recent development and one that has the potential to make a noteworthy contribution to Enoch studies should be presented. Several scholars have identified a number of the very small cave 7 fragments as coming from a Greek translation of the Epistle of Enoch. In the initial publication of the cave 7 fragments in 1962, the editor was able to assign just two of them to known texts (7Q1 [Exodus] and 7Q2 [The Letter of Jeremiah; see below]), while 7Q3-18 were listed as unidentified.[55] Later studies have, however, defended these identifications:

7Q4 frg. 1 + 7Q12 + 7Q14 + 7Q8 + 7Q13 = *1 En.* 103:3-4, 7-8, 15 (3 successive columns)
7Q11 = *1 En.* 100:12 (?)[56]

The script of 7Q4 is apparently to be dated to ca. 100 B.C.E.[57] If that is true, the traditional dating for the Aramaic original of the Epistle of Enoch — near the end of the second century B.C.E. — is almost certainly wrong,

---

53. Milik, *The Books of Enoch*, 7.

54. E.g., J. C. VanderKam, *Enoch and the Growth of an Apocalyptic Tradition* (CBQMS 16; Washington: Catholic Biblical Association of America, 1984); G. W. E. Nickelsburg, *1 Enoch 1: A Commentary on the Book of 1 Enoch, Chapters 1–36; 81–108* (Hermeneia; Minneapolis: Fortress, 2001).

55. Baillet, DJD 3:142-46.

56. E. Muro, "The Greek Fragments of Enoch from Qumran Cave 7 (7Q4, 7Q8, & 7Q12 = 7QEn gr = Enoch 103:3-4, 7-8)," *RevQ* 18/70 (1997): 307-12; É. Puech, "Sept fragments de la Lettre d'Hénoch (1 Hén 100, 103, et 105) dans la grotte 7 de Qumrân (= 7QHén gr)," *RevQ* 18/70 (1997): 313-23 (he thinks 7Q4 frg. 2 contains letters from 105:1). See also G. W. Nebe, "7Q4 — Möglichkeit und Grenze einer Identifikation," *RevQ* 13/52 (1988): 629-33; and Puech, "Notes sur les fragments grecs du manuscrit 7Q4 = 1 Hénoch 103 et 105," *RB* 103 (1996): 592-600.

57. This is the conclusion of C. H. Roberts, as cited by Baillet, DJD 3:142, 144.

since it would very likely have taken some time for a work to establish itself to such an extent that a person fluent in both Aramaic and Greek would have taken the trouble to translate it.

The presence of these fragments in Greek implies that there was someone in the scrolls communities who could read this part of the Enoch literature in Greek. Also, it is at least intriguing that, apart from Leviticus, Numbers, and Deuteronomy, only the Epistle of Enoch, it seems, is attested in its original Semitic form and in a Greek translation among the hundreds of texts found at Qumran. Perhaps this says something about its status.

Epistle of Jeremiah

One small work that should also be mentioned is the Epistle of Jeremiah, which is often included as the sixth chapter in the book of Baruch. Baillet maintained that 7Q2, written on a papyrus piece with Greek writing, preserved words and letters from vv. 43b-44 of the one-chapter book.[58] An obvious problem with any identification is that so little of the text is preserved. A grand total of twenty-two letters can be read on the fragment, and they are distributed over five lines, with the result that only two complete words are legible ("therefore" [οὖν] in line 3 and "them" [αὐτούς] in line 4). If one assumes, nevertheless, that the identification of the small piece is correct, then one may well ask what the people of the scrolls would have found of value in this short (seventy-three verses) composition. The book purports to be a letter sent by Jeremiah to the captives who were about to be exiled to Babylon; in it he writes a scathing attack on idolatry — a familiar theme in biblical literature. A number of Qumran works are addressed to people who considered themselves to be in a state of exile (4Q383-91; see also the first column of the *Damascus Document*), and some of these texts are connected with Jeremiah, just as this letter is.

Psalms 151, 154, 155

One of the other surprises served up by the first Psalms scroll from cave 11 is the presence on it of the Hebrew text of Psalms 151 (col. 28:3-14), 154 (col.

---

58. DJD 3:143.

18), and 155 (col. 24:3-17). It should be noted that these psalms are not seg-
regated in the scroll but are scattered: Psalm 154 follows Psalm 145 and precedes the poem called Plea For Deliverance; Psalm 155 follows Psalm 144
and precedes Psalm 142, while Psalm 151 is the final one on the scroll (following Psalm 134), just as it is in the Greek Psalters. These psalms were
known previously in several witnesses. Psalm 151 is included in the Greek
copies of the Bible and was thus a familiar unit in the history of the Psalter.
Psalms 154-55 were, however, less well known. They are included in several
later Syriac witnesses but were not considered part of the standard biblical
text in that language (they are designated Syriac Psalms 2 and 3, while
Psalm 151 is Syriac Psalm 1).

From his comparison of Psalm 151 in the scroll with the Greek version,
Sanders concluded that "[t]hough LXX Ps 151 is by no means a translation
of QPs 151, it is abundantly clear that it depends ultimately on the latter."[59]
The first five verses of the psalm provide a more meaningful text in the Hebrew version, but the next words on the scroll are problematic. They are
separated on the Qumran manuscript from what precedes by a line that is
almost completely blank and deal with the Goliath episode, as do verses
6-7 in the Greek poem. In other words, one has in this section of the
Psalms scroll from cave 11 "the Hebrew psalms, at least all of the first and
the beginning of the second, which lie behind the amalgam which is LXX
Ps 151."[60] In his study of the *Syriac Apocryphal Psalms*, H. F. van Rooy concluded regarding Psalm 151 that more than one Hebrew version of it existed: one of them is reflected in the 11Q Psalms scroll, and in the Septuagint there is another version that lies behind the Syriac form of the text. He
also thinks it possible that "the original unity of Psalm 151 was broken at
Qumran by the creation of two Psalms: 151 A, dealing with David's election
and anointment, and 151 B, dealing with his fight with Goliath."[61]

Sanders noted regarding Psalm 154 that the Qumran text preserves
verses 3-17 and parts of verses 18-19 of the psalm, which in Syriac has
twenty verses. He found that there was nothing distinctively Qumranian
about the vocabulary or ideas in it (although יחד occurs). He suggested
that it "may be proto-Essenian, or Hasidic, from the period of the 'separation' of the dissident group, an early poetic expression of the 'calling out'

---

59. DJD 4:59.
60. DJD 4:63.
61. H. F. van Rooy, *Studies on the Syriac Apocryphal Psalms* (JSSSup 7; Oxford: Oxford University Press, 1999), 109 (see 90-109 for his detailed analysis).

of the sect and its *raison d'être* as it was then understood."[62] Part of the same psalm is present also on 4Q448, where it shares the surface of the fragment with the well-known Prayer for King Jonathan.[63] The editors of 4Q448 compared the two Hebrew copies of the psalm and pointed to some small differences between them.[64] Van Rooy analyzed the different versions of the psalm in detail and came to the conclusion that the Syriac copies are from a single tradition and that its *Vorlage* differed from the text of the cave 11 manuscript.[65] He found no similar evidence for a "proto-Essenian provenance" for Psalm 155, whose language sounds quite biblical.[66] From his comparison of all copies of this psalm, von Rooy inferred that there were three text traditions for it: one is found in the Hebrew, and two are reflected in Syriac copies (they may preserve a tradition older than the Qumran tradition).[67]

The texts surveyed above show that the Qumran library contained a number of works that had been known before but for which the caves offer the earliest texts in their original languages. In all of these cases (perhaps with some hesitation for Psalm 154) the compositions in question were probably older works, copies of which were brought to Qumran at a later time when the site was occupied. They are, therefore, also evidence of how the people of the scrolls inherited literature and used it for their reading, listening, and study. But for the modern student of early Judaism, the greatest value of the new copies lies in the textual data that they provide and the new questions and answers they offer for the study of these compositions and of the scrolls communities.

---

62. DJD 4:70 (cf. 75).

63. E. Eshel, H. Eshel, and A. Yardeni, "Apocryphal Psalm and Prayer," in E. Eshel et al., eds., J. C. VanderKam and M. Brady, consulting eds., *Qumran Cave 4: VI, Poetical and Liturgical Texts, Part 1* (DJD 11; Oxford: Clarendon, 1998), 403-25.

64. DJD 11:409-10.

65. Van Rooy, *Studies on the Syriac Apocryphal Psalms*, 133-47.

66. Van Rooy, *Studies on the Syriac Apocryphal Psalms*, 74.

67. Van Rooy, *Studies on the Syriac Apocryphal Psalms*, 148-61.

CHAPTER 5

Groups and Group Controversies in the Scrolls

The Dead Sea Scrolls have made a number of contributions to modern-day knowledge about early Judaism. As explained in the previous chapters, they furnish the oldest manuscripts of the books that were to become the constituents of the Hebrew Bible, document the textual diversity that prevailed at the time, and give a strong indication of how important these works were. The scrolls also reveal information about their authors, who most experts think were members — a small branch — of the much larger Essene movement.[1] From the scrolls the reader learns something, however little, about the group's (groups') way of life and about their ways of thinking. They were people who studied the scriptures intensely and learned from them their own place and duties in God's plan for all time, particularly the last days in which they thought they were living. Those scriptures they tried most energetically to obey, as they attempted to serve the Lord who, they believed, remained in covenant with them, the remnant of his people.

Another area in which the scrolls are instructive is in furnishing information about contemporary Judaism, especially about other Jewish groups and how the authors/copyists/owners of the scrolls assessed them. Before the scrolls discoveries, students of early Judaism were not, of course, ignorant about the Jewish groups in the late Second Temple period, as there are several sources of information that have been available for many centuries.[2] In the first instance, there are the historical works of

---

1. For a recent defense of the Essene identification, see K. Atkinson and J. Magness, "Josephus's Essenes and the Qumran Community," *JBL* 129 (2010): 317-42.

2. Nineteenth- and early-twentieth-century readers could expect to find in the

Josephus, who reports in both his *Jewish War* and *Jewish Antiquities* that among the Jews in the last centuries of the second temple there were three groups: Pharisees, Sadducees, and Essenes. He mentions other groups as well, such as the Zealots and Sicarii, but they, for the most part, play roles in his narratives only toward the end of the Second Temple period. To some extent another source — the New Testament — reinforces what Josephus reports, in that it pictures Jesus and his early followers coming into contact with Pharisees and Sadducees (among many examples, see Matt 15:1-9; 16:5-12; Acts 4–5), though other groupings of people are mentioned (e.g., scribes). When reflecting on earlier times, some rabbinic texts also mention Pharisees, Sadducees (for both see, for instance, *m. Yad.* 4:6-8), and others (e.g., Boethusians; *m. Menaḥ.* 10:3 is one passage where they appear). All of these sources — Josephus, the New Testament, rabbinic literature — whatever their value, share the defect that they come from later times and, of course, give voice to the points of view adopted by their writers or tradents. And, only the latest of these (rabbinic literature), was recorded in the more commonly used Semitic languages of the area rather than in Greek, as were Josephus's writings and the New Testament. So texts that talk *about* the Second Temple groups have been available for a long time; but most experts today agree that no text clearly *by* a Pharisee[3] or a Sadducee has survived to give a firsthand account of what they thought, unless Josephus was a Pharisee. Even if he was, he does not disclose much about, say, the legal convictions of the Pharisees or about their way of life.

Into this less than ideal situation the Dead Sea Scrolls have entered and furnished a fresh, contemporary, and distinctive witness to the time of early Judaism, and they are Hebrew texts primarily (ca. 750 of them), with fewer in Aramaic (ca. 125). They allow modern readers, one might almost say, to be Peeping Toms into the ancient Jewish culture, seeing phenomena from a proximity and an angle not accessible before the discoveries in the 1940s and 1950s. Naturally, the texts from Qumran are not free from bias (far from it!), and many of them relate to a body of people withdrawn from temple fellowship, so that they are not representative of Judaism at

---

standard introductions detailed treatment of the ancient groups identified by Josephus — or at least of the Pharisees and Sadducees; an important example is E. Schürer's *Geschichte des jüdischen Volkes im Zeitalter Jesu Christi* (2 vols.; Leipzig: Hinrichs, 1886-1890).

3. Some have suggested that the *Psalms of Solomon* are Pharisaic, but the matter is disputed; see G. W. E. Nickelsburg, *Jewish Literature Between the Bible and the Mishnah* (2nd ed.; Minneapolis: Fortress, 2005), 246-47.

large; but they have advantages of time, language, and place over the source material previously available. And if the scrolls communities were Essene, the manuscripts provide for the first time (nonnarrative) texts authored by members of one of Josephus's three groups.

Once the scrolls were available for study, experts attempted to align or correlate the evidence in them regarding the larger Jewish context with the details the other sources disclosed. In the scrolls one never meets the words "Pharisee," "Sadducee" (although caution is in order about the name), and, experts often claim, one does not encounter the word "Essene" either. The failure to use group names is consistent with a larger pattern in the scrolls authored and used by members of the communities: they rarely call persons or social entities by their real names, preferring to designate individuals and groups with nicknames, not to say insults. So, the leading opponent of the Teacher of Righteousness was the Wicked Priest; another enemy is called the Liar or Scoffer.[4] Though they normally do not use names for people and groups recognizable to modern readers, the scrolls, according to many scholars, do name and deal with the three primary groups identified by Josephus — Pharisees, Sadducees, and Essenes.

THE THREE GROUPS

A widely held theory holds that Josephus's parties or groups can be identified behind these epithets: (1) The writers and copyists of the scrolls found in the caves in the area of Qumran were Essenes; they used for themselves, among other self-designations, the name "Judah." (2) Their primary antagonists were Pharisees, whom they dubbed the "ones who look for smooth things," "Ephraim," and "Builders of the Wall." (3) Others whom the people of the scrolls opposed they named "Manasseh"; these may be Sadducees.[5] The evidence on which the theory rests should now be examined.

4. Regarding the phenomenon of the sorts of names used in the scrolls, see H. Bengtsson, *What's in a Name? A Study of Sobriquets in the Pesharim* (Uppsala: Uppsala University, 2000).

5. D. Flusser, "Pharisees, Sadducees, and Essenes in Pesher Nahum," in *Judaism of the Second Temple Period,* vol. 1: *Qumran and Apocalypticism* (Grand Rapids: Eerdmans and Jerusalem: Magnes and Jerusalem Perspective, 2007), 214-57.

Essenes

"Essene" remains the most plausible identification for the authors and copyists of the texts associated with the group(s) that resided in the area of Qumran and for their wider movement. The fundamental arguments for the position have been rehearsed many times and are essentially just two in number.[6] First, the views and actions of the groups represented in the scrolls match far better with the ancient descriptions of the Essenes than they do with any other group attested in the classical sources. The argument still stands strong today and need not be defended here — as long as one phrases it in an appropriately cautious way by saying the groups behind the texts are more similar to the Essenes than to any other fellowship about which the ancient writers report. The second supporting argument is Pliny the Elder's location of a settlement of Essenes north of En-gedi (*Natural History* 5.73).[7] There have been several attempts to read his comments differently (a much-debated point concerns what he might have meant by *infra hos* in the phrase "beneath these was En-gedi"), but none of the other hypotheses is as convincing as the thesis that the Essenes he describes lived somewhere north of En-gedi and near the coast of the Dead Sea — a description that, however brief, is consistent with the location of Qumran.[8] It is also true that the short account of the Essenes Pliny provides fits well with what the scrolls disclose about those who used the site of Qumran.

6. The first expert to maintain that the people of the scrolls were Essenes was Eleazer Sukenik, who made the suggestion already in 1948 when only a few of the scrolls were available. The *Rule of the Community* was the scroll that made him think of the Essenes; *Hidden Scrolls* (Jerusalem: Bialik, 1948), 16; *The Dead Sea Scrolls of the Hebrew University* (Jerusalem: Magnes, 1955), 29 (both works are in Hebrew). André Dupont-Sommer advanced the thesis in publications beginning in 1950; see, e.g., *The Dead Sea Scrolls: A Preliminary Survey* (trans. E. M. Rowley; Oxford: Blackwell, 1952), 85-96.

7. For these two "pillars" of the Essene hypothesis, see J. C. VanderKam, *The Dead Sea Scrolls Today* (2nd ed.; Grand Rapids: Eerdmans, 2010), 97-126.

8. See J. E. Taylor, "On Pliny, the Essene Location and Kh. Qumran," *DSD* 16 (2009): 1-21. She provides an overview of what scholars have written on the topic and thinks Pliny is speaking about an Essene region "west of the northern part of the Dead Sea" (20) — an area that includes Qumran. For one of the interpretations that understands the passage in Pliny much differently, cf. R. A, Kraft, "Pliny on Essenes, Pliny on Jews," *DSD* 8 (2001): 255-61. For a summary of the evidence and debates about it, see T. S. Beall, "Pliny the Elder," in *EDSS*, 2:677-79.

One at times reads that, if indeed the people associated with the scrolls were a small branch of the larger and more dispersed Essene fellowship, it is odd that the writers never saw fit to refer to themselves as Essenes. True, the scrolls writers usually do not, as noted above, give groups their proper or popular names, but would the scrolls folk not refer to at least themselves by their name a few times? It is somewhat odder still that the same scholars also claim that the Hebrew/Aramaic word for Essene is unknown. *Essene* is attested in Latin and Greek sources, not in Semitic ones — maybe. So there is, on the view of some, the curious situation that the Hebrew word for Essene is unknown but that, whatever it was, it is not present in the scrolls.[9] As argued below, it is more likely that the writers do refer to themselves by the Semitic word that gave rise to the Greek and Latin transcriptions: they are the doers (of the Torah).[10]

The meaning of "Essene" has attracted attention since antiquity, with Philo suggesting it perhaps had some connection with ὁσιότης ("holiness") and that it was given to them because of their holy way of living in God's service (*Good Person* 12.75). As it seems unlikely a group in Judea would be given a Greek name, most have attempted to explain it on the basis of a Hebrew or Aramaic term. One suggestion has been that it is related to a word known in Eastern Aramaic — חסי, חסיא — an adjective meaning "holy."[11] A form of the word is now attested in 4Q213a, one of the copies of *Aramaic Levi*, widely thought to be a text written well before the time of the Qumran settlement. There one reads: "the name of his *holy one* will not be blotted out from all her people forever" (frgs. 3-4, line 6).[12] The

---

9. See, e.g., K. H. Rengstorf, *Ḥirbet Qumran and the Problem of the Library of the Dead Sea Scrolls* (Leiden: Brill, 1963), 15; M. Goodman, "A Note on the Qumran Sectarians, the Essenes and Josephus," *JJS* 46 (1995): 161-66.

10. The thesis has a long pedigree, going back at least to Azariah di Rossi and Philip Melanchthon. See the studies by S. Goranson, "'Essenes': Etymology from עשׂה," *RevQ* 11/44 (1984): 483-98; "Others and Intra-Jewish Polemic as Reflected in Qumran Texts," in J. C. VanderKam and P. W. Flint, eds., *The Dead Sea Scrolls after Fifty Years: A Comprehensive Assessment* (2 vols.; Leiden: Brill, 1998-99), 2:537-40. For this paragraph and the following section, see also VanderKam, "Identity and History of the Community," in *The Dead Sea Scrolls after Fifty Years*, 2:490-97.

11. Among those who have advocated this derivation is Dupont-Sommer, *The Dead Sea Scrolls*, 86-87. It had been the most common explanation before the scroll discoveries.

12. F. M. Cross, who has long supported this derivation of *Essene,* noted the occurrence of the term in 4Q213a in his *The Ancient Library of Qumran* (3rd ed.; Minneapolis: Fortress, 1995), 183.

word rendered "holy one" is indeed חסיא, but it is not used as a group designation in this text and thus does not appear to be relevant to the issue.

Geza Vermes has championed the idea that the name Essene reflects the Aramaic word אסיא ("physician, healer"). He points to the use by Philo of the words θεραπευταί and θεραπεία in connection with the Essenes (that is, Philo talks about some Essene-like people whom he calls *Therapeutai*). Vermes understands the word to have dual senses, both appropriate for these people — they were worshippers who were healers.[13] The same objection holds for this more widely held position: *the scrolls* do not use the term for the group. It figures in the *Genesis Apocryphon* and in the book of Tobit, but hardly as the name for a body of people.

J. T. Milik tried to relate the word to Hebrew חסידים or Aramaic חסידין and maintained that he had located support for the suggestion in a letter from the Wadi Murabbaʿat (45 line 6) where there is reference to what he took to be "the fortress of the pious [חסדין]."[14] His interpretation of the phrase and the word has been shown to be unlikely.[15]

A more compelling derivation is found in an old proposal that has been revived since the scrolls were discovered. It comes closer to explaining the Greek and Latin forms of the names, although it too does not solve every difficulty with the transcriptions. The proposal is that the name derives from the expression עושי התורה = "the doers of Torah."[16] It, like the other proposals, would be appropriate for the Essenes as depicted in the sources, but it has the advantage that it is actually used by them — something neither of the others can claim. The letter *n* of the form, used at times by Josephus (in Greek) and by Pliny the Elder (in Latin), would reflect the Aramaic form of the participle (ending in -*în*), while the ending -*aioi* in Greek spellings would arise from the Aramaic plural -*ayyā'* (something proponents of all the proposals maintain). The first vowel of the word in most of the representations (an "e") could be a product of an

---

13. G. Vermes, "The Etymology of 'Essenes,'" *RevQ* 2/7 (1960): 427-43. In addition to defending his view, Vermes here surveys a range of other proposals.

14. He made the argument in his edition of the text, "45. Lettre," in P. Benoit, Milik, and R. de Vaux, eds., *Les grottes de Murabbaʿât* (DJD 2; Oxford: Clarendon, 1961), 163-64.

15. See É. Puech, "La 'Forteresse des Pieux' et Kh. Qumrân: A Propos du Papyrus Murabbaʿât 45," *RevQ* 16/63 (1994): 469. VanderKam, "Identity and History of the Community," 2:493-94.

16. Goranson, "'Essenes,'" 488; "Essenes," in E. Meyers, ed., *The Oxford Encyclopedia of Archaeology in the Near East* (5 vols.; New York: Oxford University Press, 1997), 2:268.

Aramaic-like pronunciation of the first vowel in the participle *(ā)*, with the gutteral *'ayin* influencing it to sound more like an "e" — perhaps especially to a nonnative speaker.[17]

If "doers of the Torah" is the Semitic phrase underlying the Greek and Latin forms of *Essene,* then it, unlike the other two suggestions, is used in the scrolls. In 1QpHab 7:10-12 it is employed as a group designation. The passage contains commentary on Hab 2:3b: "If it seems to tarry, wait for it; it will surely come, it will not delay." The delay in God's decisive response to evil is likely to have been a concern for the people of the community. The *pesher* explains the scriptural words: "Interpreted, this concerns the men of truth who keep the Law [עושי התורה], whose hands shall not slacken in the service of truth when the final age is prolonged." ("The men of the truth" could also be a group designation; it or similar phrases are fairly frequent in the scrolls, at times in sectarian contexts; see 1QS 4:5, 6; 1QM 17:8; and 1QHᵃ, e.g., 6:2; 14:29; 17:35; 18:27; 19:11.) A little farther along in the same sectarian text, when commenting on Hab 2:4 ("but the righteous live by their faith"), the exegete writes: "Interpreted, this concerns all those who observe the Law [עושי התורה] in the House of Judah, whom God will deliver from the House of Judgement because of their suffering and because of their faith in the Teacher of Righteousness" (8:1-3). The passage designates the people around the Teacher as "doers of the law," thus yielding a tie-in with the groups represented in the *Damascus Document* — which mentions the Teacher — and the texts found at Qumran. When commenting on Hab 2:17 ("For the violence done to Lebanon will overwhelm you; the destruction of the animals will terrify you — because of human bloodshed and violence to the earth, to cities and all who live in them"), the expositor writes: "Interpreted, this saying concerns the Wicked Priest, inasmuch as he shall be paid the reward which he himself tendered to the Poor. For *Lebanon* is the Council of the Community, and the *beasts* are the simple of Judah who keep the Law [עושה התורה]" (12:2-5).[18]

17. VanderKam, "Identity and History of the Community," 2:495-96.

18. The spelling of the participle indicates it is singular in form ("doer of the Torah"), but, as the singular and plural would be pronounced in the same way and the term that the participle modifies ("the simple") is plural, the word is probably a plural, as Vermes translates it. M. P. Horgan (*Pesharim: Qumran Interpretations of Biblical Books* [CBQMS 8; Washington: Catholic Biblical Association of America, 1979], 53) thinks a scribal error occurred and that an attempt was made to write a *yod* (for the plural) over the *he* of the singular form. The ink of the letter is indeed darker than for the others in the word.

("Poor ones" may also be a sectarian designation in the *Hodayot* and else-where [e.g., 4Q171 1-2 ii 9: "congregation/community of the poor"; also in the same text 1+3-4 iii 10; 4Q491 11 i 11.) Note too the use of "Judah" for the "doers of the Torah" in this passage.

Pesher Habakkuk is not the only work that so designates the group, as 4QpPs[a] does the same. The first reference comes in a comment on Ps 37:12-13: "The wicked plot against the righteous, and gnash their teeth at them; but the LORD laughs at the wicked, for he sees that their day is coming." The *pesher* says: "Interpreted, this concerns the violent of the Covenant who are in the House of Judah, who have plotted to destroy those who practise the Law [עושי התורה], who are in the Council of the Community. And God will not forsake them to their hands" (frgs. 1-2 ii 13-15). Here there appears to be an expression of innergroup conflict (see the reference to Ephraim and Manasseh in line 18). Interestingly, the doers of the Torah are in the council of the community — a term familiar from the *Rule of the Community*. In the same column, when dealing with Ps 37:16 ("Better is a little that the righteous person has than the abundance of many wicked"), the commentator declares in the course of his explanation (the context is fragmentarily preserved) that the righteous person of the verse represents "the doers of the law" (עושי התורה) (frgs. 1-2 ii 23). The same Psalms *pesher* interprets "those who wait for the LORD shall inherit the land" (Ps 37:9b) as "the Congregation of His elect who do His will [עושי רצונו]" (frgs. 1-2 ii 5) — another expression employing the participle of the verb "do."

In light of this evidence, perhaps some of the expressions used to de-scribe the goals of members of the community — e.g., to do as he com-manded — purposely play with the verb עשה. Here it is fitting to recall a comment made by William Brownlee in one of his studies of *Pesher Habakkuk*:

> ... the verb "do" (*'āśāh*) is constantly in use in the Society Manual (1QS) to express the purpose of the Qumrân Community (i,2,5,6f.,16; v,3,20,22; viii,2,15; ix,13,15,20,23); and the members un-dergo annual examination as to their progress in "understanding and deeds" (v,21,23; vi,17f.). One of the numerous etymologies for Essene is "doer." This would be especially appropriate to explain an-cient spellings of Essene with *Omicron* rather than *Epsilon* in the first syllable, as in Hippolytus, Philosophumena 9:4 (18*a*-28*a*). Cf. also Philo's derivation of the name from ὅσιος . . . , which (instead

of being a translation of *ḥāsā'* = *ḥᵃsîd* ["pious or faithful"]) might be a verbal play on *'ōśēh.* In Rabbinic Hebrew, the plural of this is often *'ôśîn*, rather than *'ôśîm*.[19]

An advantage of an etymology from "doers (of the Torah)" is that the title would express very well the centrality of the Torah in the life and teaching of the people behind the scrolls. It was definitional for them.[20]

Sadducees

The second group to consider is the Sadducees: The designation "Manasseh" is supposed to be a name for them, and there are, it is claimed, some correspondences between ancient descriptions of Sadducees and what is said in the scrolls about Manasseh (they are leading people who ruled, for example).[21] It does seem, however, that there is not much force to the argument and that Manasseh, rarely mentioned in the scrolls (twelve times), has by default been interpreted as a designation for Sadducees. That is, if Ephraim refers to Pharisees, the corresponding term, Manasseh (often paired with Ephraim in the tribal lists in the Hebrew Bible), must refer to the Sadducees. The inference may be correct, but there is very little evidence on which to base a verdict.[22] This issue is complicated to a certain extent because at times a set of people in the scrolls, members of the scrolls

19. W. H. Brownlee, *The Midrash Pesher of Habakkuk* (SBLMS 24; Missoula: Scholars, 1979), 119.

20. Bengtsson (*What's in a Name?*, 217-34), after surveying and analyzing the relevant passages, concludes that the doers of the law are a faction within the Yahad (= "community"), rather than a designation for all Essenes. His view seems not to be justified by the texts cited above. That they are the simple of Judah in 1QpHab need not mean they are part of the group called Judah.

21. The suggestion seems to go back to J. D. Amusin (Amoussine), "Éphraïm et Manassé dans le Péshèr de Nahum (4 Q p Nahum)," *RevQ* 4/15 (1963-64): 389-96. He wrote that if the term Ephraim means the Pharisees, then it is natural to suppose that Manasseh is used for the Sadducees (395). He thought the commentary on Nahum described the struggles between Pharisees and Sadducees in the days of Alexander Jannaeus and Alexandra (103-67 B.C.E.).

22. See the summary of the evidence and the discussions of it by H. Eshel, "Ephraim and Manasseh," in *EDSS*, 1:253-54; and by G. Doudna, *4Q Pesher Nahum: A Critical Edition* (JSPSup 35; Copenhagen International Series 8; London: Sheffield Academic, 2001), 579-99), who comes to a negative conclusion about the equation Manasseh = Sadducees in *Pesher Nahum*.

groups, are called "the sons of Zadok," and the name "Zadok" may lie be-hind *Sadducee*. As members of the tradition represented in the scrolls, these sons of Zadok, because of their views, are not very likely to be the Sadducees pictured by the New Testament or Josephus.

That the scrolls writers refer to Sadducees by dubbing them Manasseh is possible but hardly demonstrated. Yet, a more interesting problem arises in connection with the Sadducees, whatever the Qumran writers may have called them (if they referred to them). As several experts have shown,[23] a small number of legal positions held by authors of scrolls are identified in rabbinic texts as Sadducean views. The best-known proof text for the posi-tion is *m. Yad.* 4:6-7, where a few opinions of the Pharisees are contrasted with those of the Sadducees, with the Sadducees always going first and the Pharisees following with convincing rebuttal. The first conflict has to do with the complicated issue regarding which written works render the hands unclean (an issue having something to do with the status of the books in question) and does not seem to be immediately relevant to the present topic, but the second is pertinent to it. In the quaint translation of Herbert Danby, the passage reads:

> The Sadducees say, We cry out against you, O ye Pharisees, for ye declare clean an unbroken stream of liquid [הנצוק]. The Pharisees say, we cry out against you, O ye Sadducees, for ye declare clean a channel of water that flows from a burial ground.[24]

(The following controversy on whether animal bones are unclean seems another case in which Sadducean and Qumran law agree.) When Joseph Baumgarten saw a citation from what is now called 4QMMT in J. T. Milik's edition of the *Copper Scroll* — a citation in which the cognate word המוצקות occurred three times — he drew attention to the use of הנצוק in *m. Yad.* 4:6-7.[25] The passage in 4QMMT is B 55-58 in the official edition,

---

23. J. M. Baumgarten, "The Pharisaic-Sadducean Controversies about Purity and the Qumran Texts," *JJS* 31 (1980): 157-70; L. H. Schiffman, "The New Halakhic Letter (4QMMT) and the Origins of the Dead Sea Sect," *BA* 53 (1990): 64-73; and Y. Sussmann, "The History of the Halakha and the Dead Sea Scrolls," in E. Qimron and J. Strugnell, eds., *Qumran Cave 4: V, Miqṣat Maʿaśe ha-Torah* (DJD 10; Oxford: Claren-don, 1994), 186-91.

24. H. Danby, *The Mishnah* (Oxford: Oxford University Press, 1933).

25. Baumgarten saw the citation in J. T. Milik, "Le rouleau de cuivre provenant de la grotte 3Q (3Q15)," in M. Baillet, Milik, and R. de Vaux, eds., *Les 'Petites Grottes' de*

and it reads: "And concerning liquid streams: we are of the opinion that they are not pure, and that these streams do not act as a separative between impure and pure (liquids). For the liquid of streams and (that) of (the vessel) which receives them are alike, (being) a single liquid."[26] The dispute in question concerns whether a liquid stream poured from a ritually clean container conveys impurity to that container when emptied into an impure receptacle (a law that had some practical applications). Here is a specific case in which a law termed Sadducean in the Mishnah and a law presented as the position of the authors in a scroll are the same — both the Sadducees and the writers of MMT infer that a stream of liquid does transmit impurity under such conditions. And, just as importantly, the Pharisees oppose it. What follows from this and a small number of similar cases?

It is certain that the authors of the scrolls could not have been Sadducees in the sense in which Josephus and the New Testament writers speak of the group, as they differ fundamentally on theological or philosophical topics. One need mention only the reports in the sources regarding the Sadducees' rejection of "fate" (*J.W.* 2.162) and their view about angels (Acts 23:8 says they believed there was no angel or spirit)[27] to see that they and the writers of the Qumran texts held positions diametrically opposed to one another. The implication of the agreements on points of law is not that the people of Qumran were Sadducees as Josephus and New Testament writers describe them but that their legal approach could be termed "Sadducean," perhaps meaning traditional and priestly. In general, it could be characterized as the harsher or more stringent interpretation of the law; the way in which they read the legislation in the Pentateuch differed in basic, particular ways from the Pharisaic stance that was usually character-

---

Qumrân (DJD 3; Oxford: Clarendon, 1962), 225. This was long before 4QMMT was officially published in DJD 10. As Baumgarten wrote, Y. Yadin had earlier noted the connection with the Mishnaic passage; *The Temple Scroll* (3 vols.; Jerusalem: Israel Exploration Society, 1977), 2:150 (Hebrew); see Baumgarten, "The Pharisaic-Sadducean Controversies," 164, n. 25.

26. The translation is the one by the editors E. Qimron and J. Strugnell as given in D. W. Parry and E. Tov, eds., *The Dead Sea Scrolls Reader*, vol. 1: *Texts Concerned with Religious Law* (Leiden: Brill, 2004), 331.

27. If Acts 23:8 claims the Sadducees denied there were angels, it would be difficult to accept because Genesis and other scriptural works mention them. J. A. Fitzmyer maintains that the passage means they thought there would be no resurrection — neither as an angel nor as a spirit; *The Acts of the Apostles* (AB 31; New York: Doubleday, 1998), 714 (translation), 719-20 (comment). Denial of a future resurrection would also place the Sadducees at odds with the writers of at least some texts found at Qumran.

reflects the very events Josephus describes.[33] Since Jannaeus and the Pharisees hated each other, the case for identifying seekers and Pharisees seems secure.

Josephus refers several times to those who fought against Jannaeus from the time they pelted him with fruit when he was officiating as high priest at the Festival of Tabernacles (*Ant.* 13.372) to the period of open warfare with him, but when he does so he uses frustratingly general terms for the opponents and never explicitly calls them Pharisees. Rather, he resorts to expressions like "the Jews." According to Josephus, Jannaeus's father John Hyrcanus had broken off his cordial relations with the Pharisees and had associated with the Sadducees, a policy that apparently continued in the time of his sons who succeeded him — Aristobulus I (104-103 B.C.E.) and Jannaeus. But Josephus does not say in so many words that the eight hundred men whom Jannaeus crucified were Pharisees. This fact has led a few scholars to conclude that, despite appearances, the events described in *Pesher Nahum* and those in Josephus's narratives about Jannaeus's brutality are not the same.[34] An implication is that one would not be able to use the correlation between the contents of *Pesher Nahum* and Josephus's histories to identify the seekers of smooth things with the Pharisees, leaving the conclusion much weaker.

That is, however, only part of the evidence. There is reason to think that Josephus does indeed indicate, if only by implication, that Jannaeus crucified Pharisees and that therefore the correlation between *Pesher Nahum* and Josephus's writings does allow one to conclude that the seekers of smooth things are Pharisees. Josephus fails to make the identification in the immediate context of describing the invasion by King Demetrius and Alexander's vicious response of crucifying his enemies, but he definitely points in this direction at a later juncture in his narratives. The place in question is the conversation between Alexander Jannaeus and his wife Alexandra at the time when Alexander was about to die.[35] On that

33. For a long survey of the passage and many opinions about it, see Doudna, *4Q Pesher Nahum*, 315-61. See also Horgan, *Pesharim*, 171-76.

34. Examples of those holding this position are C. Rabin, "Alexander Jannaeus and the Pharisees," *JJS* 7 (1956): 3-11; A. J. Saldarini, *Pharisees, Scribes and Sadducees in Palestinian Society: A Sociological Approach* (Wilmington: Glazier, 1988, 279-80; repr. BRS; Grand Rapids: Eerdmans and Livonia: Dove, 2001).

35. For the arguments given here, see VanderKam, "Pesher Nahum and Josephus," 304-11 (where there is also consideration of scholarly debates about the pictures of Pharisees in Josephus's two histories).

occasion he gave instructions to his wife, who, unusually enough, was to succeed him as monarch, though the couple had two grown sons. Josephus, in *J.W.* 1.110-14, chides Alexandra for her excessive reliance on the Pharisees, who became very powerful during her reign. He mentions the case of a certain Diogenes, whom the Pharisees executed while she was queen. He had been a friend of Jannaeus, but the Pharisees accused him "of having advised the king to crucify his eight hundred victims" (113). Pharisees, therefore, were the ones who, when the political climate changed, set out to punish the ones responsible for Jannaeus's decision to crucify the eigiht hundred opponents. This is not the same as saying the eight hundred were Pharisees, but it does show that Pharisees were the people who were anxious to gain for the dead a measure of justice, however belated.[36]

In the parallel account in Josephus's *Antiquities,* there is similar material but more. Josephus entertains the reader with a deathbed scene in which Jannaeus urges Alexandra to allow the Pharisees greater power in her kingdom. If she did this, he predicted, the Pharisees, who strongly influenced the masses, would dispose the nation favorably toward her, in marked contrast to their hatred for him. In the speech Jannaeus admits both the power of the Pharisees and that he "had come into conflict with the nation because these men had been badly treated by him" (13.402). Jannaeus, says Josephus, added a macabre suggestion about the treatment of his body after his death:

> "And so," he said, "when you come to Jerusalem, send for their [= the Pharisees'] partisans [text: "soldiers"], and showing them my dead body, permit them, with every sign of sincerity, to treat me as they please, whether they wish to dishonour my corpse by leaving it unburied because of the many injuries they have suffered at my hands, or in their anger wish to offer my dead body any other form of indignity." (13.403)

Alexandra turned his body over to the Pharisees (what they did with it Josephus does not say), and they became her allies, somehow even managing to praise her departed husband.

The story about Jannaeus's body furnishes some warrant for identifying the eight hundred crucified men as Pharisees. Alexander had mis-

---

36. See A. I. Baumgarten, "Seekers after Smooth Things," in *EDSS,* 2:858.

treated the bodies of the men he executed on crosses; here the king gives his (or Josephus's) most explicit confession about Jannaeus's abusing the bodies of his enemies. In fact, this is the only case in which Jannaeus makes such an allowance. Only for the eight hundred whom he crucified does one learn the way in which they died. In death Jannaeus allowed their fellow Pharisees to avenge his brutality by turning his corpse over to them, to treat it as they wished. The gesture seems a *quid pro quo:* he invited surviving Pharisees to mistreat his body as he had abused the bodies of their eight hundred colleagues whom he had crucified.

Naturally, questions arise about the factuality of the conversation between the king and queen — it appears only in *Antiquities,* not in *War.*[37] How would Josephus have learned about the royal instructions, and are not speeches prime occasions for ancient historians to interfere and cause mischief? There is no way to prove the conversation took place or to demonstrate that Jannaeus said what Josephus reports, but it is reasonable to think something of the sort occurred, or at least that Josephus leaves a signal for his readers to this effect. The Pharisees, according to both of Josephus's histories, became the effective power in Alexandra's administration (76-67 B.C.E.) and took steps to punish those responsible for crucifying the eight hundred victims. The drastic switch in allegiance by the Pharisees — from armed resistance to Alexander to enthusiastic support for Alexandra — must have had some cause. If the men who avenged the eight hundred were Pharisees as Josephus says, then it is quite possible that the executed group were also Pharisees. If the story about Alexander's corpse is true, the case is stronger yet. Hence, if the eight hundred whom Alexander crucified were Pharisees and *Pesher Nahum* calls them "ones who look for smooth things," then these seekers are Pharisees.

The conclusion harmonizes with other data in the scrolls. In some of them one finds a set of names that the scroll writers apply to opponents; all of them are related to "the ones who look for smooth things" and thus seem to refer to the same group and its leader.[38] "The Scoffer" (e.g., CD 1:14) and "the Liar" are two titles for the leader, and the theme of rejection of the law is associated with both epithets. The authors may also have pilloried this leader with the name "Spouter/Preacher of Lies," an insulting

---

37. Experts have drawn very different conclusions about the matter. See VanderKam, "Pesher Nahum and Josephus," 309, for some of them.

38. For the evidence in greater detail, see VanderKam, "Those Who Look for Smooth Things," 471-75.

title for a person who has connections with a group called "the builders of the wall." These builders, who follow the Spouter of Lies, were "caught in fornication," according to the *Damascus Document* (CD 4:19-20). Included in their sexual misconduct was the practice of niece marriage (5:6-11). The writer forbade such unions because he thought the Torah, by implication, prohibited them, while rabbinic sources report that the practice was permitted.[39] So, this too may well have been, at an earlier time, a Pharisaic position. If so, the other titles tied to the seekers of smooth things would also be ones by which the writers heaped scorn on Pharisees.

An eye-catching passage occurs at a later point in *Pesher Nahum* where the text identifies "the ones who look for smooth things" as *Ephraim*. The relevant lines read: "Woe to the city of blood; it is full of lies and rapine (iii, 1a-b). Interpreted, this is the city of Ephraim, those who seek smooth things during the last days, who walk[40] in lies and falsehood" (3-4 ii 1-2). If the two titles — "seekers" and "Ephraim" — refer to the same people, as seems to be the case, *Pesher Nahum* 3-4 ii 8 becomes intriguing: "Interpreted, this concerns those who lead Ephraim astray, who lead many astray through their false teaching [בתלמוד שקרם], their lying tongue, and deceitful lips. . . ." Since Pharisees are probably under consideration here, the word *talmud* attracts one's attention. In the passage there are three expressions that parallel one another, and these are placed between two phrases regarding misleading. The parallels are:

Their false teaching (their lying *talmud*)
Their lying tongue
Deceitful lips

39. The rules in Leviticus 18 are formulated from a male point of view, but the writer of the *Damascus Document* argues that the same principles apply to women as well: "And each man marries the daughter of his brother or sister, whereas Moses said, *You shall not approach your mother's sister; she is your mother's near kin* (Lev. xviii, 13). But although the laws against incest are written for men, they also apply to women" (CD 5:7-10). On the passage, see L. Ginzburg, *An Unknown Jewish Sect* (Moreshet 1; New York: Ktav, 1970), 23-24, where he cites the pertinent rabbinic texts; cf. also Shemesh, *Halakhah in the Making*, 80-95.

40. The writer may purposely be using a form of the verb הלך, which is related to the noun *halakhah*; so L. H. Schiffman, "Pharisees and Sadducees in Pesher Nahum," in M. Brettler and M. Fishbane, eds., *Minḥah le-Naḥum: Biblical and Other Studies Presented to Nahum M. Sarna in Honour of His 70th Birthday* (JSOTSup 154; Sheffield: Sheffield Academic, 1993), 276.

The parallels suggest that "tongue" and "lips" should clarify the meaning of *talmud*.[41] It seems that the commentator is here criticizing a particular manner of oral teaching by using the word *talmud*. It is unlikely that anything written is meant, certainly not something like the talmuds, those vast collections of rabbinic discussions compiled centuries later.

The orality repeatedly referenced naturally reminds one of a trait that the sources attribute to the Pharisees — their practice of transmitting their traditional, extrabiblical teachings by word of mouth, not in writing.[42] In fact, much of the biting criticism of these people in the scrolls has to do with speech. Examples are the words for spouting, scoffing, lies, deceit. One should not infer too much, but it is at least worth mentioning that the critique in the scrolls emphasizes the verbal aspect of the ways in which their opponents, seemingly the Pharisees, misled people. Perhaps no more should be expected for an oral society, but it is a fact that the scrolls consistently employ speech terms when dealing with the ones who look for smooth things. The sources indicate that the Pharisees were known for extrascriptural regulations that were passed along. As Josephus says in explaining a difference between them and the Sadducees: ". . . the Pharisees had passed on to the people certain regulations handed down by former generations and not recorded in the Laws of Moses, for which reason they are rejected by the Sadducaean group, who hold that only those regulations should be considered valid which were written down (in Scripture), and that those which had been handed down by former generations need not be observed" (*Ant.* 13.297).

The evidence from the several scrolls surveyed allows one to conclude that the primary Jewish opponents of the scrolls communities were Pharisees. They are, for instance, mentioned far more frequently than the group dubbed Manasseh. About the Pharisees under the guise of various epithets the texts noted above say nothing positive; rather, they picture them as prime candidates for divine judgment, deserving recipients of the covenantal curses (so CD 1). The conflict is strong and bitter and may reflect one of the reasons why some chose to separate from the larger society and to find a place of refuge in the wilderness, if indeed the Pharisees exercised as much sway in Jewish society as Josephus suggests they did (*Ant.* 18.15-17).

---

41. B. Z. Wacholder, "A Qumran Attack on the Oral Exegesis? The Phrase *'šr btlmwd šqrm* in 4Q Pesher Nahum," *RevQ* 5/20 (1966): 576-77.

42. For a fuller statement of the evidence, see VanderKam, "Those Who Look for Smooth Things," 475-77.

The Pharisees come off poorly in the scrolls, and in the New Testament they fare no better. Think, for instance, of the string of woes Jesus pronounces upon the scribes and Pharisees in Matthew 23 or controversy stories such as the one in Matt 15:1-9, where Jesus is quoted as saying to Pharisees and scribes: "'And why do you break the commandment of God for the sake of your tradition?'" (v. 3). Or, in the same context, he declares: "So, for the sake of your tradition, you make void the word [variants: 'laws,' 'commandments'] of God" (v. 6; vv. 7-9 apply Isa 29:13 to them). The Pharisees are opponents in both the scrolls and the New Testament, but they are attacked from decidedly different angles. In the scrolls they are pictured as people who look for the easy way out, avoiding the full force of the law's requirements; but in the New Testament they come across as legalistic, as teachers who miss the point of the divine law for the sake of trivial details.

It is a pity that only texts written by their opponents have survived and apparently none written by Pharisees in the period under consideration. The texts document the level of hostility between groups that Josephus mentioned (in *Ant.* 13.171-73), but they leave the modern student in a difficult situation, as s/he attempts to learn historical information from robustly biased texts.[43] It would be challenging to write an account of late Second Temple Pharisees from the extant sources. Albert Baumgarten has written:

> The state of our sources on the Pharisees is such that we have much evidence concerning the way they were seen by others, but little indication of how they saw themselves or wanted to be viewed. As a group, they are therefore even more exposed than usual to being perverted by the tendentious motives of modern scholars who write about them — a tendentiousness that is near at hand given their connection with the rabbis, and thus with traditional Jewish identity — so that Jewish scholars of varying persuasions regularly present the Pharisees as the epitome of their personal version of Judaism, while many Christian scholars continue the polemic of the New Testament against the Pharisees, in modern guise.[44]

---

43. The collection of essays edited by Neusner and Chilton mentioned above *(In Quest of the Historical Pharisees)* attempts to gather and examine all the evidence regarding them.

44. A. I. Baumgarten, "Pharisees," in *EDSS*, 2:658.

Even with the evidence of the scrolls, the resulting picture of Judaism in the late Second Temple period is not as full as one would like. For a long time the Essenes seemed the most mysterious of Josephus's three groups. Now, ironically, there has been an inundation of texts from a branch or rather branches of those Essenes. They are wonderful and yet frustrating to read and ponder. It would be so good if someone could find a library of Pharisaic works, if they wrote them down, or of Sadducean compositions — or, better yet, of both. At least then there would be more sources to provide balance in modern assessments of the Jewish groups.

CHAPTER 6

The Dead Sea Scrolls
and the New Testament Gospels

The topic of this chapter needs some contextualizing. Most experts who work with the Dead Sea Scrolls have concluded that they are Jewish texts and that none of them is a Christian composition. However, there have been a few who have studied the scrolls and have concluded just the opposite: they are Christian texts. The individuals who have offered the latter assessment have maintained that one has to read the scrolls in an unusual way to understand them as Christian works, and these scholars have had a very small following. They also take a different approach to dating the material: the scrolls generally have to be later in date than the evidence suggests for their theories to work (they could hardly be from the first century B.C.E. and also be Christian).[1]

The approach taken in the present chapter is to side with the overwhelming majority by holding that the scrolls were written, copied, and/or owned by people who were Jewish and did not acknowledge Jesus of Nazareth as the Messiah, if they were even aware he existed. If that is the case, why should one think they have anything to do with Jesus and his earliest disciples? After all, the scrolls never mention Jesus, not even John the Bap-

---

1. Among the few who have viewed the texts found at Qumran as Christian rather than Jewish are: J. L. Teicher, "The Dead Sea Scrolls — Documents of the Jewish-Christian Sect of Ebionites," *JJS* 3 (1951): 67-99; B. E. Thiering in several books, including *The Gospels and Qumran: A New Hypothesis* (Australian and New Zealand Studies in Theology and Religion; Sydney: Theological Explorations, 1981); and R. Eisenman, also in several books such as *James the Brother of Jesus: The Key to Unlocking the Secrets of Early Christianity and the Dead Sea Scrolls* (New York: Viking, 1997).

executed or imprisoned; cf. Acts 21:38). These were not the only individuals who had such aspirations.[8]

The Dead Sea Scrolls supplement the picture of Jewish messianic beliefs entertained at the time.[9] One of the very first scrolls to be found, 1QS (the best-preserved copy of the *Rule of the Community*), contains a passage that is the most familiar and remains the clearest statement of the group's expectations in this regard. As the composition in which it occurs is a kind of constitution for the community that it describes and for which it prescribes, it is an official statement of sorts, a formulation of belief from a group and not one expressing the thought of just an individual. In the place where the text speaks about establishing a community of "the men of perfect holiness" and about the need to separate from the men of injustice, it adds: "They shall depart from none of the counsels of the Law to walk in all the stubbornness of their hearts, but shall be ruled by the primitive precepts in which the men of the Community were first instructed until there shall come the Prophet and the Messiahs of Aaron and Israel" (9:9-11).

The plural "Messiahs" (distinguished from the singular form only by the small letter *yod*) naturally caught the attention of expositors from the time it was first read. The expression "the Messiahs of Aaron and Israel" reminded experts of a phrase that occurs four times in the *Damascus Document,* a work found in several copies among the scrolls but copies of which had been discovered in the storage room for old manuscripts (a Genizah) in the Ezra synagogue in Old Cairo more than fifty years before the first finds at Qumran. In the *Damascus Document,* also a kind of constitutional composition although seemingly not for a withdrawn group, the expression takes a singular form: "the messiah of Aaron and Israel"

---

8. The movements associated with these individuals have been subjected to many studies. See, e.g., R. A. Horsley, "'Messianic' Figures and Movements in First-Century Palestine," in J. H. Charlesworth, ed., *The Messiah: Developments in Earliest Judaism and Christianity* (Minneapolis: Fortress, 1992), 276-95; R. Gray, *Prophetic Figures in Late Second Temple Palestine* (Oxford: Oxford University Press, 1993), 112-44.

9. There is a detailed but brief treatment of the texts by G. Vermes, "Appendix B: The Qumran Messiahs and Messianism," in E. Schürer, *The History of the Jewish People in the Age of Jesus Christ* (3 vols.; rev. and ed. Vermes, F. Millar, and M. Black; Edinburgh: T. & T. Clark, 1973-1987), 2:550-54. See also Collins, *The Scepter and the Star,* specifically 77-109; L. H. Schiffman, "Messianic Figures and Ideas in the Qumran Scrolls," in Charlesworth, *The Messiah,* 116-29; and J. C. VanderKam, "Messianism in the Scrolls," in E. Ulrich and VanderKam, eds., *The Community of the Renewed Covenant: The Notre Dame Symposium on the Dead Sea Scrolls* (Christianity and Judaism in Antiquity 10; Notre Dame: University of Notre Dame Press, 1994), 211-34.

(CD 12:23; 14:19; 19:10; the near parallel "messiah from Aaron and from Israel" occurs at 20:1). The wording had occasioned much discussion before 1947, with some maintaining that one messiah was meant and others believing that the writer thought of two, one from Aaron, that is, a priestly messiah, and one from Israel, probably a Davidic messiah.[10] The evidence from 1QS makes one think that the proper understanding of the *Damascus Document* references may well be to take it as plural.[11] One could also consider the possibility that there was development in messianic thinking in the communities behind the scrolls, say, from an expectation of one messiah to a hope for two.[12] The discussion about the phrase "the messiahs of Aaron and Israel" has become more complicated over the years because the relevant section (not just the material in 1QS 9:9-11) is absent from the oldest copy of the *Rule of the Community,*[13] but its presence in 1QS, which dates from 100-75 B.C.E., indicates that it was a belief adopted by the people behind the text at an early point.

The idea that there would be two messiahs is unusual for the period under consideration. Perhaps it was influenced by texts in the Hebrew Bible that talk of the postexilic period, when the Jewish people were ruled by two leaders, a prince (like Zerubbabel, from the line of David) and a high priest (like Joshua, from the old high-priestly family) — a diumvirate attested in the books of Ezra, Haggai, and Zechariah. It is the case, however, that the scrolls do not tie the belief directly to such texts (Num 24:17 is explicitly connected with it; see below). Whatever the origins of the double

10. L. Ginzberg, *An Unknown Jewish Sect* (Moreshet 1; New York: Ktav, 1970), 222-56. He several times expresses his view that two messiahs are meant by the expressions against the idea of other writers that one messiah is intended.

11. See the discussion of the issues in Collins, *The Scepter and the Star,* 77-87. He also favors the two-messiah reading of the expressions from the *Damascus Document.*

12. Oddly, however, in one of the earliest overviews of messianism in the scrolls, J. Starcky hypothesized that at first the group did not expect a messiah (phase 1; at least there is no evidence for such an expectation), then it expected two of them (phase 2), only to change to a hope for one from Aaron and Israel (phase 3) and back again to two, especially a Davidic messiah; "Les quatre étapes du messianisme à Qumrân," *RB* 70 (1963): 481-505.

13. The copy in question, 4Q259 (4QS^e), has in col. 3 material paralleling 1QS 8:10-15, directly after which it has text corresponding with 1QS 9:12 (on the same line, line 2), thus lacking the intervening section including the statement about the prophet and the two messiahs. For the official publication of the text, see P. S. Alexander and G. Vermes, eds., *Qumran Cave 4: XIX, Serek Ha-Yaḥad and Two Related Texts* (DJD 26; Oxford: Clarendon, 1998), 129-52, with pls. 14-16, esp. 144-49.

expectation, there is a series of other passages in the scrolls where one messiah or the other (not necessarily together) put in appearances and where they carry out appropriate functions in the eschatological war.

The messiah of Israel or of David also appears under the titles Branch of David and Prince of the Congregation.[14] One text in which he figures and which for a time generated much excitement is *The Rule of War* (4Q285) — a composition that may mention both messiahs:

[As it is written in the book of] Isaiah the Prophet, [The thickets of the forest] will be cut [down with an axe and Lebanon by a majestic one will f]all. And there shall come forth a shoot from the stump of Jesse [. . .] the Branch of David and they will enter into judgement with [. . .] and the Prince of the Congregation, the Br[anch of David] will kill him [. . . by strok]es and by wounds. And a Priest [of renown(?) will command [. . . the s]lai[n] of the Kitti[m . . .]. (frg. 7)[15]

The scene, based on Isaiah 11, which assists in identifying some of the allusions, appears to be one in which the Branch of David is fighting against the forces of evil (the Kittim) and killing someone. Present too is a priest, although he is not given a recognizable messianic title in the legible parts of the text (though Geza Vermes capitalizes "Priest"). This is the picture encountered in the *War Scroll*, which speaks at length about the final war between the good and the wicked, "the sons of light" and "the sons of darkness." In it the Prince of the Congregation leads the battle (5:1; cf. 11:6-7, where Num 24:17-19 is quoted),[16] and a priest carries out scriptural duties of Aaron and his successors in times of war (1QM 10:2; 13:1-6; 15:4; 16:13; 18:5; 19:1).

The *Rule of the Congregation* (1QSa), a text that names as its subject the end of days (1:1), contains a scene that has both fascinated and frustrated interpreters. Of a meeting in those last days, the author writes:

14. For the relevant passages, see VanderKam, "Messianism in the Scrolls," 216-18; Collins, *The Scepter and the Star*, 62-67.

15. The official edition of the text is P. S. Alexander and G. Vermes, "285. 4QSefer ha-Milḥamah," in Alexander et al., eds., J. C. VanderKam and M. Brady, consulting eds., *Qumran Cave 4: XXVI, Miscellanea, Part 1* (DJD 36; Oxford: Clarendon, 2000), 228-46, with pls. 12-13. See their comments esp. on p. 239.

16. See Y. Yadin, *The Scroll of the War of the Sons of Light Against the Sons of Darkness* (trans. B. and Ch. Rabin; Oxford: Oxford University Press, 1962), 278-79; Collins, *The Scepter and the Star*, 64-67.

When God engenders (the Priest-)Messiah, he shall come with them [at] the head of the whole congregation of Israel, with all [his brethren, the sons] of Aaron the Priests, [those called] to the assembly, the men of renown; and they shall sit [before him, each man] in the order of his dignity. And then [the Mess]iah of Israel shall [come], and the chiefs of the [clans of Israel] shall sit before him, [each] in the order of his dignity, according to [his place] in their camps and marches. And before them shall sit all the heads of [family of the congreg]ation, and the wise men of [the holy congregation,] each in the order of his dignity.

And [when] they shall gather for the common [tab]le, to eat and [to drink] new wine, when the common table shall be set for eating and the new wine [poured for] drinking, let no man extend his hand over the firstfruits of bread and wine before the Priest; for [it is he] who shall bless the firstfruits of bread and wine, and shall be the first [to extend] his hand over the bread. Thereafter, the Messiah of Israel shall extend his hand over the bread, [and] all the congregation of the Community [shall utter a] blessing, [each man in the order] of his dignity.

A meal involving bread and wine with a messiah present can hardly fail to be of interest to readers of the Gospels, yet much about the passage is difficult. One issue concerns the translation "When God engenders (the Priest-)Messiah" (note that Vermes supplies the parenthetical words "the Priest" in his rendering; they are not in the text). The verb is not at all easy to read, but a defensible suggestion is "when God reveals."[17] The reference here is probably to the messiah of Israel, the only person explicitly termed a messiah in this passage. The priest is present to perform the task of blessing the ingredients of the meal.[18]

17. See VanderKam, "Messianism in the Scrolls," 221-22; Collins, *The Scepter and the Star*, 81-82, for the alternatives such as "when God sends the messiah," "when the messiah assembles" (the latter is the interpretation of J. Licht, *The Rule Scroll: A Scroll from the Wilderness of Judaea 1QS · 1QSa · 1QSb: Text, Introduction and Commentary* [Jerusalem: Bialik, 1965 (Hebrew)], 267-69; L. H. Schiffman, *The Eschatological Community of the Dead Sea Scrolls: A Study of the Rule of the Congregation* [SBLMS 38; Atlanta: Scholars, 1989], 53-54).

18. Collins, *The Scepter and the Star*, 82 (he thinks the priest in the passage is the messianic priest, though he is not given the title messiah in the text). The much-discussed issue of whether mention of the priest before the messiah of Israel entails a

The scrolls, then, provide information about communities that believed two messiahs, a priestly and nonpriestly one, would be present in the last days and during the final conflict. In fact, their arrival marks the end of the present age. Other than their roles in the final conflict, the texts divulge little about what they will do. It has been suggested, and plausibly, that the distribution of the two offices — ruler and priest — to two messiahs was directed against the Hasmoneans, who combined the top political office with the high-priestly position in one person.[19]

In the New Testament, unlike the scrolls, there is just one messiah, and, as for others at the time who thought a messiah would come, he was of the Davidic line. In that sense, there is an important difference between the two literatures. It is worth remembering, however, that the New Testament presentation of Jesus as messiah is more complex than simply depicting him as a special descendant of David. Primarily in the book of Hebrews he takes on priestly qualities; there he is a priest after the order of Melchizedek, one who officiates in the heavenly sanctuary.[20] As a result, the notion of a priestly messiah is not foreign to the New Testament. Unlike the messianic teachings in the scrolls, Jesus in the New Testament combines in his one person some aspects of the two messiahs expected in Qumran texts.

THE WORKS OF THE MESSIAH

Another topic related to the subject of messianism in the scrolls and in the New Testament should also be treated. According to Luke 7, after Jesus healed a centurion's servant and raised the widow of Nain's son, John's disciples reported the amazing events to their master. John then dispatched two of his disciples to Jesus to ask him a question: "'Are you the one who is

---

higher rank for him seems beside the point. The priest appears first because of his function in the scene — he blesses the food and wine before anyone may partake of it.

19. See, e.g., P. W. Flint, "*4Qpseudo-Daniel ar^c* (4Q245) and the Restoration of the Priesthood," *RevQ* 17/65-68 (1996): 137-50. The Hasmoneans held the top political and priestly offices in the nation beginning with Jonathan in 152 B.C.E., although Aristobulus I (104-103) is supposed to have been the first who adopted the title of king.

20. H. Anderson, "The Jewish Antecedents of the Christology in Hebrews," in Charlesworth, *The Messiah*, 512-35; E. F. Mason, '*You Are a Priest Forever': Second Temple Jewish Messianism and the Priestly Christology of the Epistle to the Hebrews* (STDJ 74; Leiden: Brill, 2008).

to come, or are we to wait for another?'" (v. 19 and v. 20, where it is re-peated). Luke writes: "Jesus had just then cured many people of diseases, plagues, and evil spirits, and had given sight to many who were blind. And he answered them, 'Go and tell John what you have seen and heard: the blind receive their sight, the lame walk, the lepers are cleansed, the deaf hear, the dead are raised, the poor have good news brought to them. And blessed is anyone who takes no offense at me'" (7:21-23). A similar passage is found in Matt 11:2-6, where John is in prison at the time of the exchange. John's question may have been motivated by some concern that Jesus did not fit the messianic expectations that he — John — entertained. Proof of Jesus' status as messiah comes through the healing miracles he performs.

The passage has received additional attention since the publication of a text named *A Messianic Apocalypse* (4Q521).[21]

> . . . [the hea]vens and the earth will listen to His Messiah, and none
> therein will stray from the commandments of the holy ones.
> Seekers of the Lord, strengthen yourselves in His service!
> All you hopeful in (your) heart, will you not find the Lord in this?
> For the Lord will consider the pious *(hasidim)* and call the righteous
> by name.
> Over the poor His spirit will hover and will renew the faithful with
> His power.
> And He will glorify the pious on the throne of the eternal Kingdom.
> He who liberates the captives, restores sight to the blind, straightens
> the b[ent]. (Ps. cxlvi, 7-8)
>
> And f[or] ever I will clea[ve to the h]opeful and in His mercy . . .
> And the fr[uit . . .] will not be delayed for anyone
> And the Lord will accomplish glorious things which have never been
> as [He . . .]
> For He will heal the wounded, and revive the dead and bring good
> news to the poor (Isa. lxi, 1). (2 ii 1-12)

21. The official publication of 4Q521 was by É. Puech, "521. 4QApocalypse messianique," in Puech, ed., *Qumrân Grotte 4: XVIII, Textes hébreux (4Q521-4Q528, 4Q576-4Q579)* (DJD 25; Oxford: Clarendon, 1998), 1-38, with pls. 1-3. He had issued a preliminary edition of it in "Une Apocalypse messianique (4Q521)," *RevQ* 15/60 (1992): 475-522; and he examined it at length in *La croyance des Esséniens en la vie future: Immortalité, résurrection, vie éternelle? Histoire d'une croyance dans le judaïsme ancien* (2 vols.; EBib 20; Paris: Gabalda, 1993), 627-92.

The text mentions a messiah in the first line and in the sequel lists several of the wonders that parallel the ones that Jesus enumerates for John's messengers. Both 4Q521 and the gospel passage are working with sections from the book of Isaiah. The first one is Isa 61:1-2, which is the text Jesus reads from the scroll of Isaiah when he is in the synagogue at Nazareth:

> When he came to Nazareth where he had been brought up, he went to the synagogue on the sabbath day, as was his custom. He stood up to read, and the scroll of the prophet Isaiah was given to him. He unrolled the scroll and found the place where it was written: "The Spirit of the Lord is upon me, because he has anointed me to bring good news to the poor. He has sent me to proclaim release to the captives, and recovery of sight to the blind, to let the oppressed go free, to proclaim the year of the Lord's favor." (Luke 4:16-19)

Actually the passage from Isaiah is not cited word for word, and it is supplemented from Isa 58:6 ("to let the oppressed go free"). Jesus follows his reading of the lectionary portion by declaring to his fellow townsfolk that the passage of scripture had been fulfilled in their hearing (4:21).

Isaiah 61:1-2 accounts for one of the items Jesus lists for John's disciples in Luke 7 but by no means for all of them. Others come from Isa 35:5-6: "Then the eyes of the blind shall be opened, and the ears of the deaf unstopped; then the lame shall leap like a deer, and the tongue of the speechless sing for joy. . . ." Below is a list of the parallel items in the two Isaiah texts, Luke 7:21-22, and 4Q521:

Isaiah 35	Isaiah 61	Luke 7	4Q521
	cured many		heal the wounded
blind eyes opened		blind see	blind see
lame leap		lame walk	
		lepers cleansed	
ears of deaf opened		deaf hear	
		dead raised	dead raised
	good news to poor	good news to poor	good news to poor

The scriptural background for most of the deeds in the list is clear enough, but the remarkable point is that Luke 7:22 and 4Q521 both add to their list — immediately before referencing good news to the poor — the subject of raising the dead, a miracle not present in either Isaianic passage. The two lists appear to be offering the same kind of reading and supplement to the Isaiah texts.[22] 4Q521 is thus one of a small number of works found in the Qumran scrolls attesting a belief that a resurrection would occur.

The messianic reference in the first line is problematic in that the term "his Messiah" appears to function as a poetic parallel to "the holy ones." Whatever is being predicated of "his messiah" here (unless it is "his messiahs" spelled defectively), the same applies to "the holy ones" in line 2. In addition, the Lord is the one who accomplishes the miraculous actions in 4Q521, not the Messiah, while in Luke 7 Jesus the Messiah is the one who performs them.

SCRIPTURAL INTERPRETATION

One of the most interesting topics in the scrolls is the way in which the writers interpret the older scriptures. As seen in Chapter 2 above, scriptural study was exceedingly important to the community. For example, the *Rule of the Community* stipulates: "And where the ten [the ten men who are mentioned in the preceding paragraph] are, there shall never lack a man among them who shall study the Law continually, day and night, concerning the right conduct of a man with his companion. And the Congregation shall watch in community for a third of every night of the year, to read the Book and to study the Law and to bless together" (6:6-8).[23] In addition, they believed God had revealed to the Teacher of Righteousness the true meaning of the prophetic books (1QpHab 2:6-10), and they wrote detailed, line-by-line commentaries (the *pesharim*) on those books.

There are some cases in which one can compare the way in which a passage from the Hebrew scriptures was understood and used in both the

---

22. A number of scholars have examined the parallels between this part of 4Q521 and Luke 7. Examples are: J. D. Tabor and M. O. Wise, "4Q521 'On Resurrection' and the Synoptic Gospel Tradition: A Preliminary Study," *JSP* 10 (1992): 149-62; J. J. Collins, "The Works of the Messiah," *DSD* 1 (1994): 98-112; and *The Scepter and the Star*, 131-41, 231-32. For an overview, see J. C. VanderKam and P. W. Flint, *The Meaning of the Dead Sea Scrolls: Their Significance for Understanding the Bible, Judaism, Jesus, and Christianity* (San Francisco: HarperSanFrancisco, 2002), 332-34.

23. On the passage, see P. Wernberg-Møller, *The Manual of Discipline* (STDJ 1; Leiden: Brill, 1957), 103: "The context is to the effect that there was always one member of the society studying the Torah; in this way the community lived up to the ideal expressed in Ps. i 2."

action when a human life is at risk. Perhaps the Pharisees would have answered Jesus' question affirmatively (though they might have wondered about its relevance to the case at hand). Yet the gospel saying fits well in its historical context in the sense that it was an issue debated at the time, as the scrolls indicate.

REBUKING

There is another parallel between the gospels and the scrolls showing that the communities behind them had similar, scripturally related ways of handling those disputes between members that inevitably arise in close-knit groups. For people like the ones occupying the area of Qumran, there were presumably plenty of opportunities for friction between individuals, just as there were in the early Christian congregations. The shared practice to be explored here is the requirement of rebuking or confronting fellow members who have committed an offense. The two literatures talk about the practice, and well they might because it is a scriptural one; and they indicate similarities in the way their authors read the ancient text and put it into practice. Rebuking was to take place when one member was offended or harmed by another, according to Matthew 18; whether it was limited to such cases at Qumran the texts do not say. These practices are based on teachings in Leviticus 19; but both communities developed the instructions of Leviticus in parallel ways. The procedures they elaborated were designed to reduce the negative effects of incidents that in some way pitted member against member and to help the individuals involved overcome any lingering feelings of hatred or resentment in order to maintain a harmonious fellowship. It is perhaps not surprising that partial parallels exist with other groups as well (e.g., the Iobacchi).[37]

Leviticus 19, a part of the Holiness Code (Leviticus 17-26), is a chapter that emphasizes the sanctity of God and often motivates the laws stated by appeal to the Lord's holiness. The law about rebuking is one of them, and it follows a series of rules meant to govern communal life. Specifically, it follows several statements that place one in a courtroom setting. Leviticus

---

37. M. Weinfeld, *The Organizational Pattern and the Penal Code of the Qumran Sect: A Comparison with Guilds and Religious Associations of the Hellenistic-Roman Period* (NTOA 2; Fribourg: Éditions Universitaires and Göttingen: Vandenhoeck & Ruprecht, 1986), 39-41.

19:15 forbids unjust judgments and deference to rich or poor; verse 16 adds prohibitions of slander and harming one's neighbor in some way. The relevant verses follow: "You shall not hate in your heart anyone of your kin; you shall reprove your neighbor, or you will incur guilt yourself. You shall not take vengeance or bear a grudge against any of your people, but you shall love your neighbor as yourself: I am the Lord" (19:17-18).[38]

Matthew 18:15-17 offers the following set of guidelines for church practice (see Luke 17:3):[39]

a. Private level: if one member sins against a second, the second one is to point this out "when the two of you are alone." If this approach succeeds, then the matter is settled ("if the member listens to you, you have regained that one"). Here the kinship language of Leviticus is continued with ἀδελφός, although it is used in a transferred sense for a fellow church member. As the offense involved only the two of them, they handle it alone in the first instance.

b. Witnesses level: if this private confrontation does not bring about the desired result, "take one or two others along with you, so that every word may be confirmed by the evidence of two or three witnesses." The number of witnesses conforms to the scriptural requirement of two or three (with the original accuser), as the citation of Deut 19:15 in Matt 18:16 shows.

c. Community level: if the offender still persists after the private confrontation and the one before witnesses, the offended party is to take the matter to the entire assembly, here called the church.

d. Expulsion: if he remains obstinate, he is to be considered in the same category as a Gentile and tax collector.

As many have observed, 1QS 5:24–6:1 offers the covenanters' parallel though differently nuanced approach to such matters.[40]

---

38. For an overview of the text and interpretations of it, including ones in the scrolls, see J. Milgrom, *Leviticus 17–22* (AB 3A; New York: Doubleday, 2000), 1646-56. As he notes, the presence of two Hebrew verbs in the expression translated "you shall reprove" was understood to mean that the rebuking was to be done before witnesses (1649-50).

39. See Luz, *Matthew 8–20*, 450-53.

40. For the subject, see Licht, *The Rule Scroll*, 136-37; L. H. Schiffman, *Sectarian Law in the Dead Sea Scrolls: Courts, Testimony and the Penal Code* (BJS 33; Chico: Scholars, 1983), 89-109.

a. It states the principle that the members "shall rebuke one another in truth, humility, charity." This was to be the spirit that prevailed when there was conflict. The immediately preceding section deals with becoming and remaining a member and the proper hierarchy in the group along with the relations that were to prevail between the different kinds of members in the community.

b. An offended person was not to hate the offender but "let him rebuke him on the very same day lest he incur guilt because of him." The provision regarding the timing of the rebuke is not echoed in Matthew. It has been suggested that it reflects the law in Num 30:5, 8, 12 where a man may nullify the oath of a daughter or wife at the very time when he hears about it, not on the next day.[41]

c. Also, a person was not to accuse another before the congregation without having first admonished him "in the presence of witnesses."

As nearly as one can tell, there are three successive stages here that resemble closely those in Matthew: personal confrontation, accusation before witnesses, and bringing the matter before the entire group. More of the overall context in which the rules were operative arises from CD 9:2-8, which quotes Lev 19:17-18, one of the scriptural bases of the practice:

> And concerning the saying, *You shall not take vengeance on the children of your people, nor bear any rancour against them* (Lev. xix, 18), if any member of the Covenant accuses his companion without first rebuking him before witnesses; if he denounces him in the heat of his anger or reports him to his elders to make him look contemptible, he is one that takes vengeance and bears rancour, although it is expressly written, *He takes vengeance upon His adversaries and bears rancour against His enemies* (Nah. i, 2). If he holds his peace towards him from one day to another [4QD (267) 9 i 1 adds: and from one month to another] and thereafter speaks of him in the heat of his anger, he testifies against himself concerning a capital matter because he has not fulfilled the commandment of God which tells him: *You shall rebuke your companion and not be burdened with sin because of him* (Lev. xix, 17).

---

41. Schiffman, *Sectarian Law in the Dead Sea Scrolls*, 90-91; Milgrom, *Leviticus 17–22*, 1649-50.

Or CD 7:2-3 says: "They shall rebuke each man his brother according to the commandment and shall bear no rancour from one day to the next" (or "from one month to the next"; see Num 30:15). Delay in handling the problem could lead to the further sins of bearing a grudge or exacting vengeance, both of which are prohibited in Lev 19:18.

Timothy Carmody has argued that, despite similarities, there is a basic difference between the instructions in Matthew and those in the Qumran texts: in Matthew the goal is the repentance of the offender, the gaining of a brother, with little attention paid to the accuser; in the Qumran literature the aim is to keep the law exactly and gain a legal conviction.[42] The conclusion appears to be unjustified. The legislation in Matthew and in the *Serekh* figures in contexts that deal with the fellowship. It is true that in Matthew there is much concern with losing no one (the preceding section is Matt 18:10-14 — the parable of the Lost Sheep), while in the *Serekh* entry into membership, the hierarchy, and duties of members are under review. But the first step in each case (the individual meeting) is phrased in such a way that the tone or nature of the confrontation is to the fore: in Matthew, the stress is on the private nature of it (just the two who are directly affected), while the *Serekh* is more explicit about the spirit in which rebuking was to be done and the immediate timing of it (which appears to be to the advantage of the accuser). The subsequent steps in both cases are more judicial in nature, with each providing for meetings with witnesses and, if needed, with the entire community. In the two texts, of course, the practice is based on a scriptural passage that ends with "you shall love your neighbor as yourself" (see also CD 6:20-21 for loving one's brother as oneself, and CD 7:1-2 for not sinning against near of kin; CD 9:2-8 fits in a context having to do with vows).

CD 9:16-20 describes the procedures obtaining for circumstances in which a sin in a capital matter is witnessed; it is to be reported to the overseer, and the witness is apparently the one who issues the rebuke in the presence of the overseer. The overseer then records it, lest it be repeated and witnessed again.[43] The process seems similar to the New Testament injunction, although Matthew does not mention the matter of keeping rec-

---

42. T. R. Carmody, "Matt 18:15-17 in Relation to Three Texts from Qumran Literature (CD 9:2-8, 16-22; 1QS 5:25–6:1)," in M. P. Horgan and P. J. Kobelski, eds., *To Touch the Text: Biblical and Related Studies in Honor of Joseph A. Fitzmyer, S.J.* (New York: Crossroad, 1989), 141-58.

43. 4Q477 is named *Rebukes Reported by the Overseer;* it is highly fragmentary but is thought to be a copy of the sort of record of which CD 9:16-20 speaks.

ords. It is worth noting, however, that the passage in Matthew is immediately followed by one asserting, "Truly I tell you, whatever you bind on earth will be bound in heaven, and whatever you loose on earth will be loosed in heaven" (18:18; see also v. 19). The passage reflects a close association between earth and heaven, perhaps not unlike the communion the covenanters of the Qumran texts felt with the angels.

The examples given above are a selection of passages in which the scrolls furnish added information that is helpful for reading the New Testament gospels. They allow the reader to see events in the lives of Jesus and those around him in their context, but in a context now known more fully because of the scrolls.

CHAPTER 7

The Dead Sea Scrolls, the Acts of the Apostles, and the Letters of Paul

As explained in the previous chapter, the Dead Sea Scrolls provide helpful backlighting so that one can read some passages in the New Testament gospels in a more informed fashion. The same is true for the book of Acts and the letters of Paul. Scholars date Luke and Acts, generally thought to have been written by the same person, to a time late in the first century, after the communities of the scrolls had disappeared from the historical record. But both books report events that happened at an earlier time, and both can be illuminated in places by the scrolls. Paul is the earliest New Testament writer. All of his authentic letters were written while the site of Khirbet Qumran was in use, and they are intensely concerned with Jewish subjects. His letters too have proved to be instructive subjects of comparison with the scrolls. Obviously it will be possible to touch upon only a few selected topics in these books. The procedure will be to follow the scriptural order, not a chronological one, and consider Acts first.

THE SCROLLS AND ACTS 1–4[1]

The first chapters of Acts show a series of significant parallels with material in the scrolls.

---

1. In his remarkable collection of parallels between the scrolls and the New Testament — *Qumran und das Neue Testament* (2 vols.; Tübingen: Mohr [Siebeck], 1966) — Herbert Braun covers the book of Acts in 1:139-68.

of the Community. Here too, as in the sources listed above, the sharing of possessions comes third as an explanation of the meaning of "might." There is no need to think the writer of this part of Acts drew his interpretation from the *Rule of the Community,* but it documents it as an understanding of "might" in Deut 6:5 well before Acts was written.

Acts 2, Pentecost, and Sinai

Communal sharing of property is perhaps the most familiar parallel between the scrolls community and the first believers in Jesus. It would be a mistake, however, to stop there and leave this part of the book of Acts in a search for meaningful parallels between the scrolls and the New Testament book. There will be more to say about the ways in which the people of the scrolls interpreted the scriptures (and see Chapter 2 above), but there is also an intriguing example of scriptural interpretation in the same context — in Acts 2. There Peter, after the pouring out of the Spirit on the disciples, counters the bystanders' charge that Jesus' followers were speaking oddly because they were drunk. "Indeed, these are not drunk, as you suppose, for it is only nine o'clock in the morning. No, this is what was spoken through the prophet Joel: 'In the last days it will be, God declares, that I will pour out my Spirit upon all flesh, and your sons and your daughters shall prophesy . . .'" (Acts 2:15-17). An instance in which an ancient prophecy is said to be actualized in a contemporary event of the community's life would have resonated with the people of the scrolls because they too read the prophets eschatologically in their commentaries, the *pesharim,* and elsewhere.[10]

In the face of such strong parallels between the Qumran scrolls and the early chapters of Acts, there is reason to search for further commonalities between them. And the story of Pentecost in Acts 2 provides even more of them.

---

10. The passage in Joel (3:1 [Eng. 2:28]) begins, in MT, with "Then afterward I will pour out my spirit on all flesh . . . ," while LXX reads: "And it shall be after these things I will pour out my spirit on all flesh . . ." (translation of G. Howard in A. Pietersma and B. G. Wright, eds., *A New English Translation of the Septuagint and the Other Greek Translations Traditionally Included under That Title* [New York: Oxford University Press, 2007]). "In the last days" seems to be from the writer of Acts, as does "God declares": "Luke thus gives to the quotation a new eschatological orientation and ascribes the prophet's words to God himself"; Fitzmyer, *The Acts of the Apostles,* 252 (note also his comment on the citation formula in v. 16).

Pentecost is a scriptural holiday, and, as practicing Jews, Jesus' disciples were celebrating it with their fellow religionists. Jews from all over the world came to Jerusalem for the pilgrimage holiday, thus accounting for the presence of visitors from so many different countries as enumerated in Acts 2:9-11. The legislation for the holiday appears in several passages in the scriptures where it is called the Festival of Weeks.[11] It received its name from the way of calculating its date: "And from the day after the sabbath, from the day on which you bring the sheaf of the elevation offering, you shall count off seven weeks; they shall be complete. You shall count until the day after the seventh sabbath, fifty days; then you shall present an offering of new grain to the LORD" (Lev 23:15-16). That the festival fell fifty days after the waving of the sheaf yielded its Greek name *Pentecost* ("fiftieth"). It was celebrated on a day in the third month of the Jewish calendar, coinciding with a time in the late spring or early summer. The holiday was hardly a minor one for Jewish people: it was one of the three pilgrimage festivals when "all your males shall appear before the LORD your God" (Exod 23:17). The result was that Jewish people in great numbers traveled to Jerusalem to the temple to carry out the scriptural mandate, even though it, unlike the other two pilgrimage festivals — Unleavened Bread and Tabernacles — was a one-day celebration only.

An oddity about a holiday as important as Weeks is that the scriptural sections detailing the legislation for it do not supply a specific date when Israel was to celebrate it. This contrasts with the other two pilgrimage holidays that are dated precisely: the Festival of Unleavened Bread runs from month one, the fifteenth day until the twenty-first. The Festival of Booths or Tabernacles comes exactly one half year later, month seven, the fifteenth through the twenty-first. There is no such date for the Festival of Weeks because the event from which the fifty-day count begins is itself not dated exactly. As a result, Jews had to decide on other grounds how to calculate the date of Pentecost, and not everyone agreed on when it was to take place.

The fact that the Torah is imprecise on a practical issue such as dating an important holiday led to disputes about when Weeks was to be observed. The source of the later controversies was the statement in Lev 23:15

11. J. Milgrom, *Leviticus 23–27* (AB 3B; New York: Doubleday, 2001), 1990-2011; J. C. VanderKam, "The Festival of Weeks and the Story of Pentecost in Acts 2," in C. A. Evans, ed., *From Prophecy to Testament: The Function of the Old Testament in the New* (Peabody: Hendrickson, 2004), 185-205; and S. Park, *Pentecost and Sinai: The Festival of Weeks as a Celebration of the Sinai Event* (LHB/OTS 342; New York: T. & T. Clark, 2008).

as to when the fifty-day count to the Festival of Weeks was to begin: "from the day after the sabbath, you shall count off seven weeks." The word thought to be ambiguous here is "sabbath," and several possibilities for interpreting it presented themselves. One option was, of course, to understand it as referring to the weekly Sabbath. In this case, the Festival of Weeks would always fall on a Sunday, seven weeks and one day after the Sabbath from which the count started. The problem with this reading was that the text did not say which Sabbath after Passover (celebrated on the first month, the fourteenth day; see Lev 23:4-8) was the one designated by the rule. One Jewish tradition (attested in *Jubilees* and the Dead Sea Scrolls) understood Lev 23:15 to designate the first Sabbath day after the completion of the eight days of Passover and the Festival of Unleavened Bread (that is, after 1/14-21). A second possibility was to take the word "sabbath" in the sense of "festival." This is not the most common meaning of the term, but it is attested in the Bible. So, for example, the Day of Atonement, which falls on the tenth day of the seventh month, whatever day of the week that may be from year to year, is termed "a sabbath of complete rest" (Lev 23:32). If the law about the Festival of Weeks is using "sabbath" in this sense, then it could refer to the first day of the Festival of Unleavened Bread (the first holiday after Passover) or the last day of the same festival (these are the two most sacred days of the seven-day celebration and are marked by special assemblies [Lev 23:7-8]). The fifty-day count would then begin from either 1/16 (the day after the sabbath = the first day of the festival) or 1/22 (the day after the last day of the festival).[12]

The Festival of Weeks is mentioned several times in Second Temple literature. The references demonstrate that, while the holiday appears not to have been especially important in the Hebrew Bible, it was regularly observed and even gained greater prominence at least for some groups later in Jewish history. It figures in the writings of Josephus, in Philo's works, and several other texts, among which are the Dead Sea Scrolls.

One tradition in early Judaism — the tradition that produced the book of *Jubilees* and the sectarian Dead Sea Scrolls — seems to have associated more themes with the Festival of Weeks than did other groups; or at least the sources, which are more abundant for this tradition, show that the holi-

---

12. For summaries of the debates, see R. H. Charles, *The Book of Jubilees, or the Little Genesis* (London: Black, 1902), 106-7, note; and M. D. Herr, "The Calendar," in S. Safrai and M. Stern, eds., *The Jewish People in the First Century* (CRINT 1.2; Assen: van Gorcum and Philadelphia: Fortress, 1976), 858-60.

day was extremely important in the minds of those who were at home in it. The book of *Jubilees,* from the mid–second century B.C.E., is the earliest witness to the enhanced importance of the Festival of Weeks.[13] As the writer of the book retells the stories in Genesis and the first half of Exodus, he deals with the Festival of Weeks in a series of noteworthy passages. A fundamental fact about the holiday as presented in *Jubilees* is that it is associated with the single ongoing covenant that God made and renewed several times with the ancestors and with his people. The first passage in which the festival and the covenant are explicitly connected is *Jub* 6:17-19, verses that pair Noah's eternal covenant in Genesis 9 and the Festival of Weeks. *Jubilees* 14 retells the story about the covenant made with Abram in Genesis 15. It says: "He got all of these [pieces of the animals for the covenant ceremony] in the middle of the month" (14:10). In *Jubilees'* 364-day calendar, the third month has thirty-one days, so that the middle would be the sixteenth day in it, but other passages demonstrate that the writer places the festival on the fifteenth of the third month (see 1:1; 44:1-5). He ties the eternal covenant of Genesis 17 to the Festival of Weeks: ". . . in the third month, in the middle of the month (= 3/15) — Abram celebrated the festival of the firstfruits of the wheat harvest" (15:1). He also reports that Isaac was born "in the third month; in the middle of the month, on the day that the Lord had told Abraham — on the festival of the firstfruits of the harvest" (16:13; for Weeks as the festival of the wheat harvest, see Exod 34:22).[14]

These are the explicit references to the Festival of Weeks in *Jubilees,* but the beginning of the book shows that the entire revelation contained in it is to be understood in light of what the holiday had come to mean. The Prologue and *Jubilees* 1 describe the setting for the meeting of God with Moses and the revelations made to him by the angel of the presence when Moses was on Mount Sinai, and *Jub* 1:1 names the date: "During the first year of the Israelites' exodus from Egypt, in the third month — on the sixteenth of the month — the Lord said to Moses: 'Come up to me on the mountain. I will give you the two stone tablets of the law and the com-

---

13. Fourteen copies of *Jubilees* have been identified among the Qumran scrolls (see Chapter 4 above). For the date of the book, see J. C. VanderKam, *Textual and Historical Studies in the Book of Jubilees* (HSM 14; Missoula: Scholars, 1977), 207-85; "The Origins and Purposes of the Book of Jubilees," in M. Albani, J. Frey, and A. Lange, eds., *Studies in the Book of Jubilees* (TSAJ 65; Tübingen: Mohr Siebeck, 1997), 3-24.

14. Translations of Jubilees come from J. C. VanderKam, *The Book of Jubilees: A Critical Text* (2 vols.; CSCO 510-11; Scriptores Aethiopic 87-88; Leuven: Peeters, 1989), vol. 2.

rael had become blissfully unified, just as the followers of Jesus described in Acts 2–4 did.[22]

Conclusions

Summing up, there is little in Acts 2 that recalls explicitly what the scriptures say about the festival of Weeks, but sundry kinds of evidence indicate that, in writing his account, the author drew upon exegetical traditions that had accumulated around the festival in some Jewish circles, including especially ones attested in Qumran texts.

a. The *Jubilees*-Qumran tradition shows that by the second pre-Christian century the festival of Weeks was intimately associated with the Sinai stories from Exodus, especially with the covenant between God and Israel. The festival of Weeks was the occasion for making and remembering the biblical covenants and for renewing the great pact made at the mountain.
b. Acts 1 uses language for Jesus' ascension that reminds one of Moses' ascent of Mount Sinai to receive the Torah and make the covenant.
c. Summaries of the ideal fellowship in the scrolls and Acts 2:42-47; 4:32 (cf. 1:14) are modeled on the notion that Israel at Sinai was harmonious, a people that accepted the Torah without dissent and lacked the defects that otherwise disrupt society. Exodus implies as much, and later sources expanded upon the theme.

There are, of course, important differences between the Sinai stories as read in some Jewish sources and the account in Acts 1–2. So, for instance, the gift at Sinai was the divine word, the Torah, while in Acts 2 it was the divine Spirit.

Not all of the elements in Acts 1–2 arose from Jewish elaborations on the Sinai chapters. There are unique elements in the New Testament account, and it is possible that other scriptural material, as later understood,[23]

22. For a sketch of the self-understanding evident in texts such as the *Rule of the Community* and references to other scholarly literature on the topic, see J. C. VanderKam, "Sinai Revisited," in M. Henze, ed., *Biblical Interpretation at Qumran* (SDSSRL; Grand Rapids: Eerdmans, 2005), 44-60.

23. One such possibility is the passage about Eldad and Medad in Num 11:26-30. Some of the targums say that the Holy Spirit rested on them as they prophesied about

contributed to the shaping of Acts 1–2. But the evidence demonstrates that in Acts 1–2 the writer was heavily influenced by Jewish traditions about the festival of Weeks, prominently including ones known from the Dead Sea Scrolls.

PAUL

The writings of the Apostle Paul have proved a rich source for comparisons with material in the scrolls. This may be surprising because of how differently Paul and the writers of the scrolls spoke about several fundamental theological topics, but it is a fact nevertheless.

Scriptural Interpretation

There are numerous examples of scriptural interpretation in the scrolls and in the New Testament, and there are also some instances in which the same text is under appeal. There is ample warrant for thinking that the scroll commentators on the scriptures and New Testament interpreters took similar approaches to authoritative texts, especially the ones they understood to be prophecies. Both groups believed such prophecies were being realized in their time though they had been written centuries earlier (see Chapter 2 above). An intense interest in the meaning of the scriptures would not have distinguished the followers of Jesus and the writers of the scrolls from other Jews, but the consequences they drew from the ancient texts might have been unusual.

At least two assumptions drove interpretation of prophecy as it comes to expression in the scrolls: the ancient prophets spoke about the latter days, and these are the latter days.[24] The commentator was convinced that he lived in the time about which the prophet was unwittingly speaking.

Joshua's succeeding Moses. See M. McNamara, *The New Testament and the Palestinian Targum to the Pentateuch* (AnBib 27; Rome: Pontifical Biblical Institute, 1966), 235.

24. These are the two highlighted by K. Elliger, *Studien zum Habakuk-Kommentar vom Toten Meer* (BHT 15; Tübingen: Mohr, 1953), 150 (see Chapter 2 above). A passage expressing these ideas is 1QpHab 7:1-5, where the commentator, explaining Hab 2:2, says that God did not tell the prophet when the events he predicted would occur but revealed such secrets to the Teacher of Righteousness who, as the *pesharim* show, applied them to his own time. See S. L. Berrin, "Pesharim," in *EDSS*, 2:644-47.

The result was that the prophecies were understood as applying to the present time for the expositor — prophecies were coming to fruition in his day or right around his time. The Teacher of Righteousness, it was believed, had been divinely empowered to understand all the mysteries written by the prophets — words that even the prophets who uttered them had not understood (1QpHab 7:1-5). So, for example, prophecies of Habakkuk, which were spoken in the seventh-sixth centuries B.C.E., were explained as references to experiences in the career of the Teacher of Righteousness and those around him. Or, in the New Testament, as seen above, Peter appealed to Joel's prophecy to explain what happened centuries later on the Pentecost celebration recorded in Acts 2. Like the people of the scrolls, the first Christians believed they had a leader who unlocked the scriptural mysteries for them: that leader was Jesus, who after his resurrection told his stunned followers: "'These are my words that I spoke to you while I was still with you — that everything written about me in the law of Moses, the prophecies, and the psalms must be fulfilled.' Then he opened their minds to understand the scriptures" (Luke 24:44-45; see also 24:27). Paul understood Jesus Christ himself as revealed by the Spirit to be the key to opening the meaning of the ancient scriptures (2 Cor 3:12-18).

A passage that illustrates well the approach of Paul and the scrolls commentators is their reading of Hab 2:4b, which the NRSV translates as: "but the righteous live by their faith." In the context preceding this passage the prophet described the horrific onslaught of the Chaldeans and wondered how a good God could tolerate such evil, however angry he was with his disobedient people. At the beginning of chapter 2 Habakkuk stations himself at his watch post, awaiting an answer to his complaint. The Lord responds and tells him the predicted vision will happen: "it speaks of the end, and does not lie. If it seems to tarry, wait for it; it will surely come, it will not delay" (2:3). Verse 4 then says: "Look at the proud! Their spirit is not right in them, but the righteous live by their faith."[25]

Although the passage comes from the book of a relatively obscure prophet, it is surprisingly well known, because for the Apostle Paul that text, along with Gen 15:6, was a key scriptural support in his presentation of a law-free grace. He cites it in both Gal 3:11 and Rom 1:17 (it is also quoted in

---

25. In MT the noun has a third person masculine singular suffix: "his/its faith/faithfulness" (LXX reads "my faith/faithfulness," i.e., God's faithfulness). J. J. M. Roberts (*Nahum, Habakkuk, and Zephaniah* [OTL; Louisville: Westminster John Knox, 1991], 107) thinks the suffix refers to the vision and translates "But the righteous person will live by its faithfulness" (105). See p. 111 for his decision to translate with "faithfulness."

Heb 10:38). In the former he writes: "Now it is evident that no one is justified before God by the law; for 'The one who is righteous will live by faith.'"

The meaning of the term translated "faith" in the NRSV (אמונה = 'ĕmûnâ) in Hab 2:4b, the quality that allows the righteous one to endure, is debated: should it be translated by "faith" or "faithfulness"? Which of the two meanings one chooses makes a difference: in the one case the text would be saying that an attitude or disposition on the part of the righteous person leads to life ("faith"); in the other a way of life would be intended ("faithfulness"), that is, acting in a faithful way through challenging times (see Heb 10:38). Paul takes the former option in his reading of the passage: life comes to the one who has faith in God's promise to Abraham that was fulfilled in Christ. It is part of his sharp contrast between the way of faith and that of doing works of the law.[26]

In *Pesher Habakkuk,* when the commentator reaches this verse, he writes: "Interpreted, this concerns all those who observe the Law in the House of Judah, whom God will deliver from the House of Judgement because of their suffering and because of their faith in the Teacher of Righteousness" (8:1-3). Geza Vermes's translation quoted here assumes that the commentator adopts both understandings of the word 'ĕmûnâ: the notion of the "faithfulness" of the righteous is expressed by referring to them as "those who observe the Law in the House of Judah" and their deliverance because of their "suffering" (cf. 4QMMT C 31-32); the idea of "faith" is embodied in the expression "and because of their faith in the Teacher of Righteousness." James A. Sanders concurs. He has written that the commentator agrees with Paul in that he understands faith to be centered in a person.[27] Not everyone accepts this explanation of the words in Pesher Habakkuk. Fitzmyer thinks it means: "Because of struggle and loyalty to the Teacher of Righteousness God will deliver them from the house of judgment."[28] The interpretation given in Vermes's translation is, one

26. See D. Lührmann, *Galatians* (CC; Minneapolis: Fortress, 1992), 59-65; J. A. Fitzmyer, *Romans* (AB 33; New York: Doubleday, 1993), 264-65 (where he also discusses the variants in the Greek witnesses). Cf. T. H. Lim, *Holy Scripture in the Qumran Commentaries and Pauline Letters* (Oxford: Clarendon, 1997), 51-53.

27. J. A. Sanders, "Habakkuk in Qumran, Paul, and the Old Testament," *JR* 39 (1959): 233.

28. J. A. Fitzmyer, "Habakkuk 2:3-4 and the New Testament," in *To Advance the Gospel: New Testament Studies* (2nd ed.; BRS; Grand Rapids: Eerdmans and Livonia: Dove, 1998), 239; *Romans,* 264-65 (he prefers to read the phrase as speaking of fidelity to the Teacher, not as faith in him). See also his essay "Paul and the Dead Sea Scrolls," in

might say, faithful to the text. What exactly such a faith in the Teacher would entail *Pesher Habakkuk* does not disclose.[29]

The passage, understood in this way, shows that Paul adopted a current interpretive option for the text, even if others understood it differently or explained it in more than one sense.

2 Corinthians 6:14–7:1

Long before the bedouin found the first scrolls in 1947, scholars of Paul's letters had commented on the strange character of 2 Cor 6:14–7:1. One reason was that it sits so awkwardly in its context. The apostle had been speaking pastorally about opening his heart to the Corinthians and theirs to him (6:11-13), and he continues the thought in 7:2 ("Make room in your hearts for us") and in a similar vein in verses 3-4. Between these "opening hearts" passages comes the problematic unit:

> Do not be mismatched with unbelievers. For what partnership is there between righteousness and lawlessness? Or what fellowship is there between light and darkness? What agreement does Christ have with Beliar? Or what does a believer share with an unbeliever? What agreement has the temple of God with idols? For we are the temple of the living God; as God said, "I will live in them and walk among them, and I will be their God, and they shall be my people. Therefore come out from them, and be separate from them, says the Lord, and touch nothing unclean; then I will welcome you, and I will be your father, and you shall be my sons and daughters, says the Lord Almighty." Since we have these promises, beloved, let us cleanse ourselves from every defilement of body and of spirit, making holiness perfect in the fear of God.

Many expositors would agree that "the intervening material is at least to some extent disruptive."[30] Besides breaking the flow of the passage, the

---

P. W. Flint and J. C. VanderKam, eds., *The Dead Sea Scrolls after Fifty Years: A Comprehensive Assessment* (2 vols.; Leiden: Brill, 1998, 1999), 2:605-6.

29. See also the survey of early views in Braun, *Qumran und das Neue Testament*, 2:171-72.

30. V. P. Furnish, *II Corinthians* (2nd ed.; AB 32A; Garden City: Doubleday, 1984), 368.

self-contained unit 6:14–7:1 has no obvious connection with the situation in Corinth and contains six important words (outside the scriptural citations) that appear nowhere else in Paul's letters — in fact, in no other place in the entire New Testament.[31] Although some defend the Pauline nature of the passage and/or think it is in its correct location (whether from Paul or an editor),[32] the conclusion that it is an interpolation is frequently drawn. Victor Furnish divides the many variant forms of the interpolation hypothesis into two basic approaches: (1) the passage is from Paul but was drawn from another of his letters and placed here; (2) it is non-Pauline or even anti-Pauline.[33]

Furnish finds three units in 2 Cor 6:14–7:1: an initial admonition (6:14-16a); affirmation, promises, and further admonitions — including a testimonia or catena of scriptural citations (6:16b-18); and a concluding appeal (7:1).[34] After examining each of these units, he assesses the non-Pauline features (e.g., the unique terms, separation from unbelievers), the anti-Pauline traits (or at least ones that some find anti-Pauline such as the emphasis on purity [see Rom 14:20; Gal 5:1–6:10]), affinities with Qumran sectarianism (e.g., the catena which includes 2 Sam 7:14, a text treated in 4QFlorilegium, separation of the clean and unclean), and Pauline features (for example, "sons of light" occurs elsewhere in Paul's letters [e.g., 1 Thess 5:5]). He concludes about the section and the theories offered to explain it:

> At the same time, one must acknowledge that there are important reasons for questioning the Pauline origin of 6:14–7:1. It is not just a matter of several non-Pauline words, or the form and content of the citations from scripture. In themselves, these things are not decisive. What must be taken seriously is the clustering of so many non-Pauline features in these few verses, the fact that so many of the ideas, including the most fundamental appeals, of the passage are not easily attributable to the apostle, and the many general and spe-

31. J. A. Fitzmyer, "Qumran and the Interpolated Paragraph in 2 Cor 6:14–7:1," in *The Semitic Background of the New Testament* (BRS; Grand Rapids: Eerdmans and Livonia: Dove, 1997), 206 (the essay appeared originally in *CBQ* 23 [1961]: 271-80).

32. P. Barnett (*The Second Epistle to the Corinthians* [NICNT; Grand Rapids: Eerdmans, 1997], 337-58), for one, maintains the passage is Pauline and, not only is it in the right place, it is the climax of "the apostolic excursus, begun at 2:14" (337).

33. Furnish, *II Corinthians*, 378-82.

34. Furnish, *II Corinthians*, 371-75; see also H. D. Betz, "2 Cor 6:14–7:1: An Anti-Pauline Fragment?" *JBL* 92 (1973): 89-99.

cific affinities between these verses and the Jewish sectarian texts from Qumran. Moreover, many of the elements cited in support of the authenticity of the passage are only superficially Pauline.[35]

A little later he adds: "What evidence there is would seem to be best satisfied by the hypothesis that the passage is of non-Pauline composition, but was incorporated by the apostle as he himself wrote this letter. One might speak of a Pauline interpolation of non-Pauline material."[36] But in the end he admits that the passage is an enigma.

The affinities of the passage with Qumran sectarian terms and teachings are a topic on which experts have been writing since the 1950s when the cave 1 texts were becoming available for study.[37] Fitzmyer enumerated five elements in 2 Cor 6:14–7:1 that suggested to him some form of contact between the contents of the Qumran texts and those of the Pauline pericope.

(1) Triple dualism: three contrasting pairs — uprightness/iniquity, light/ darkness (for two classes of people, an ethical dualism), and Christ/ Beliar. The name Beliar (Belial) occurs only here in the New Testament but a number of times in Qumran and related texts (e.g., 1QM 13:1-4).[38] In these respects he believes "it is difficult to deny the reworking of Qumran expressions and ideas" in 2 Cor 6:14–7:1.[39]

(2) Opposition to idols: The same attitude is expressed in the question "What agreement has the temple of God with idols?" as in 1QS 2:16-17: "He shall be cut off from the midst of all the sons of light, and because he has turned aside from God on account of his idols and his stumbling-block of sin, his lot shall be among those who are cursed forever."

35. Furnish, *II Corinthians*, 382.

36. Furnish, *II Corinthians*, 383. On this page he calls the passage an enigma.

37. Braun, *Qumran und das Neue Testament*, 1:201-3, covers the early discussions of the issue.

38. The name is found in other compositions besides the Qumran literature and related works (e.g., *Jubilees*), but one meets it most frequently in this tradition (88 times in Qumran texts). When this fact is coupled with the remaining features isolated by Fitzmyer and others, the combination constitutes a strong argument — one perhaps not always properly appreciated by defenders of the Pauline character of 2 Cor 6:14–7:1 (see, e.g., Barnett, *The Second Epistle to the Corinthians*, 338, n. 4).

39. Fitzmyer, "Qumran and the Interpolated Paragraph," 213. This first element he treats on pp. 208-13.

(3) Temple of God: The declaration that "we are the temple of the living God" recalls those passages in the *Rule of the Community* in which the group is described as a sanctuary (examples are 1QS 8:4-6; 9:5-7).

(4) Separation from all impurity: The commands to separate from others and not to touch any unclean thing echo the teachings found through-out the sectarian texts (among the passages Fitzmyer mentions are CD 6:17; 1QS 4:5; 5:13-14; 9:8-9).

(5) Concatenation of Old Testament texts: The chain-like citation of forms of Lev 26:12 with Ezek 37:27; Isa 52:11; Ezek 20:34; and 2 Sam 7:14 resembles 4QTestimonia, and the citation formula "as God said" (only here in the New Testament) is paralleled in CD 6:13; 8:9.[40]

Fitzmyer concludes from the evidence he has adduced:

> Not all the points in this comparison are of equal importance or value, but the cumulative effect of so many of them within such a short passage is the telling factor. We are faced with a paragraph in which Qumran ideas and expressions have been reworked in a Christian cast of thought. Some of the contacts can be shown to ex-ist also in genuinely Pauline passages, e.g., the temple of God, the idea of the 'lot', the *testimonia*-form. But when the total Qumran influence is considered along with the other reasons (the inter-rupted sequence of the surrounding context, the self-contained unit and the strange vocabulary), the evidence seems to total up to the admission of a Christian reworking of an Essene paragraph which has been introduced into the Pauline letter. The problem of how it got there remains unsolved.[41]

Those experts who consider the passage strange in its context (and they confess they do not know why it appears where it does) seem to make a more convincing case, regardless whether it is Pauline. It does break the

---

40. For points (2)-(5), see Fitzmyer, "Qumran and the Interpolated Paragraph," 213-16.

41. Fitzmyer, "Qumran and the Interpolated Paragraph," 216-17. Betz ("2 Cor 6:14–7:1") noted many parallels with texts from Qumran but thought the passage expresses the views of opponents of Paul such as the ones he confronted in Galatia, though it ad-dresses Jewish Christians, not the Gentile Christians Paul combated in Galatia: "In any case, it must be assumed that the redactor of the Pauline corpus, for reasons unknown to us, has transmitted a document among Paul's letters which in fact goes back to the movement to which Paul's opponents in Galatia belonged" (108).

Bibliography

Abegg, M. G., Jr. "4QMMT, Paul, and 'Works of the Law.'" In Flint, *The Bible at Qumran*, 203-16.

Abegg, M. G., Jr., P. W. Flint, and E. Ulrich. *The Dead Sea Scrolls Bible*. San Francisco: HarperSanFranciso, 1999.

Alexander, P. S., and G. Vermes, eds. *Qumran Cave 4: XIX, Serek Ha-Yaḥad and Two Related Texts*. DJD 26. Oxford: Clarendon, 1998.

————. "285. 4QSefer ha-Milḥamah." In Alexander et al., eds., J. C. VanderKam and M. Brady, consulting eds., *Qumran Cave 4: XXVI, Miscellanea, Part 1*. DJD 36. Oxford: Clarendon, 2000, 228-46, with pls. 12-13.

Allegro, J. M. "Further Light on the History of the Qumran Sect." *JBL* 75 (1956): 89-95.

————, ed. *Qumran Cave 4: I (4Q158-4Q186)*. DJD 5. Oxford: Clarendon, 1968.

Amusin (Amoussine), J. D. "Éphraïm et Manassé dans le Péshèr de Nahum (4 Q p Nahum)." *RevQ* 4/15 (1963-64): 389-96.

Anderson, H. "The Jewish Antecedents of the Christology in Hebrews." In Charlesworth, *The Messiah*, 512-35.

Atkinson, K. *I Cried to the Lord: A Study of the Psalms of Solomon's Historical Background and Social Setting*. JSJSup 84. Leiden: Brill, 2004.

Atkinson, K., and J. Magness. "Josephus's Essenes and the Qumran Community." *JBL* 129 (2010): 317-42.

Attridge, H. W. *The Interpretation of Biblical History in the* Antiquitates Judaicae *of Flavius Josephus*. HDR 7. Missoula: Scholars, 1976.

Baillet, M., J. T. Milik, and R. de Vaux, eds. *Les 'Petites Grottes' de Qumrân*. DJD 3. Oxford: Clarendon, 1962.

————. "Remarques sur le manuscrit du Livre des Jubilés de la grotte 3 de Qumran." *RevQ* 5/19 (1964-66): 423-33.

Barnett, P. *The Second Epistle to the Corinthians*. NICNT. Grand Rapids: Eerdmans, 1997.

Barthélemy, D., and J. T. Milik, eds. *Qumran Cave I*. DJD 1. Oxford: Clarendon, 1955.

Barton, J. *Oracles of God: Perceptions of Ancient Prophecy in Israel after the Exile*. London: Darton, Longman, and Todd, 1986.

Baumgarten, A. I. "Pharisees." In *EDSS*, 2:657-63.

————. "Seekers after Smooth Things." In *EDSS*, 2:857-59.

Baumgarten, J. M. "The Pharisaic-Sadducean Controversies about Purity and the Qumran Texts." *JJS* 31 (1980): 157-70.

————. "Purification after Childbirth and the Sacred Garden in 4Q265 and Jubilees." In Brooke and García Martínez, *New Qumran Texts and Studies*, 3-10.

————. "Gentiles." In *EDSS*, 1:304-6.

————, ed. *Qumran Cave 4: XIII, The Damascus Document (4Q266-273)*. DJD 18. Oxford: Clarendon, 1996.

Baumgarten, J. M., et al., eds. *Qumran Cave 4: XXV, Halakhic Texts*. DJD 35. Oxford: Clarendon, 1999.

Beall, T. S. *Josephus' Description of the Essenes Illustrated by the Dead Sea Scrolls*. SNTSMS 58. Cambridge: Cambridge University Press, 1988.

————. "Pliny the Elder." In *EDSS*, 2:677-79.

Beckwith, R. *The Old Testament Canon of the New Testament Church and Its Background in Early Judaism*. Grand Rapids: Eerdmans, 1985.

Beentjes, P. C. *The Book of Ben Sira in Hebrew: A Text Edition of All Extant Hebrew Manuscripts and a Synopsis of All Parallel Hebrew Ben Sira Texts*. VTSup 68. Leiden: Brill, 1997.

Bengtsson, H. *What's in a Name? A Study of Sobriquets in the Pesharim*. Uppsala: Uppsala University, 2000.

Benoit, P., J. T. Milik, and R. de Vaux, eds. *Les Grottes de Murabba'ât*. DJD 2. Oxford: Clarendon, 1961.

Bergsma, J. S. *The Jubilee from Leviticus to Qumran: A History of Interpretation*. VTSup 115. Leiden: Brill, 2007.

Bernstein, M. J. "4Q252: From Re-Written Bible to Biblical Commentary." *JJS* 45 (1994): 1-27.

————. "Introductory Formulas for Citation and Re-citation of Biblical Verses in the Qumran Pesharim." *DSD* 1 (1994): 30-70.

————. "Interpretation of Scriptures." In *EDSS*, 1:376-83.

Berrin, S. L. "Pesharim." In *EDSS*, 2:644-47.

Betz, H. D. "2 Cor 6:14–7:1: An Anti-Pauline Fragment?" *JBL* 92 (1973): 88-108.

Beyer, K. *Die aramäischen Texte vom Toten Meer*. Göttingen: Vandenhoeck & Ruprecht, 1984.

————. *Die aramäischen Texte vom Toten Meer: Ergänzungsband*. Göttingen: Vandenhoeck & Ruprecht, 1994.

Bonani, G., et al. "Radiocarbon Dating of the Dead Sea Scrolls." *Atiqot* 20 (1991): 27-32.

Braun, H. *Qumran und das Neue Testament.* 2 vols. Tübingen: Mohr (Siebeck), 1966.

Brooke, G. J. "Qumran Pesher: Towards the Redefinition of a Genre." *RevQ* 10/40 (1981): 483-503.

———. "Isaiah 40:3 and the Wilderness Community." In Brooke and García Martínez, *New Qumran Texts and Studies,* 117-32.

———. "252. 4QCommentary on Genesis A." In Brooke et al., eds., VanderKam, consulting ed., DJD 22, 185-207, with pls. 12-13.

Brooke, G. J., et al., eds., J. C. VanderKam, consulting ed. *Qumran Cave 4: XVII, Parabiblical Texts, Part 3.* DJD 22. Oxford: Clarendon, 1996.

Brooke, G. J., and F. García Martínez, eds. *New Qumran Texts and Studies: Proceedings of the First Meeting of the International Organization for Qumran Studies, Paris 1992.* STDJ 15. Leiden: Brill, 1994.

Brown, R. E. *The Gospel According to John.* 2 vols. AB 29-29A. Garden City: Doubleday, 1966-1970.

Brownlee, W. H. "Biblical Interpretation among the Sectaries of the Dead Sea Scrolls." *BA* 14 (1951): 54-76.

———. *The Text of Habakkuk in the Ancient Commentary from Qumran.* JBLMS 11. Philadelphia: SBL, 1959.

———. *The Midrash Pesher of Habakkuk.* SBLMS 24. Missoula: Scholars, 1979.

Bruns, G. L. "Canon and Power in the Hebrew Scriptures." In R. von Hallberg, ed., *Canons.* Chicago: University of Chicago Press, 1984, 65-83.

Cameron, R., and A. J. Dewey, trans. *The Cologne Mani Codex (P. Colon. inv. nr. 4780).* SBLTT 15. Missoula: Scholars, 1979.

Campbell, J. G. *The Exegetical Texts.* CQS 4. London: T. & T. Clark, 2004.

Carmignac, J. "Le Document de Qumrân sur Melkisédeq." *RevQ* 7/27 (1969-1971): 343-78.

Carmody, T. R. "Matt 18:15-17 in Relation to Three Texts from Qumran Literature (CD 9:2-8, 16-22; 1QS 5:25–6:1)." In M. P. Horgan and P. J. Kobelski, eds., *To Touch the Text: Biblical and Related Studies in Honor of Joseph A. Fitzmyer, S.J.* New York: Crossroad, 1989, 141-58.

Charles, R. H. *The Book of Jubilees, or the Little Genesis.* London: Black, 1902.

Charlesworth, J. H., ed. *The Messiah: Developments in Earliest Judaism and Christianity.* Minneapolis: Fortress, 1992.

Charlesworth, J. H., et al., eds., J. C. VanderKam and M. Brady, consulting eds. *Miscellaneous Texts from the Judaean Desert.* DJD 38. Oxford: Clarendon, 2000.

Childs, B. S. *Introduction to the Old Testament as Scripture.* Philadelphia: Fortress, 1979.

Collins, J. J. *Daniel: A Commentary on the Book of Daniel.* Hermeneia. Minneapolis: Fortress, 1993.

————. "The Works of the Messiah." *DSD* 1 (1994): 98-112.

————. *The Scepter and the Star: The Messiahs of the Dead Sea Scrolls and Other Ancient Literature.* 2nd ed. Grand Rapids: Eerdmans, 2010.

Cranfield, C. E. B. *The Gospel according to Saint Mark.* CGTC. Cambridge: Cambridge University Press, 1963.

Cross, F. M. "The Evolution of a Theory of Local Texts." In Cross and Talmon, *Qumran and the History of the Biblical Text,* 306-20.

————. *The Ancient Library of Qumran.* 3rd ed. Minneapolis: Fortress, 1995.

Cross, F. M., D. W. Parry, R. J. Saley, and E. Ulrich, eds. *Qumran Cave 4: XII, 1-2 Samuel.* DJD 17. Oxford: Clarendon, 2005.

Cross, F. M., and S. Talmon, eds. *Qumran and the History of the Biblical Text.* Cambridge, Mass.: Harvard University Press, 1975.

Danby, H. *The Mishnah.* Oxford: Oxford University Press, 1933.

Dimant, D. "The 'Fallen Angels' in the Dead Sea Scrolls and in the Apocryphal and Pseudepigraphic Books Related to Them." Diss., Hebrew University of Jerusalem, 1974. (Hebrew)

————. "Not Exile in the Desert but Exile in Spirit: The Pesher of Isa. 40:3 in the *Rule of the Community* and the History of the Qumran Community." In *Connected Vessels: The Dead Sea Scrolls and the Literature of the Second Temple Period.* Jerusalem: Bialik, 2010, 40-53. (Hebrew)

Doudna, G. L. "Dating the Scrolls on the Basis of Radiocarbon Analysis." In Flint and VanderKam, *The Dead Sea Scrolls after Fifty Years,* 1:430-71.

————. *4Q Pesher Nahum: A Critical Edition.* JSPSup 35. Copenhagen International Series 8. London: Sheffield Academic, 2001.

Drawnel, H. *An Aramaic Wisdom Text from Qumran: A New Interpretation of the Levi Document.* JSJSup 86. Leiden: Brill, 2004.

Dunn, James D. G. "Works of the Law and Curse of the Law (Galatians 3.10-14)." *NTS* 31 (1985): 523-42.

————. "4QMMT and Galatians." *NTS* 43 (1997): 147-53.

————. *The New Perspective on Paul.* Rev. ed. Grand Rapids: Eerdmans, 2005.

Dupont-Sommer, A. *The Dead Sea Scrolls: A Preliminary Survey.* Trans. E. M. Rowley. Oxford: Blackwell, 1952.

Eisenman, R. *James the Brother of Jesus: The Key to Unlocking the Secrets of Early Christianity and the Dead Sea Scrolls.* New York: Viking, 1997.

Elizur, S. "Two New Leaves of the Hebrew Version of Ben Sira." *DSD* 17 (2010): 13-29.

Elledge, C. D. "Exegetical Styles at Qumran: A Cumulative Index and Commentary." *RevQ* 21/82 (2003): 165-208.

Elliger, K. *Studien zum Habakuk-Kommentar vom Toten Meer.* BHT 15. Tübingen: Mohr, 1953.

Eshel, E., H. Eshel, and A. Yardeni. "Apocryphal Psalm and Prayer." In E. Eshel et al., eds., J. C. VanderKam and M. Brady, consulting eds., *Qumran Cave 4: VI, Poetical and Liturgical Texts, Part 1*. DJD 11. Oxford: Clarendon, 1998, 403-25.

Eshel, H. "Ephraim and Manasseh." In *EDSS*, 1:253-54.

Evans, C. A. "The Dead Sea Scrolls and the Canon of Scripture in the Time of Jesus." In Flint, *The Bible at Qumran*, 67-79.

―――. "The Scriptures of Jesus and His Earliest Followers." In McDonald and Sanders, *The Canon Debate*, 185-95.

Falk, D. K. *The Parabiblical Texts: Strategies for Extending the Scriptures among the Dead Sea Scrolls*. CQS 8. LSTS 63. London: T. & T. Clark, 2007.

Fine, G., ed. *The Oxford Handbook of Plato*. New York: Oxford University Press, 2008.

Fishbane, M. *Biblical Interpretation in Ancient Israel*. Oxford: Clarendon, 1985.

Fitzmyer, J. A. "The Use of Explicit Old Testament Quotations in Qumran Literature and in the New Testament." *NTS* 7 (1960-61): 297-333. Repr. in *The Semitic Background of the New Testament*, 3-58.

―――. *The Gospel according to Luke X–XXIV*. AB 28A. Garden City: Doubleday, 1985.

―――. *Romans*. AB 33. New York: Doubleday, 1993.

―――. "The Aramaic and Hebrew Fragments of Tobit from Qumran Cave 4." *CBQ* 57 (1995): 655-75.

―――. "Tobit." In M. Broshi et al., eds., J. C. VanderKam, consulting ed., *Qumran Cave 4: XIV, Parabiblical Texts, Part 2*. DJD 19. Oxford: Clarendon, 1995, 1-76.

―――. "Qumran and the Interpolated Paragraph in 2 Cor 6:14–7:1." In *The Semitic Background of the New Testament*, 205-17.

―――. *The Semitic Background of the New Testament*. BRS. Grand Rapids: Eerdmans and Livonia: Dove, 1997.

―――. *The Acts of the Apostles*. AB 31. New York: Doubleday, 1998.

―――. "Habakkuk 2:3-4 and the New Testament." In *To Advance the Gospel: New Testament Studies*. 2nd ed. BRS. Grand Rapids: Eerdmans and Livonia: Dove, 1998, 236-46.

―――. "Paul and the Dead Sea Scrolls." In Flint and VanderKam, *The Dead Sea Scrolls after Fifty Years*, 2:599-621.

Flint, P. W. "4Qpseudo-Daniel ar^c (4Q245) and the Restoration of the Priesthood." *RevQ* 17/65-68 (1996): 137-50.

―――. "'Apocrypha,' Other Previously Known Writings, and 'Pseudepigrapha' in the Dead Sea Scrolls." In Flint and VanderKam, *The Dead Sea Scrolls after Fifty Years*, 2:24-66.

―――. "Noncanonical Writings in the Dead Sea Scrolls: Apocrypha, Other Previously Known Writings, Pseudepigrapha." In *The Bible at Qumran*, 80-126.

―――. "The Biblical Scrolls and the Text of the Hebrew Bible/Old Testament." In VanderKam and Flint, *The Meaning of the Dead Sea Scrolls*, 103-53.

————, ed. *The Bible at Qumran: Text, Shape, and Interpretation.* SDSSRL. Grand Rapids: Eerdmans, 2001.

Flint, P. W., and E. Ulrich, eds. *Qumran Cave 1: II, The Isaiah Scrolls.* 2 vols. DJD 32. Oxford: Clarendon, 2010.

Flint, P. W., and J. C. VanderKam, eds. *The Dead Sea Scrolls after Fifty Years: A Comprehensive Assessment.* 2 vols. Leiden: Brill, 1998-99.

Flusser, D. "Melchizedek and the Son of Man." In *Judaism and the Origins of Christianity.* Jerusalem: Magnes, 1988, 186-92.

————. "Pharisees, Sadducees, and Essenes in Pesher Nahum." In *Judaism of the Second Temple Period.* Vol. 1: *Qumran and Apocalypticism.* Grand Rapids: Eerdmans and Jerusalem: Magnes and Jerusalem Perspective, 2007, 214-57.

Fuller, R. E. "The Twelve." In E. Ulrich et al., eds., *Qumran Cave 4: X, The Prophets.* DJD 15. Oxford: Clarendon, 1997, 221-318 and pls. 40-64.

Furnish, V. P. *II Corinthians.* 2nd ed. AB 32A. Garden City: Doubleday, 1984.

García Martínez, F. "Temple Scroll." In *EDSS*, 2:927-33.

García Martínez, F., E. J. C. Tigchelaar, and A. S. van der Woude, eds. *Qumran Cave 11: II, 11Q2-18, 11Q20-31.* DJD 23. Oxford: Clarendon, 1998.

Ginzburg, L. *An Unknown Jewish Sect.* Moreshet 1. New York: Ktav, 1970.

Goldstein, J. A. "The Date of the Book of Jubilees." *PAAJR* 50 (1983): 63-86.

Goodman, M. "A Note on the Qumran Sectarians, the Essenes and Josephus." *JJS* 46 (1995): 161-66.

Goranson, S. "'Essenes': Etymology from עשה." *RevQ* 11/44 (1984): 483-98.

————. "Essenes." In E. M. Meyers, ed., *The Oxford Encyclopedia of Archaeology in the Near East.* 5 vols.; New York: Oxford University Press, 1997, 2:268-69.

————. "Others and Intra-Jewish Polemic as Reflected in Qumran Texts." In Flint and VanderKam, *The Dead Sea Scrolls after Fifty Years,* 2:534-51.

Gray, R. *Prophetic Figures in Late Second Temple Palestine.* Oxford: Oxford University Press, 1993.

Greenfield, J. C., and M. E. Stone. "Aramaic Levi Document." In Brooke et al., eds., VanderKam, consulting ed., DJD 22, 1-72.

Greenfield, J. C., M. E. Stone, and E. Eshel. *The Aramaic Levi Document: Edition, Translation, Commentary.* SVTP 19. Leiden: Brill, 2004.

Grundmann, W., F. Hesse, M. de Jonge, and A. S. van der Woude. "χρίω κτλ." *TDNT* 9:493-580.

Haran, M. *The Biblical Collection: Its Consolidation to the End of the Second Temple Times and Changes of Form to the End of the Middle Ages.* 3 vols. Jerusalem: Bialik Institute and Magnes, 1996-2008. (Hebrew)

Hempel, C. "Community Structures in the Dead Sea Scrolls: Admission, Organization, Disciplinary Procedures." In Flint and VanderKam, *The Dead Sea Scrolls after Fifty Years,* 2:67-92.

Henning, W. B. "The Book of Giants." *BSO(A)S* 11 (1943-46): 52-74.

Herr, M. D. "The Calendar." In S. Safrai and M. Stern, eds., *The Jewish People in the*

First Century. CRINT 1.2. Assen: van Gorcum and Philadelphia: Fortress, 1976, 834-64.

Horgan, M. P. *Pesharim: Qumran Interpretations of Biblical Books.* CBQMS 8. Washington: Catholic Biblical Association of America, 1979.

Horsley, R. A. "'Messianic' Figures and Movements in First-Century Palestine." In Charlesworth, *The Messiah,* 276-95.

Jackson, D. R. *Enochic Judaism: Three Defining Paradigm Exemplars.* LSTS 49. London: T. & T. Clark, 2004.

Janzen, J. G. *Studies in the Text of Jeremiah.* HSM 6. Cambridge, Mass.: Harvard University Press, 1973.

Josephus. Trans. H. St. J. Thackeray et al. 10 vols. LCL. New York: Putnam, 1926-1981.

Kister, M. "Newly-Identified Fragments of the Book of Jubilees: Jub 23:21-23, 30-31." *RevQ* 12/48 (1987): 529-36.

———, ed. *The Qumran Scrolls and Their World.* Between Bible and Mishnah. 2 vols. Jerusalem: Yad Ben-Zvi, 2009. (Hebrew)

Knibb, M. A. "Jubilees and the Origins of the Qumran Community." Inaugural Lecture in the Department of Biblical Studies, King's College, London, 17 January 1989.

Kobelski, P. J. *Melchizedek and Melchireša'.* CBQMS 10. Washington: Catholic Biblical Association of America, 1981.

Koester, H. *Introduction to the New Testament.* 2 vols. Hermeneia. Minneapolis: Fortress and Berlin: de Gruyter, 1982.

Kraft, R. A. "Pliny on Essenes, Pliny on Jews." *DSD* 8 (2001): 255-61.

Kraus, H.-J. *Psalms 60–150.* CC. Minneapolis: Augsburg, 1989.

Kugel, J. L. "Levi's Elevation to the Priesthood in Second Temple Writings." *HTR* 86 (1993): 1-64.

———. *Traditions of the Bible: A Guide to the Bible As It Was at the Start of the Common Era.* Cambridge, Mass.: Harvard University Press, 1998.

Kugler, R. A. *From Patriarch to Priest: The Levi-Priestly Tradition from Aramaic Levi to Testament of Levi.* SBLEJL 9. Atlanta: Scholars, 1996.

Larson, E., and L. H. Schiffman. "478. 4QpapFragment Mentioning Festivals." In Brooke et al., eds., VanderKam, consulting ed., DJD 22, 295-96.

Leiman, S. Z. *The Canonization of Hebrew Scripture: The Talmudic and Midrashic Evidence.* Transactions of the Connecticut Academy of Arts and Sciences 47. Hamden: Archon, 1976.

———. "Josephus and the Canon of the Bible." In L. H. Feldman and G. Hata, eds., *Josephus, the Bible, and History.* Leiden: Brill, 1989, 50-58.

Licht, J. *The Thanksgiving Scroll: A Scroll from the Wilderness of Judaea.* Jerusalem: Bialik, 1957. (Hebrew)

———. *The Rule Scroll: A Scroll from the Wilderness of Judaea 1QS · 1QSa · 1QSb: Text, Introduction and Commentary.* Jerusalem: Bialik, 1965. (Hebrew)

Lim, T. H. *Holy Scripture in the Qumran Commentaries and Pauline Letters.* Oxford: Clarendon, 1997.

―――. *Pesharim.* CQS 3. London: Sheffield Academic, 2002.

Loader, W. *Jesus' Attitude towards the Law: A Study of the Gospels.* Grand Rapids: Eerdmans, 2002.

Lockshin, M. I., ed. and trans. *Rashbam's Commentary on Exodus: An Annotated Translation.* BJS 310. Atlanta: Scholars, 1997.

Lührmann, D. *Galatians.* CC. Minneapolis: Fortress, 1992.

Luz, U. *Matthew 8–20.* Hermeneia. Minneapolis: Fortress, 2001.

Marcus, J. *Mark 1–8.* AB 27. New York: Doubleday, 2000.

Mason, E. F. *'You Are a Priest Forever': Second Temple Jewish Messianism and the Priestly Christology of the Epistle to the Hebrews.* STDJ 74. Leiden: Brill, 2008.

Mason, S. "Josephus and His Twenty-Two Book Canon." In McDonald and Sanders, *The Canon Debate,* 110-27.

McCabe, D. R. "How to Kill Things with Words: Ananias and Sapphira Under the Apostolic-Prophetic Speech-Act of Divine Judgment (Acts 4:32–5:11)." Diss., Edinburgh, 2008.

McDonald, L. M., and J. A. Sanders, eds. *The Canon Debate.* Peabody: Hendrickson, 2002.

McNamara, M. *The New Testament and the Palestinian Targum to the Pentateuch.* AnBib 27. Rome: Pontifical Biblical Institute, 1966.

Meier, J. P. *A Marginal Jew: Rethinking the Historical Jesus.* 4 vols. ABRL. New York: Doubleday, 1991-2009.

―――. "Is There *Halaka* (the Noun) at Qumran?" *JBL* 122 (2003): 150-55.

Metso, S. *The Textual Development of the Qumran Community Rule.* STDJ 21. Leiden: Brill, 1997.

Milgrom, J. *Leviticus.* 3 vols. AB 3, 3A, 3B. New York: Doubleday, 1991-2001.

Milik, J. T. "Le Testament de Lévi en araméen: Fragment de la grotte 4 de Qumrân." *RB* 62 (1955): 398-406.

―――. *Ten Years of Discovery in the Wilderness of Judea.* SBT 26. London: SCM, 1959.

―――. "Milkî-ṣedeq et Milkî-reša' dans les anciens écrits juifs et chrétiens." *JJS* 23 (1972): 95-144.

―――. *The Books of Enoch: Aramaic Fragments of Qumrân Cave 4.* Oxford: Clarendon, 1976.

Montgomery, J. A. *A Critical and Exegetical Commentary on the Book of Daniel.* ICC. Edinburgh: T. & T. Clark, 1927.

Muro, E. "The Greek Fragments of Enoch from Qumran Cave 7 (7Q4, 7Q8, & 7Q12 = 7QEn gr = Enoch 103:3-4, 7-8)." *RevQ* 18/70 (1997): 307-12.

Murphy, C. M. *Wealth in the Dead Sea Scrolls and in the Qumran Community.* STDJ 40. Leiden: Brill, 2002.

Nakman, D. "*Tefillin* and *Mezuzot* at Qumran." In Kister, *The Qumran Scrolls and Their World*, 1:143-55. (Hebrew)

Nebe, G. W. "7Q4 — Möglichkeit und Grenze einer Identifikation." *RevQ* 13/52 (1988): 629-33.

Neusner, J. *The Tosefta Translated from the Hebrew with a New Introduction.* 2 vols. Peabody: Hendrickson, 2002.

———. *The Babylonian Talmud: A Translation and Commentary.* 22 vols. Peabody: Hendrickson, 2005.

Nickelsburg, G. W. E. *1 Enoch 1: A Commentary on the Book of 1 Enoch, Chapters 1–36; 81–108.* Hermeneia. Minneapolis: Fortress, 2001.

———. *Jewish Literature Between the Bible and the Mishnah.* 2nd ed. Minneapolis: Fortress, 2005.

Nickelsburg, G. W. E., and J. C. VanderKam. *1 Enoch: A New Translation.* Minneapolis: Fortress, 2004.

Oegema, G. S. *The Anointed and His People: Messianic Expectations from the Maccabees to Bar Kochba.* JSPSup 27. Sheffield: Sheffield Academic, 1998.

Park, S. *Pentecost and Sinai: The Festival of Weeks as a Celebration of the Sinai Event.* LHB/OTS 342. New York: T. & T. Clark, 2008.

Parry, D. W., and E. Tov, eds. *The Dead Sea Scrolls Reader.* 6 vols. Leiden: Brill, 2004-5.

Pietersma, A., and B. G. Wright, eds. *A New English Translation of the Septuagint and the Other Greek Translations Traditionally Included under That Title.* New York: Oxford University Press, 2007.

Potin, J. *La fête juive de la Pentecôte: Étude des texts liturgiques.* 2 vols. LD 65-65a. Paris: Cerf, 1971.

Puech, É. "Une Apocalypse messianique (4Q521)." *RevQ* 15/60 (1992): 475-522.

———. "Fragments d'un apocryphe de Lévi et le personnage eschatologique: 4QTestLevi^{c-d}(?) et 4QAJa." In J. Trebolle Barrera and L. Vegas Montaner, eds., *The Madrid Qumran Congress.* 2 vols. Leiden: Brill and Madrid: Editorial Complutense, 1992, 2:449-501.

———. *La croyance des Esséniens en la vie future: Immortalité, résurrection, vie éternelle? Histoire d'une croyance dans le judaïsme ancien.* 2 vols. EBib 20. Paris: Gabalda, 1993.

———. "La 'Forteresse des Pieux' et Kh. Qumrân: A Propos du Papyrus Murabba'ât 45." *RevQ* 16/63 (1994): 463-71.

———. "Notes sur les fragments grecs du manuscrit 7Q4 = 1 Hénoch 103 et 105." *RB* 103 (1996): 592-600.

———. "Sept fragments de la Lettre d'Hénoch (1 Hén 100, 103, et 105) dans la grotte 7 de Qumrân (= 7QHén gr)." *RevQ* 18/70 (1997): 313-23.

———, ed. *Qumrân Grotte 4: XVIII, Textes Hébreux (4Q521-4Q528, 4Q576-4Q579).* DJD 25. Oxford: Clarendon, 1998.

Qimron, E., and J. Strugnell, eds. *Qumran Cave 4: V, Miqṣat Maʿaśe ha-Torah*. DJD 10. Oxford: Clarendon, 1994.

———. "Improving the Editions of the Dead Sea Scrolls." *Meghillot* 1 (2003): 135-45. (Hebrew)

Rabin, C. "Alexander Jannaeus and the Pharisees." *JJS* 7 (1956): 3-11.

Ravid, L. "The Book of Jubilees and Its Calendar — A Reexamination." *DSD* 10 (2003): 371-94.

Reeves, J. C. *Jewish Lore in Manichaean Cosmogony: Studies in the* Book of Giants *Traditions*. HUCM 14. Cincinnati: Hebrew Union College Press, 1992.

Rengstorf, K. H. *Ḥirbet Qumran and the Problem of the Library of the Dead Sea Scrolls*. Leiden: Brill, 1963.

Ringgren, H. *The Faith of Qumran: Theology of the Dead Sea Scrolls*. Philadelphia: Fortress, 1963.

Roberts, J. J. M. *Nahum, Habakkuk, and Zephaniah*. OTL. Louisville: Westminster John Knox, 1991.

Rofé, A. "The Acts of Nahash according to 4QSam[a]." *IEJ* 32 (1982): 129-33.

Roo, J. C. R. de. *'Works of the Law' at Qumran and in Paul*. New Testament Monographs 13. Sheffield: Sheffield Phoenix, 2007.

Rooy, H. F. van. *Studies on the Syriac Apocryphal Psalms*. JSSSup 7. Oxford: Oxford University Press, 1999.

Ruiten, J. T. A. G. M. van. "The Rewriting of Exodus 24:12-18 in Jubilees 1:1-4." *BN* 79 (1995): 25-29.

Ryle, H. E. *The Canon of the Old Testament*. 2nd ed. London: Macmillan, 1909.

Saldarini, A. J. *Pharisees, Scribes and Sadducees in Palestinian Society: A Sociological Approach*. Wilmington: Glazier, 1988. Repr. BRS. Grand Rapids: Eerdmans and Livonia: Dove, 2001.

Sanders, E. P. *Jewish Law from Jesus to the Mishnah: Five Studies*. Philadelphia: Trinity, 1990.

Sanders, J. A. "Habakkuk in Qumran, Paul, and the Old Testament." *JR* 39 (1959): 232-44.

———, ed. *The Psalms Scroll of Qumrân Cave 11 (11QPs[a])*. DJD 4. Oxford: Clarendon, 1965.

Schiffman, L. H. *Sectarian Law in the Dead Sea Scrolls: Courts, Testimony and the Penal Code*. BJS 33. Chico: Scholars, 1983.

———. *The Eschatological Community of the Dead Sea Scrolls: A Study of the Rule of the Congregation*. SBLMS 38. Atlanta: Scholars, 1989.

———. "The New Halakhic Letter (4QMMT) and the Origins of the Dead Sea Sect." *BA* 53 (1990): 64-73.

———. "The Septuagint and the Temple Scroll: Shared 'Halakhic' Variants." In G. J. Brooke and B. Lindars, eds., *Septuagint, Scrolls and Cognate Writings*. SBLSCS 33. Atlanta: Scholars, 1992, 277-97.

————. "Messianic Figures and Ideas in the Qumran Scrolls." In Charlesworth, *The Messiah*, 116-29.

————. "Pharisees and Sadducees in Pesher Naḥum." In M. Brettler and M. Fishbane, eds., *Minḥah le-Naḥum: Biblical and Other Studies Presented to Nahum M. Sarna in Honour of His 70th Birthday.* JSOTSup 154. Sheffield: Sheffield Academic, 1993, 272-90.

————. *Reclaiming the Dead Sea Scrolls.* Philadelphia: Jewish Publication Society, 1994.

————. "Phylacteries and Mezuzot." In *EDSS*, 2:675-77.

————. *The Courtyards of the House of the Lord: Studies on the Temple Scroll.* STDJ 75. Leiden: Brill, 2008.

————, and J. C. VanderKam, eds. *Encyclopedia of the Dead Sea Scrolls.* 2 vols. New York: Oxford University Press, 2002.

Schofield, A. *From Qumran to the Yaḥad: A New Paradigm of Textual Development for the Community Rule.* STDJ 77. Leiden: Brill, 2009.

Schrenk, G. "γράφω." *TDNT* 1 (1964): 742-73.

Schürer, E. *Geschichte des jüdischen Volkes im Zeitalter Jesu Christi.* 2 vols. Leipzig: Hinrichs, 1886-1890.

————. *The History of the Jewish People in the Age of Jesus Christ.* 3 vols. Rev. and ed. G. Vermes, F. Millar, and M. Black. Edinburgh: T. & T. Clark, 1973-1987.

Segal, M. "Biblical Exegesis in 4Q158: Techniques and Genre." *Text* 19 (1998): 45-62.

Shemesh, A. *Halakhah in the Making: The Development of Jewish Law from Qumran to the Rabbis.* Taubman Lectures in Jewish Studies 6. Berkeley: University of California Press, 2009.

————. "4Q265 and the Authoritative Status of Jubilees at Qumran." In G. Boccaccini and I. Ibba, eds., *Enoch and the Mosaic Torah: The Evidence of Jubilees.* Grand Rapids: Eerdmans, 2009, 247-60.

Skehan, P. W., and A. A. Di Lella. *The Wisdom of Ben Sira.* AB 39. New York: Doubleday, 1987.

Smith, J. Z. "Sacred Persistence: Toward a Redescription of Canon." In *Imagining Religion: From Babylon to Jonestown.* Chicago Studies in the History of Judaism. Chicago: University of Chicago Press, 1982, 36-52.

Starcky, J. "Les quatre étapes du messianisme à Qumrân." *RB* 70 (1963): 481-505.

Stone, M. E. "The Dead Sea Scrolls and the Pseudepigrapha." *DSD* 3 (1996): 270-95.

Strugnell, J. "Notes en marge du volume V des 'Discoveries in the Judaean Desert of Jordan.'" *RevQ* 7/26 (1970): 163-276.

Stuckenbruck, L. T. *The Book of Giants from Qumran: Texts, Translation, and Commentary.* TSAJ 63. Tübingen: Mohr Siebeck, 1997.

Sukenik, E. L. *Hidden Scrolls.* Jerusalem: Bialik, 1948. (Hebrew)

————, ed. *The Dead Sea Scrolls of the Hebrew University.* Jerusalem: Magnes, 1955. (Hebrew)

Sussmann, Y. "The History of the Halakha and the Dead Sea Scrolls." In Qimron and Strugnell, eds., DJD 10, 179-200.

Tabor, J. D., and M. O. Wise. "4Q521 'On Resurrection' and the Synoptic Gospel Tradition: A Preliminary Study." *JSP* 10 (1992): 149-62.

Talmon, S. "The Textual Study of the Bible — A New Outlook." In Cross and Talmon, *Qumran and the History of the Biblical Text,* 321-400.

———. *Hebrew Fragments from Masada.* Masada VI: Yigael Yadin Excavations 1963-1965: Final Reports. Jerusalem: Israel Exploration Society, Hebrew University of Jerusalem, 1999, 31-97.

Talshir, Z. "Biblical Texts from the Judaean Desert." In Kister, *The Qumran Scrolls and Their World,* 1:109-42. (Hebrew)

Taylor, J. E. "On Pliny, the Essene Location and Kh. Qumran." *DSD* 16 (2009): 1-21.

Teicher, J. L. "The Dead Sea Scrolls — Documents of the Jewish-Christian Sect of Ebionites." *JJS* 3 (1951): 67-99.

Thiering, B. E. *The Gospels and Qumran: A New Hypothesis.* Sydney: Theological Explorations, 1981.

Toorn, K. van der. *Scribal Culture and the Making of the Hebrew Bible.* Cambridge, Mass.: Harvard University Press, 2007.

Tov, E. *Textual Criticism of the Hebrew Bible.* 2nd rev. ed. Minneapolis: Fortress and Assen: Van Gorcum, 2001.

———. *Revised Lists of the Texts from the Judaean Desert.* Leiden: Brill, 2010.

———, ed. *The Greek Minor Prophets Scroll from Naḥal Ḥever (8ḤevXIIgr).* The Seiyâl Collection 1. DJD 8. Oxford: Clarendon, 1990. Repr. with corrections 1995.

Trebolle Barrera, J. "4QChr." In Ulrich, Cross et al., eds., DJD 16, 295-97, with pl. 38.

Ulrich, E. C. *The Qumran Text of Samuel and Josephus.* HSM 19. Missoula: Scholars, 1978.

———. "4QEzra." In Ulrich, Cross et al., eds., DJD 16, 291-93 and pl. 38.

———. *The Dead Sea Scrolls and the Origins of the Bible.* SDSSRL. Grand Rapids: Eerdmans, 1999.

———. "The Notion and Definition of Canon." In McDonald and Sanders, *The Canon Debate,* 21-35.

———. "The Non-attestation of a Tripartite Canon in 4QMMT." *CBQ* 65 (2003): 202-14.

———. "Two Perspectives on Two Pentateuchal Manuscripts from Masada." In S. Paul et al., eds., *Emanuel: Studies in Hebrew Bible, Septuagint, and Dead Sea Scrolls in Honor of Emanuel Tov.* VTSup 94. Leiden: Brill, 2003, 453-64.

———. *The Biblical Qumran Scrolls: Transcriptions and Textual Variants.* VTSup 134. Leiden: Brill, 2010.

———. "The Evolutionary Production and Transmission of the Scriptural Books." In S. Metso, H. Najman, and E. Schuller, eds., *The Dead Sea Scrolls:*

Transmission of Traditions and Production of Texts. STDJ 92. Leiden: Brill, 2010, 209-25.

─────. "The Jewish Scriptures: Texts, Versions, Canons." In J. J. Collins and D. C. Harlow, eds., *The Eerdmans Dictionary of Early Judaism*. Grand Rapids: Eerdmans, 2010, 97-119.

Ulrich, E. C., F. M. Cross et al., eds. *Qumran Cave 4: IX, Deuteronomy, Joshua, Judges, Kings*. DJD 14. Oxford: Clarendon, 1995.

─────. *Qumran Cave 4: XI, Psalms to Chronicles*. DJD 16. Oxford: Clarendon, 2000.

VanderKam, J. C. *Textual and Historical Studies in the Book of Jubilees*. HSM 14. Missoula: Scholars, 1977.

─────. *Enoch and the Growth of an Apocalyptic Tradition*. CBQMS 16. Washington: Catholic Biblical Association of America, 1984.

─────. *The Book of Jubilees*. 2 vols. CSCO 510-11. Scriptores Aethiopic 87-88. Leuven: Peeters, 1989.

─────. "John 10 and the Feast of the Dedication." In H. W. Attridge, J. J. Collins, and T. H. Tobin, eds., *Of Scribes and Scrolls: Studies on the Hebrew Bible, Intertestamental Judaism, and Christian Origins*. College Theology Society Resources in Religion 5. Lanham: University Press of America, 1990, 203-14.

─────. "The Scrolls, the Apocrypha, and the Pseudepigrapha." *HS* 34 (1993): 35-47.

─────. "Messianism in the Scrolls." In E. Ulrich and VanderKam, eds., *The Community of the Renewed Covenant: The Notre Dame Symposium on the Dead Sea Scrolls*. Christianity and Judaism in Antiquity 10. Notre Dame: University of Notre Dame Press, 1994, 211-34.

─────. *Enoch: A Man for All Generations*. Columbia: University of South Carolina Press, 1995.

─────. "'Jubilees' Exegetical Creation of Levi the Priest." *RevQ* 17/65-68 (1996): 359-73.

─────. "The Origins and Purposes of the Book of Jubilees." In M. Albani, J. Frey, and A. Lange, eds., *Studies in the Book of Jubilees*. TSAJ 65. Tübingen: Mohr Siebeck, 1997, 3-24.

─────. "Authoritative Literature in the Dead Sea Scrolls." *DSD* 5 (1998): 382-402.

─────. *Calendars in the Dead Sea Scrolls: Measuring Time*. London: Routledge, 1998.

─────. "Identity and History of the Community." In Flint and VanderKam, *The Dead Sea Scrolls after Fifty Years*, 2:487-533.

─────. "The Judean Desert and the Community of the Dead Sea Scrolls." In B. Kollmann, W. Reinbold, and A. Steudel, eds., *Antikes Judentum und Frühes Christentum: Festschrift für Hartmut Stegemann zum 65. Geburtstag*. BZNW 97. Berlin: de Gruyter, 1999, 159-71.

─────. "Studies on 'David's Compositions' (11QPs^a 27:2-11)." In B. A. Levine et al., eds., *Frank Moore Cross Volume*. Eretz Israel 26. Jerusalem: Israel Exploration Society, 1999, 212*-20*.

———. *From Revelation to Canon: Studies in the Hebrew Bible and Second Temple Literature*. JSJSup 62. Leiden: Brill, 2000.

———. "Sabbatical Chronologies in the Dead Sea Scrolls and Related Literature." In T. H. Lim, ed., *The Dead Sea Scrolls in Their Historical Context*. Edinburgh: T. & T. Clark, 2000, 159-78.

———. "Studies on the Prologue and *Jubilees* 1." In R. A. Argall, B. A. Bow, and R. A. Werline, eds., *For a Later Generation: The Transformation of Tradition in Israel, Early Judaism and Early Christianity*. Harrisburg: Trinity Press International, 2000, 266-79.

———. *The Book of Jubilees*. GAP. Sheffield: Sheffield Academic, 2001.

———. "Questions of Canon Viewed through the Dead Sea Scrolls." In McDonald and Sanders, *The Canon Debate*, 91-109.

———. "Those Who Look for Smooth Things, Pharisees, and Oral Law." In S. M. Paul et al., eds., *Emanuel: Studies in Hebrew Bible, Septuagint, and Dead Sea Scrolls in Honor of Emanuel Tov*. VTSup 94. Leiden: Brill, 2003, 465-77.

———. "The Festival of Weeks and the Story of Pentecost in Acts 2." In C. A. Evans, ed., *From Prophecy to Testament: The Function of the Old Testament in the New*. Peabody: Hendrickson, 2004, 185-205.

———. "Pesher Nahum and Josephus." In A. J. Avery-Peck, D. Harrington, and J. Neusner, eds., *When Christianity and Judaism Began: Essays in Memory of Anthony J. Saldarini*. 2 vols. JSJSup 85; Leiden: Brill, 2004, 299-311.

———. "Scripture in the Astronomical Book of Enoch." In E. G. Chazon, D. Satran, and R. A. Clements, eds., *Things Revealed: Studies in Early Jewish and Christian Literature in Honor of Michael E. Stone*. JSJSup 89. Leiden: Brill, 2004, 89-103.

———. "Sinai Revisited." In M. Henze, ed., *Biblical Interpretation at Qumran*. SDSSRL. Grand Rapids: Eerdmans, 2005, 44-60.

———. "The Apocrypha and Pseudepigrapha at Qumran." In J. H. Charlesworth, ed., *The Bible and the Dead Sea Scrolls*, vol. 2: *The Dead Sea Scrolls and the Qumran Community*. Waco: Baylor University Press, 2006, 469-91.

———. "Adam's Incense Offering (Jubilees 3:27)." *Meghillot* 5-6 (2007): *141-56.

———. "The Pharisees and the Dead Sea Scrolls." In J. Neusner and B. D. Chilton, eds., *In Quest of the Historical Pharisees*. Waco. Baylor University Press, 2007, 225-36.

———. *The Dead Sea Scrolls Today*. 2nd ed. Grand Rapids: Eerdmans, 2010.

———. "Moses Trumping Moses: Making the Book of *Jubilees*." In S. Metso, H. Najman, and E. Schuller, eds., *The Dead Sea Scrolls: Transmission of Traditions and Production of Texts*. STDJ 92. Leiden: Brill, 2010, 25-44.

———. "The Wicked Priest Revisited." In D. C. Harlow et al., *The "Other" in Sec-*

ond Temple Judaism: Essays in Honor of John J. Collins. Grand Rapids: Eerdmans, 2011, 350-67.

————. "The Common Ownership of Property in Essene Communities." In A. M. Maeir, J. Magness, and L. H. Schiffman, eds., *"Go Out and Study the Land" (Judges 18:2): Archaeological, Historical and Textual Studies in Honor of Hanan Eshel.* JSJSup 148. Leiden: Brill, forthcoming.

————, consulting ed. *Qumran Cave 4: XVII, Parabiblical Texts, Part 3.* DJD 22. Oxford: Clarendon, 1996.

VanderKam, J. C., and P. W. Flint. *The Meaning of the Dead Sea Scrolls: Their Significance for Understanding the Bible, Judaism, Jesus, and Christianity.* San Francisco: HarperSanFrancisco, 2002.

VanderKam, J. C., and J. T. Milik. "Jubilees." In H. Attridge et al., eds., VanderKam, consulting ed., *Qumran Cave 4: VIII, Parabiblical Texts, Part I.* DJD 13. Oxford: Clarendon, 1994, 1-140.

Vermes, G. "The Etymology of 'Essenes.'" *RevQ* 2/7 (1960): 427-43.

————. *Scripture and Tradition in Judaism: Haggadic Studies.* 2nd rev. ed. StPB 4. Leiden: Brill, 1973.

————. *The Religion of Jesus the Jew.* Minneapolis: Fortress, 1993.

————. *The Complete Dead Sea Scrolls in English.* New York: Penguin, 1997.

Vermes, G., and M. D. Goodman, eds. *The Essenes: According to the Classical Sources.* Sheffield: JSOT, 1989.

Wacholder, B. Z. "A Qumran Attack on the Oral Exegesis? The Phrase *'šr btlmwd šqrm* in 4Q Pesher Nahum." *RevQ* 5/20 (1966): 575-78.

Wagner, J. R., *Heralds of the Good News: Isaiah and Paul "In Concert" in the Letter to the Romans.* NovTSup 101. Leiden: Brill, 2002.

Webster, B. "Chronological Index of the Texts from the Judaean Desert." In E. Tov, ed., *The Texts from the Judaean Desert: Indices and an Introduction to the Discoveries in the Judaean Desert Series.* DJD 39. Oxford: Clarendon, 2002, 351-446.

Weinfeld, M. *The Organizational Pattern and the Penal Code of the Qumran Sect: A Comparison with Guilds and Religious Associations of the Hellenistic-Roman Period.* NTOA 2. Fribourg: Éditions Universitaires and Göttingen: Vandenhoeck & Ruprecht, 1986.

Wernberg-Møller, P. *The Manual of Discipline.* STDJ 1. Leiden: Brill, 1957.

Wise, M. O. "A Note on 4Q196 (papTob ar^a) and Tobit i 22." *VT* 43 (1993): 566-69.

Würthwein, E. *The Text of the Old Testament.* 2nd ed. Grand Rapids: Eerdmans, 1995.

Yadin, A. *Scripture as Logos: Rabbi Ishmael and the Origins of Midrash.* Philadelphia: University of Pennsylvania Press, 2004.

Yadin, Y. *The Scroll of the War of the Sons of Light Against the Sons of Darkness.* Trans. B. and Ch. Rabin. Oxford: Oxford University Press, 1962.

————. *The Ben Sira Scroll from Masada*. Jerusalem: Israel Exploration Society and Shrine of the Book, 1965.

————. *The Temple Scroll*. 3 vols. Jerusalem: Israel Exploration Society, 1983.

Yarbro Collins, A., and J. J. Collins. *King and Messiah as Son of God: Divine, Human, and Angelic Messianic Figures in Biblical and Related Literature*. Grand Rapids: Eerdmans, 2008.

Zahn, M. M. *Rethinking Rewritten Scripture: Composition and Exegesis in the 4QReworked Pentateuch Manuscripts*. STDJ 95. Leiden: Brill, 2011.

Index

Exodus, 3, 4, 6, 21, 33-35, 39-43, 66, 70, 76-77, 153-55
Ezekiel, 3, 6, 67, 70
Ezra, 2, 3, 52, 67, 124

Fitzmyer, Joseph A., 90-91, 145, 158, 161-62, 164
Flint, Peter W., 16
Fuller, Russell E., 2-3
Furnish, Victor P., 160-61

Gabriel, 30
Galatians, 53, 163-66
Genesis, 3, 4, 6, 21, 31-35, 39-40, 44-46, 54, 66, 70, 76-77
Genesis Apocryphon, 101
Gilgamesh, 82-83
Greenfield, Jonas C., 78-80

Habakkuk, 2, 5, 23-24, 70, 157
Habakkuk, Commentary on (Pesher Habakkuk), 5, 23-24, 36-38, 156n.24, 158-59; and "doers of the law," 102-4
Haggai, 124
Hakatuv, 57
Hanukkah, 56
Haplography, 19-20, 23
Hasmoneans, 52, 127
Hebrews, Letter to the, 46, 127
Henning, Walter B., 81
Hodayot, 103, 109
Hosea, 70
Hymn to the Creator, 68

Idols, 161
Isaiah, 3, 4, 6, 28, 32, 66, 67, 70, 76, 108, 129, 131
Ishmael, Rabbi, 57

Jacob, 39-40, 108
Jeremiah, Book of, 3, 12-14, 70; use in Daniel, 28-30
Jeremiah, Epistle of (Baruch 6). *See* Epistle of Jeremiah
Jesus, 116, 118, 119, 129, 153, 157; ascension, 153, and Pharisees, 53-54, 121-22,

133-34; and scriptures, 53-54, 56-57, 62-64, 69
Job, 3, 4
Joel, 157
John Hyrcanus, 111
John the Baptist, 118-19, 127-28, 131
John, Gospel of, 56-57, 131
Jonathan (Hasmonean ruler), 127n.19
Joseph, 36
Josephus, 101, 122-23, 143-44, 149; on Alexander Jannaeus, 110-13; on Essenes, 26-27, 143-44; on Jewish and Greek historical works, 58-60; on messiah(s), 122; on Nahash and Jabesh-gilead episode, 18-20; on Pharisees, 110-13, 115; on Sadducees, 106, 111, 115; and three Jewish groups, 96-98
Joshua (high priest), 124
Joshua, Book of, 3, 6
Josiah, 51
Jubilee Year, 34, 46
Jubilees, 8, 21, 30, 31, 45, 67, 70, 73-77, 80; 4Q216, 75-76; chronology, 34, 150-51; date of composition, 75-76; Festival of Weeks and covenant, 34-35, 149-51; Qumran copies, 74-76; relationship to *Aramaic Levi,* 35
Jude, Epistle of, 70
Judges, 3, 6

Kings (1-2), 3, 28, 51
Kittim, 125

Lamentations, 3
Latter/last days, 37, 125-27
"Law and the prophets," 52, 61-66, 71
Leningradensis, Codex, 8n.16
Levi, 35, 80
Leviticus, 3, 4, 6, 30, 43-45, 66, 70, 93, 137-38
"Liar" ("Scoffer"), 98, 109, 113
Luke, Gospel of, 63-64, 65, 129, 131, 134

Maccabees (1-2), 51-52
Malachi, 70
Mani, 81-84